P9-AGQ-079

# The Teaching for Social Justice Series

The White Architects of Black Education:
Ideology and Power in America, 1865–1954
WILLIAM H. WATKINS

The Public Assault on America's Children:
Poverty, Violence, and Juvenile Injustice
VALERIE POLAKOW, Editor

Construction Sites:
Excavating Race, Class, and Gender Among Urban Youths
LOIS WEIS and MICHELLE FINE, Editors

Walking the Color Line:
The Art and Practice of Anti-Racist Teaching
MARK PERRY

A Simple Justice:
The Challenge of Small Schools
WILLIAM AYERS, MICHAEL KLONSKY, and GABRIELLE H. LYON, Editors

Holler If You Hear Me:
The Education of a Teacher and His Students
GREGORY MICHIE

# The White Architects of Black Education

## IDEOLOGY AND POWER IN AMERICA, 1865–1954

### William H. Watkins

#### FOREWORD BY ROBIN D. G. KELLEY

Teachers College, Columbia University
New York and London

Published by Teachers College Press, 1234 Amsterdam Avenue, New York, NY 10027

Excerpts from *The Education of Blacks in the South, 1860–1935*, by James D. Anderson, reprinted from *The Education of Blacks in the South, 1860–1935* by James D. Anderson. Copyright © 1988 by the University of North Carolina Press. Used by permission of the publisher.

Excerpts from *Origins of the Modern Social Studies Curriculum 1900–1916*, by Michael D. Lybarger (unpublished doctoral dissertation, University of Wisconsin–Madison), copyright © 1981 by Michael D. Lybarger. Used with permission.

Excerpts from *Philanthropy and Cultural Imperialism*, edited by Robert F. Arnove (G. K. Hall, 1980; reprint, Indiana University Press, 1982), copyright © 1980 by Robert F. Arnove. Reprinted with permission.

Excerpts from *The Booker T. Washington Papers* reprinted from *The Booker T. Washington Papers*, vol. 2, edited by Louis R. Harlan et al., courtesy University of Illinois press.

Excerpts from *An American Citizen: The Life of William Baldwin, Jr.,* by J. Brooks, reprinted by permission of Ayer Company Publishers.

Excerpts from W. E. B. Du Bois's writings in *The Crisis* magazine reprinted with permission. The author wishes to thank The Crisis Publishing Co., Inc., the publisher of the magazine of the National Association for the Advancement of Colored People, for the use of this work.

*Library of Congress Cataloging-in-Publication Data*

Watkins, William H. (William Henry), 1946–
    The White architects of Black education : ideology and power in America, 1865–1954 /
William H. Watkins ; foreword by Robin D. G. Kelley.
        p.   cm. — (The teaching for social justice series)
    Includes bibliographical references and index.
    ISBN 0-8077-4043-8 (cloth : alk. paper) — ISBN 0-8077-4042-X (pbk. : alk. paper)
    1. Afro-Americans—Education—History—19th century.   2.
Afro-Americans—Education—History—20th century.   I. Title.   II. Series.
LC2741 .W38   2001
371.829'96073—dc21                                                                    00-053620

ISBN 0-8077-4042-X (paper)
ISBN 0-8077-4043-8 (cloth)

Printed on acid-free paper
Manufactured in the United States of America

08   07   06   05   04   03   02   01      8   7   6   5   4   3   2

# Contents

# Series Foreword

TEACHING FOR SOCIAL JUSTICE might be thought of as a kind of popular education—of, by, and for the people—something that lies at the heart of education in a democracy, education toward a more vital, more muscular democratic society. It can propel us toward action, away from complacency, reminding us of the powerful commitment, persistence, bravery, and triumphs of our justice-seeking forebears—women and men who sought to build a world that worked for us all. Without them, liberty would today be slighter, poorer, weaker—the American flag wrapped around an empty shell—a democracy of form and symbol over substance.

Rousseau argues in regard to justice that equality "must not be understood to mean that degrees of power and wealth should be exactly the same," but only that with respect to *power*, equality renders it "incapable of all violence" and only exerted in the interest of a freely developed and participatory law, and that with respect to *wealth*, "no citizen should be so opulent that he can buy another, and none so poor that he is constrained to sell himself." The quest for equality and social justice over many centuries is worked out in the open spaces of that proclamation, in the concrete struggles of human beings constructing and contesting all kinds of potential meanings within that ideal. Nothing is settled once and for all, but a different order of question presents itself: Who should be included? What do we owe one another? What is fair and unfair?

This series gathers together examples of popular education being practiced today, as well as clear and new thinking concerning issues of democracy, social justice, and educational activism. Many contributions will be grounded in practice and will, we hope, focus on the complexities built into popular education: difficulties, setbacks, successes, steps forward—work that reminds us of what Bernice Johnson Reagon calls "the sweetness of struggle." We seek as well, developing theoretical work that might push us all forward, to grasp anew the meaning of democracy in changing times, the demands of justice, and the imperatives of social change. We want to encourage new voices and new ideas, and in all cases to contribute to a serious, grounded, thoughtful exchange about the enduring questions in education: Education for what? Education for whom? Education toward what kind of social order?

If society cannot be changed under any circumstances, if there is nothing to be done, not even small and humble gestures toward something better, well, that about ends all conversation. Our sense of agency shrinks, our choices diminish. What more is there to say? But if a fairer, more sane, and just social order is both desirable and possible, that is, if some of us can join one another to imagine and build a participatory movement for justice, a public space for the enactment of democratic dreams, our field opens slightly. There would still be much to be done, for nothing would be entirely settled. We would still need to stir ourselves from passivity, cynicism, and despair; to reach beyond the superficial barriers that wall us off from one another; to resist the flattening effects of consumerism and the blinding, mystifying power of the familiar social evils (such as racism, sexism, and homophobia); to shake off the anesthetizing impact of most classrooms, most research, and of the authoritative, official voices that dominate the airwaves and the media; and to, as Maxine Greene says, "release our imaginations" and act on behalf of what the known demands, linking our conduit firmly to our consciousness. We would be moving, then, without guarantees, but with purpose and with hope.

Education is an arena of struggle as well as hope—struggle because it stirs in us the need to look at the world anew, to question what we have created, to wonder what is worthwhile for human beings to know and experience—and hope because we gesture toward the future. Education is where we ask how we might engage, enlarge, and change our lives, and it is, then, where we confront our dreams and fight out notions of the good life, where we try to comprehend, apprehend, or possibly even change the world. Education is contested space, a natural site of conflict—sometimes restrained, other times in full eruption—over questions of justice.

The work, of course, is never done. Democracy is dynamic, a community always in the making. Teaching for social justice continues the difficult task of constructing and reinvigorating a public. It broadens the table, so that more may sit together. Clearly, we have a long, long way to go. And we begin.

William Ayers, Series Editor
Therese Quinn, Associate Series Editor

# Foreword

"THE TENDENCY IS HERE," wrote W. E. B. DuBois nearly a century ago, "born of slavery and quickened to renewed life by the crazy imperialism of the day, to regard human beings as among the material resources of a land to be trained with an eye single to future dividends. . . . [W]e daily hear that an education that encourages aspiration, that sets the loftiest ideals and seeks as an end culture and character rather than bread-winning, is the privilege of white men and the danger and delusion of black." DuBois is speaking of a critical moment in world history—a moment marked by the consolidation of an educational policy toward black people that, in theory, would ensure the reproduction of a race of "hewers of wood and drawers of water." DuBois understood better than most that the end of slavery, the expansion of imperialism, the birth of Jim Crow, and the emergence of monopoly capitalism were one and the same process, and that at the fulcrum of this global economic transformation lay the "Negro." What do we do about black labor, the ex-slave, the colonial subject? How do we discipline, exploit, and civilize the Negro? These were the burning questions of the day.

The men who stepped forward to offer a solution to these questions are the subjects of this remarkable book. Working at the intersection of intellectual history, political economy, and educational sociology, William Watkins takes us to the boardrooms, backrooms, and classrooms where black educational policy was being debated and made. With clarity and insight, Watkins destroys the myth that the debate between DuBois and Booker T. Washington over the character of schooling actually determined the future of educational policy toward African Americans. Important as they might have been, these men were minor players in the formation of black schooling and the philosophy that lay behind it. Watkins cuts to the very heart of the matter, drawing our attention to the real power brokers: Thomas Jesse Jones, Franklin Giddings, J. L. M. Curry, William Baldwin, and Robert Ogden, among others.

These men represented a class of modern elites, the visionaries of laissez-faire capitalism who were most concerned about building profits, maintaining working-class peace in the South, and "uplifting" the Negro to his or her proper place in the wheel of modern industry. Working in the best tradition of DuBoisian scholarship, Watkins understands the formation of this class and their ideas as a global process. Many were directly involved in developing colonial policies in Africa, and every one of these "architects" recognized the direct links between the construction of the color line on a world scale and the flow of capital. They did not always agree, nor were they anything close to a monolithic group. But their policies and ideas profoundly shaped twentieth-century public education, race relations, and the development of modern racism—not to mention colonial rule.

THE WHITE ARCHITECTS OF BLACK EDUCATION is a study of power and the political economy of education. And yet it is hardly a "top down" history. Always attuned to the dialectical character of historical movements, Watkins reveals how these men were shaped as much by black struggles for freedom as by philanthropic idealism, New South ideology, Social Darwinism, Protestant beliefs, and liberal capitalist thought. He reminds us that newly freed black folk regarded education, along with land and citizenship, as the key to their liberation. And so did the ruling classes, which is why during the antebellum era virtually every Southern state passed laws prohibiting slaves from learning to read and write. Once formal slavery was destroyed, black people enthusiastically embraced education as a weapon to ensure their emancipation. Knowledge was power, the cornerstone of democracy. They envisioned a Reconstructed nation in which education was a basic right and schools afforded to the laborer as much knowledge as their former masters enjoyed. Their struggle for universal public education created opportunities not only for freed people but for poor whites throughout the South. Furthermore, the "black architects" of black education displayed a broader vision of democracy than did the original framers of the Constitution, for, unlike the founders, the masses of freed people regarded education as a basic right.

In the end, however, the black architects were defeated. How and why this happened is the subject of this book. The consequences of such a defeat are still with us, however, and the lessons this book has to offer are as urgent and prescient for the twenty-first century as DuBois's insights were for the twentieth. The difference is that while the architects of the late nineteenth century sought to turn a mass of determined, independent black people into cheap wage labor, the contemporary ruling architects are developing ways to deal with an increasingly redundant, unskilled, and by some accounts "unemployable" urban labor force. Look around today and what do we see? A crisis-ridden public education system characterized by massive budget cuts, crumbling buildings, overcrowded classrooms, and a curriculum that measures success by standardized tests. A book arguing for a correlation between race and intelligence (guess who has the lowest IQ?) on the best seller list. The swift dismantling of affirmative action programs, especially on college campuses. A *Democratic* welfare "reform" law that excludes higher education in its definition of work or "training programs" and, instead, limits welfare recipients to vocational programs. A record 2 million inmates (two thirds of whom are nonviolent offenders) in a country that spends more to build prisons than on universities. In fact, between 1988 and 1998, New York State's prison budget increased by $761 million, while its expenditures on public universities declined by $615 million. In New York alone, there are twice as many black men in prison as are enrolled in the entire state university system. Nationwide, approximately one out of three young black males are under the administrative arm of the criminal justice system.

To paraphrase the final lines of DuBois's magnificent *Black Reconstruction in America*, "This is education in the [twenty-first century]; this is modern and exact social science; this is the university course in 'History 12.'" And this is what we have inherited from the original edifice designed and constructed by the white architects of education. The lesson I take from Watkins is this: If we are to create new models of pedagogy and intellectual work and become architects of our own education, then we cannot simply repair the structures that have been passed down to us. We need to dismantle the old architecture so that we might begin anew.

Robin D. G. Kelley

# Acknowledgments

THIS BOOK HAS BEEN a long time in the making. I am eternally grateful to my family, friends, colleagues, and co-workers, who have supported and encouraged my work. I could not even begin to thank the scores of librarians, archivists, typists, and computer technicians who assisted and tolerated me in times of tribulation and tears. I'm hard pressed for some kind of order in which to thank people.

First, I thank our—and my—ancestors, who struggled against insurmountable odds to survive centuries of cruel and barbarous treatment. I dare to speak boldly for those who have been and continue to be enslaved, oppressed, and exploited. It is my wish to see a world where equality, peace, and justice triumph over hatred and avarice.

To my many friends and comrades in the struggle: We have spent many years protesting, picketing, organizing, boycotting, and leafletting against inhumanity. Our labors shall not be in vain.

I first conceived and drafted this work while a junior professor at the University of Utah. To my former faculty colleagues Nick Burbules, Donna Dehyle, Andrew Gitlin, Harvey Kantor, Frank Margonis, and Audrey Thompson, and the many graduate students who attended the Friday afternoon sessions, especially Georgia Johnson, Larry Johnson, and Sharon LaSalle, I owe many thanks for providing the most intellectually rich and stimulating group of academics to be found anywhere.

In recent times I have imposed on many individuals to read chapter drafts, edit, react to ideas, and provide me comfort. Those individuals have been indispensable to this effort. I wish to first thank my son, William J. Watkins, an accomplished writer himself, for his help. Additionally, I'm indebted to Dr. Audrey P. Watkins, Dr. Rochelle Brock, Sheilah Garland-Olaniran, and Dr. Eileen M. Hayes. Special thanks to my manuscript editor, Mrs. Julie Moore, for her exceptional grasp of grammar and language, and for her countless suggestions.

Perhaps the most challenging part of this work has been negotiating the computer and its many uncertainties. I'm grateful to Christine Olson, of the University of Illinois at Chicago computer support department, for preventing me from committing computercide.

Faculty colleagues William H. Schubert, William Ayers, and Annette Henry have been sources of daily support and friendship in recent times.

I am indebted to the Schömberg Center for Research in Black Culture of the New York Public Library, Library of Congress, Hampton University Archives, Rockefeller Archive Center, Rare Book and Manuscript Library of Columbia University, Wisconsin State Historical Society, Alabama Department of Archives and History, and Phelps Stokes Fund.

I thank the University of North Carolina Press, Professor Michael Lybarger, Professor Robert Arnove, *Crisis* magazine, the University of Illinois Press, and Arno Press-Ayer Publications for allowing me to reprint material from their publications.

# Introduction

THIS BOOK FLOWS from my lifelong interest in Black America's politics, education, and oppression. As an undergraduate political science student during the tumultuous 1960s, I was attracted to questions of power and discrimination affecting people, especially people of color. Later, as an educator, my interests were drawn to the political role of education in the larger scheme of oppression of Blacks in America. I have come to understand what people in power have long known—education can be used both to oppress and to liberate. Ideas are indeed powerful things.

I further came to understand that America's colonization of Blacks employed the textbook as often as the bullet. As Carter G. Woodson declared, when you can control a person's thinking you can control that person. Colonial education in America was designed to control, pacify, and socialize subject people. The education of Black Americans has always been inextricably connected to state politics and the labor market.

Substantial accounts of Black education in America have been written in the twentieth century. Among them, the following stand out: James D. Anderson's *The Education of Blacks in the South, 1860–1935* (1988), Kenneth King's *Pan Africanism and Education: A Study of Race Philanthropy and Education in the Southern States of America and East Africa* (1971), Henry Bullock's *A History of Negro Education in the South: From 1619 to Present* (1967), and Horace Mann Bond's *The Education of the Negro in the American Social Order* (1934). Additionally, the exhaustive volumes on Booker T. Washington edited by Louis Harlan et al. (1972) provide rich sources of information.

Anderson's (1988) work places Black education into a broader context. He demonstrates that industrial education fulfilled the objectives of those who wanted an orderly South. Anderson's themes on the politics and power surrounding Black education in the crucial Reconstruction and post-Reconstruction periods in the South represent rich historical inquiry. He has helped frame the issues and problems addressed in this book.

This book explores the body of ideas that undergird social, economic, racial, and educational beliefs about Black education in America; it is an ideological study. The objective is to investigate the ideological construction of colonial Black education by examining the views, politics, and practices of the White architects that funded, created, and refined it. A body of ideas may serve to rationalize and justify any political, educational, or economic system, but ideology helps *organize* our world and explains it in relation to power and vested interests.

The White architects represented great power and wealth. Most often they stood for the interests of northern capital and White southern expediency. Colonial education in the South must never be confused with the educational agenda of Blacks in the South. In fact, these agendas conflicted.

This book began with my (1986) doctoral dissertation on colonial education in Nigeria, West Africa. In the course of that research, I discovered that many of the individuals, missionary societies, philanthropic foundations, and other purveyors of colonial education in Africa were American or tied to America. After considerable reading, I decided on a more in-depth examination of this history.

Over the years I have become fascinated by biography. Beyond the events and accomplishments of a life, however, I have become interested in the ideas of important, and not so important, people who have shaped the social, political, economic, and cultural arrangements of our world. Thus, the biographies I present are of a certain variety. They explore the subjects' lives in order to tell the story of their ideas and activities. I have tried to capture the ideological and sociopolitical environments in which my subjects, the architects, were shaped. In turn, I have tried to exhibit their deeds and misdeeds.

The subjects were chosen because of their importance to Black education. These people were in an important place at an important time. They were all part of a hegemonic order striving to (re)organize a nation torn by civil war, regionalism, and strife. All were forward-seeking people, that is, leaders, who understood that their actions would have great consequences. All understood that "solving" the "Negro question" was the key to reuniting the country and facilitating the opening of the new corporate industrial order for the twentieth century. All demonstrated extraordinary social, political, and personal skills.

This group in no way exhausts the considerable list of architects of Black education, but this is an ideologically representative group. I have tried to profile individuals whose roles and impact have been obscured in the education literature. Until the past few years, Thomas Jesse Jones had escaped the examination befitting his major role in twentieth-century Black education. Recent dissertations and articles cited in this work have reversed that omission. William Baldwin and Robert Ogden likewise have not been given significant treatment in educational or curriculum literature. Despite his voluminous writings and major presence in Columbia University's sociology department, Franklin H. Giddings is almost never mentioned in critical educational discourses. Most of the scholarship on J. L. M. Curry explores his role as a confederate leader and ideologue.

Well-known Black educator Booker T. Washington worked in league with the White architects and has a shadowy presence in virtually every aspect of this inquiry; however, I did not give him exhaustive attention. Washington has been researched and re-researched extensively and is a frequent topic in educational history and inquiry.

In researching this work, I relied on both primary and secondary sources. The primary sources allowed me to get firsthand narratives. To this end, lengthy quotations occasionally are included in the text. In some cases, these quotations appear in print for the first time. In other instances, they are provided to offer in-depth understanding of the individual's outlooks and vision.

Secondary sources draw from a treasury of historical, sociological, and "critical" scholarship, which has been accumulating since the turn of the twentieth century. This work might be viewed as the continuation of the appraisals begun by DuBois, Woodson, and others. The book is organized to connect the general to the particular, the political to the personal, and the theoretical to the practical. However, it is not presented in a strict chronological sequence. It is hoped that a broad understanding emerges of overlapping lives and institutions of a period.

## OVERVIEW OF BOOK

The book consists of two parts. Part I, Chapters 1 and 2, provides background, conceptual framework, and perspective. As a practicing curriculum sociologist, I have accumulated a treasury of experiences. Like any investigator, I employ certain tools of inquiry. My tools include sociohistorical, conflict, and critical analysis. I attempt to explain phenomena within a contextual framework. I believe history and social development proceed dialectically, where thesis confronts antithesis and position confronts opposition. Conflict, contradiction, and change are universal. Some contradictions are irreconcilable; others are not. All societal interactions occur in a context of power and vested interests.

Chapter 1 introduces and sets up the study and provides a conceptual framework within which to understand the story/stories. The chapter situates the construction of colonial Black education within the unfolding political context. That context finds a country in transition from regionalism and agrarianism to a mighty corporate-industrial state. Within this drama, power was shifting and new conforming institutions were being forged. An ideology likewise was evolving to rationalize the new social stratifications and arrangements. These new ideas, theorems, and propositions were both funded and constructed by corporate philanthropists and the theorists sympathetic to their cause. The ideas undergirding colonial Black education were brokered in the process.

This same chapter establishes the explanatory power of critical social science to explore colonial education. The terms *political sociology* and *political economy* are used to methodologically frame the inquiry. Political sociology allows the interrogation of human actions and interactions within the context of power. Power is viewed in terms of wealth, property, access, inheritance, and privilege. Political economy connects the analysis of power to wealth. It suggests that unequal wealth fosters unequal power. Furthermore, political economy joins the discussion of race to issues of labor expropriation, the wage system, and the distribution of wealth. The presumption is that vested interests frequently explain actions. Beyond power, political sociology allows the investigation of both societal and individual ideology in the posing and opposing of ideas. A central thesis of this work holds that the study of ideology provides a framework to explain a social system.

Finally, Chapter 1 concludes by raising some of the broader questions and issues underlying this study: How is great wealth wielded in the public sphere? How are political, educational, and racial ideas brokered in our society? What, in the final analysis, does it mean to have private interests making public policy? Who benefits? How have corporate foundations influenced both education and the racial politics of this country since the Civil War?

Chapter 2 provides an overview of the popular "scientific" racism of the nineteenth and early twentieth centuries, which provided the intellectual rationale for the modern social sciences and eventually a Black educational system. Notions of "color coding," skull measuring, and classification dominated views of race and intelligence. Beginning with the work of Linnaeus (1735/1964), the chapter reviews two centuries of race theorizing. In the process "science," medicine, politics, and economics converged to create the big lie of genetic and hereditary intelligence, the roots of the genetic and pathological arguments on racial inferiority.

Part II consists of the seven biographies. The aforementioned analyses are embedded in each chapter.

Chapter 3 examines the life and ideas of General Samuel Chapman Armstrong, founder of Hampton Institute, and prominent architect of colonial education in America. While he was Principal at Hampton, Armstrong wrote extensively on matters of race, education, politics, and national unity. He was among the first to understand and articulate "solutions" for a country wracked by war, regionalism, and uncertainty.

This discussion seeks to challenge the notion that Armstrong was a humble military man who became a schoolmarm. Armstrong's ideas and activities, in fact, were of enormous consequence. His construction of accommodationist politics and education provided a program of national salvation. It was Armstrong who demonstrated that solving the "Negro question" was the key to national reconciliation. Armstrong is cast as far more than an educator. He was a colonial theorist, social engineer, nation builder, and patriot of the highest order.

Chapter 4 explores the role of Dr. Franklin H. Giddings in shaping social theory underlying Black education. Seldom included in educational histories, Giddings was one of America's preeminent sociologists at the turn of the twentieth century. As the first full-time professor of sociology in the United States,

Giddings helped infuse social studies and educational discourses with the principles of "scientific sociology" and White supremacy. Giddings was the quintessential curricularist, providing ideological propositions for citizenship education. His work was applied to the education concocted for minorities and immigrants.

Giddings is cast as an important theorist. He was both a mentor of Dr. Thomas Jesse Jones and a powerful intellectual influence in the social science community. Beyond social scientist and educator, he was an important ideologist in the architecture of Black education.

Chapter 5 offers a look at the powerful Phelps Stokes family and their philanthropic activities. In the early part of the twentieth century, the Phelps Stokes Fund was perhaps the most influential force in funding and administering Black education. This family bridged the gap between missionary and corporate philanthropy. In the process, it contributed to the ideologies of both. Anson, Olivia, James, and other members of the Phelps Stokes family provided first the abolitionist then the "liberal" outlook to colonial Black education. This philanthropy might be seen as a leading foundation for Black education at a critical juncture in the country's history.

Chapter 6 describes the life and work of Dr. Thomas Jesse Jones, who is in many ways the centerpiece of this book. During his life, Jones was settlement house worker, federal government employee, Hampton professor, theologian, sociologist, and, most important, corporate foundation administrator. In his many roles, Jones was perhaps, for a time, the most important White educator of Blacks in the country and, ultimately, in the world. Recent papers, dissertations, and discussions of Jones have finally situated him within the discourse. Chapter 6 not only deconstructs Jones's views but also provides a comprehensive investigation into his background, activities, and monumental historical impact.

Chapter 7 provides a glimpse of the educational activities of the ubiquitous Rockefeller family and its special role in the education of Black Americans. As the keepers and protectors of a great deal of America's wealth, this family set about to guarantee that the country could reunite and move forward into the industrial age. Given the family's extensive involvement in business, it is remarkable that members dedicated so much energy to Black education. The establishment by the Rockefellers of the General Education Board and their considerable funding activities signify how important Black education was as a political and policy initiative. This chapter illuminates the efforts of a private family to influence public policy.

Chapter 8 takes a look at the role of influential northern businessmen Robert Ogden and William Baldwin in the construction of Black education. Both individually and in tandem, they sat on every important policy-making board concerned with the education of Black people. Their participation highlights the involvement of the corporate community in these activities and demonstrates the monumental importance of Black education to the corporate and, ultimately, the political communities.

Finally, Chapter 9 represents an original, extensive discussion of Jabez Curry within the context of Black education. Long known as the arch segregationist of his time, this northern-educated, flamboyant orator and scholar of the Confederacy was an important actor in Black education and segregation. Curry represented the ultimate southern voice of reason upon finding that no other viable option existed for the South. His words and deeds were indispensable to the rebuilding of the nation.

Chapter 9 also presents a sidebar discussion on the role of George Peabody, who established the first major corporate philanthropy concerned with Black education. It was his Peabody Fund that allowed Curry and others to mold and ideologically control this undertaking that would influence millions of lives.

## POLITICIZING BLACK EDUCATION

The "Negro question" is at the very heart of American history and American educational history. The new and experimental country called America had no idea how to organize its disparate populations or its newfound wealth. The accumulations of nearly 250 years of unpaid wages to slaves, and another 100 years of sharecropping, provided America the financial reserves to industrialize and become a (the) world power. No other country was in that position at that time.

The establishment of Black education was much more than teaching the ABCs to little children of color. It was a political proposition. Black education helped define and forge the race relations that shaped the entire twentieth century and beyond.

This examination of the White architects of Black education will demonstrate that they operated in a politically driven environment. They were political operatives as much as or more than educators and curricularists. Their curriculum for accommodationist education evolved to be as much a primer for citizenship and obedience as for school subjects.

# PART I

## *Historical Context*

# 1

## Toward a Political Sociology
## of Black Education

A CENTURY AGO, sociologist Emile Durkheim raised the question of how societies hold together. That question is more relevant than ever in a world of conflicting interests, increasing maldistribution of wealth, and retreat to the tribalism and
ethnic loyalties of a bygone era. Durkheim, in his groundbreaking work, *Education and Sociology* (1899), attempted to explore and understand the role of education in the emerging and complex twentieth-century world. He understood that
education operated in a social context and fulfilled a social mission. Education,
he declared, was an eminently "social" thing.

Building upon Durkheim's thesis, in modern society, education is also an
eminently political thing. A central thesis of this book suggests that education,
that is, schooling, in the modern corporate-industrial society has emerged as
central to state political and ideological management. Political and ideological
management involves ideation, which in this context means the imparting and
reinforcement of ideas and values that support the current economic and social
order.

## IDEOLOGY AND EDUCATION IN THE INDUSTRIAL ORDER

Ideology is not left to chance. Modern industrial society sought out ideas that
supported it (Wade, Thompson, & Watkins, 1994). Hence, ideology becomes the
currency of those dominating the culture. Ideology is imparted subtly and made
to appear as though its partisan views are part of the "natural order." The dominating
ideology is a product of dominant power.

Recognizing the importance of examining politics and ideology in education
and the school curriculum, I and those whose work I draw from are guided by
several questions: What meaning does education (schooling) have in the modern industrial world? How has the curriculum been brokered? By whom? What
political ideology is reflected in the school curriculum? What racial, class, and
gender ideology is associated with what political outlooks? What is "Black

education"? What are its origins, purposes, and outlooks? Who were the architects of Black education? What has been the historical significance of Black education?

The dynamics of power, control, racial subservience, and class conflict shape and construct education, particularly the curriculum, politically and ideologically. In recent decades education scholars have looked more closely at the role of ideology in the curriculum. Michael Apple (1979), who has been in the forefront of this inquiry, writes:

> We need to examine critically not just how a student acquires more knowledge (the dominant question in our efficiency minded field), but why and how particular aspects of the collective culture are presented in school as objective, factual knowledge. How, concretely, may official knowledge represent ideological configurations of the dominant interests in a society? How do schools legitimate these limited and partial standards of knowing as unquestioned truths? (p. 14)

Further,

> We have tended to perceive knowledge as a relatively neutral "artifact." We have made of it a psychological "object" or a psychological "process" (which it is in part, of course). In so doing, however, we have nearly totally depoliticized the culture that schools distribute. Yet there is a growing body of curriculum scholars and sociologists of education who are taking much more seriously the questions of "whose culture?" "What social group's knowledge?" and "In whose interest is certain knowledge (facts, skills, and propensities and dispositions) taught in cultural institutions like schools?" (p. 16)

Education has been romanticized to the extent that, like religion, it appears disconnected from the world of power, partisanship, and the shaping of the social order. Humankind's thirst for knowledge, like the quest to understand its existence, provides the ideal terrain for this to occur. Organized education, much like organized religion, has long been influenced by the forces of the power structure, the state, and those with an ideological agenda.

In the realm of political sociology, Marxian and radical theorists explain that the predominating economic system greatly influences and shapes the culture, ideas, and institutions that surround it. Societal institutions thus are tied to the means and relationships of production. Ideas and institutions that do not conform to the dominant relationships of production receive little or no support within the system. Thus, the culture of individualism and property rights is inextricably connected to capitalist society. Institutions of the state, of association, and of worship, to be sanctioned, must conform to the economic base. This is not to deny that oppositionist cultures and institutions emerge; they simply do not receive the support of the established order.

Education thus becomes a most important component within modern society. It includes both a developmental and a sociopolitical mission. Developmentally, industrial and technological society requires a level of cognitive and intellectual performance not required in feudal and agrarian society. Socially and politically, those who hold power attempt to forge a society ideologically accepting of their economic and cultural agenda, which is often inimical to the vast majority who remain propertyless. Public education becomes a useful ideological tool in creating social consensus.

Students of capitalist education such as Bowles and Gintis (1976) explore reproduction theory. Reproduction theory holds that schools reproduce capitalist social relationships conforming to a base and superstructure framework. Liston, in his work *Capitalist Schools* (1988), examines Marxist and radical views of schools in the corporate order:

> Schools produce minimally skilled workers for wage labor, and these educational institutions educate workers to an ideology of compliance. . . . Basically, the premise is that schools are necessary elements in the reproduction of a capitalist economy. (p. 16)

Since schools perform an ideological function in modern society, it is important to understand what that ideology is. Issues and questions surrounding the education of Blacks date to 1619. Still, after nearly four centuries, the "Negro question" or "Negro problem" remains at the heart of the social and educational conundrum.

## On Race, Ethnicity, and Education in Early America

Following the European example of expansionism in the modern period, American policy evolved its own colonialism. This colonialism touched every aspect of social life. The educational program devised for minorities represented classical colonialism.

The seventeenth, eighteenth, and nineteenth centuries, a time of nation building, witnessed the great aligning and defining of people in the emerging American polyglot. The free settlers, mostly European, stood in stark contrast to the steadily arriving boatloads of African slaves and other people of color who profoundly affected the future of America's racial and ethnic landscape. America became an uneasy mix of immigrants alongside colonized and dominated minority groups (Blauner, 1972). The challenges of the frontier, differentiated labor, and slavery became significant issues.

Architects of colonial, racial, and ethnic ideology, such as the respected Dr. Benjamin Rush, declared American Indians as unclean and "strangers to the obligations both of morality and decency" (Takaki, 1990, p. xx). Further, Indians were not only "too lazy to work but even to think" (p. xx). As for Blacks, Rush associated their skin color with leprosy, wrote of their "morbid insensitivity of the nerves" (p. xx), and repeatedly proclaimed them diseased.

During the nineteenth century, America's racial and ethnic attitudes hardened. More than 2 centuries of slavery, territorial conquest, and international isolation fed notions of White supremacy, ethnocentrism, and great-nation chauvinism. The concept of morality came to be associated with the triumphant White American character. Morality recurred as a defining theme within ethnic literature. Amazingly, social scientists and educators alike came to utilize morality as a defining quality of race.

## American Slavery and Education: A Political and Economic Glimpse

Although much has been written about slavery, too few scholars have emphasized slavery's contribution to the emergence of America's rise to world power. We all know of the cruelty, displacement, family breakup, and cultural genocide accompanying the "peculiar institution" (Stampp, 1956), but we don't always explore its political economy.

America's slavery was inextricably connected to commodity production and international trade. The "cotton kingdom" created in the American South catapulted America to a place of great prominence in the developing industrial Western world. Countless millions and billions of dollars in unpaid wages provided accumulations of wealth unprecedented in human history. American slavery should be viewed not simply as a cruel and inhuman drama, but as the foundation for nineteenth- and twentieth-century industrial capitalism.

Beyond its role in capital accumulation, southern slavery also forged social and racial relationships for the next several centuries. Shaped and entrenched during the epoch of slavery were notions of economic and social privilege standing alongside racial subservience.

Helping to perpetuate this subservience was the fact that most states had no provisions for educating slaves prior to the Civil War. In fact, education was anathema to the interests of keepers of chattel slaves. Pronouncements that people of African descent were incapable of formal learning, masked plans for cultural genocide.

Efforts at slave education consisted most often of self-help or assistance from abolitionist-minded Christian humanists (Anderson, 1988). Various missionary societies and similarly inclined families also contributed to the education of slaves.

Henry Bullock (1967) describes slave education that resulted unintentionally. Favored slaves were drawn into the business practices of the plantation, such as record keeping, purchasing provisions, and so on. Bullock uses the phrase "slave aristocracy" to refer to those slaves who were educated in the course of their enslavement. Booker T. Washington called the plantation an industrial school, suggesting that the slaves received a kind of education by virtue of their lives and work.

Efforts to expand slavery throughout the country were unacceptable to many northern farmers and wage laborers alike. Reconciliation between the systems of slavery in the South and emergent industrialization in the North was not possible through negotiation. The coming conflict determined the destiny of chatteled Black Americans.

## The Civil War and Beyond: Toward a New Industrial Order

Without question the Civil War was the defining event in the shaping of industrial America. It represented at once an end to outdated agriculturalism, semifeudal social relationships in the South, divisive regional governments, and international isolation.

The victory of the North created the conditions needed for northern industrialists to expand without political opposition from southern planters. The "robber baron" capitalists now found a huge national market in which to expand their fledging oil, steel, textile, and railroad industries. They organized commerce within the structures of corporations, banks, holding companies, interlocking directorates, and trusts. The business of America truly became business.

The amount of wealth expropriated by business magnates around this time was unprecedented. Cornelius Vanderbilt, for example, had accumulated a personal fortune of $105 million at the time of his death in 1889. His heirs soon increased that figure sevenfold with investments in 73 transportation (mostly railroad) and industrial corporations. Jay Gould of Union Pacific Railroad had a fortune exceeding $50 million in the 1870s. John Blair, founder of Lackawanna Coal & Iron Co., had a fortune of between $50 and $100 million by 1899, as well as interests in Lackawanna Railroad.

Many among the new elite established corporate philanthropies, became patrons of the arts, or built great monuments. Among those were philanthropist Russell Sage, who accumulated more than $100 million. Leland Stanford, a U. S. senator from California earning $5,000 a year, possessed railroad and real estate holdings earning $1 million annually, and built a university. J. P. Morgan had banking, railroad, industrial, and mineral interests exceeding $1 billion before the turn of the twentieth century. John D. Rockefeller (and his Standard Oil Trust) was also worth more than $1 billion in his time. He too built a university to rival the great learning institutions of Europe. Andrew Carnegie's steel and other investments placed his fortune near the $1 billion range (Myers, 1936).

Although not all of the new elite were visible in public life, most supported a reordering of society, a redistribution of wealth, and a new economic power base in society. Those who got directly involved in political ideation, such as Rockefeller, Carnegie, and others, most often spoke for the new class of plutocrats. The subsequent corporate ordering of society would subjugate and/or influence the legislative, cultural, and social dynamics of the entire nation.

A major test for the new industrialists was their approach to race relations in general, along with a clear policy on what to do with millions of newly freed slaves. Among the options were isolation, deportation, or integration. In many ways the realities of the South and the aftermath of the Civil War provided answers. Northern industrialists quickly and expeditiously determined that their dominance could proceed without disturbing the racial arrangements of the South. Reconstruction served the historical destiny of northern dominance.

## Reconstruction and the Education of Black Americans

Historians have long viewed Reconstruction as a period of adjustment during which the South licked its wounds and the North moved to establish its political and economic supremacy. The temporary "democratization" of the South in which Black Americans participated in the electoral and political processes was unquestionably part of the new adjustment.

But Reconstruction was more than a period in which Blacks voted and elected representatives to high office for the first time. It was also a turning point in the dynamics of governance and control. The heavily invested industrialists left nothing to chance. They asserted and inserted themselves into the cultural, intellectual, and political unfolding of the country.

As northern corporate industrialists emerged as the undisputed power brokers of the period, they also came to be concerned with the ideological shaping of the then-fragmented population. Ideology would be as important as order in the post–Civil War period. With the future of the country hanging in the balance, the industrialists turned considerable attention to education.

The growing popularity of mass schooling, combined with the demand of Blacks for social participation, helped highlight the dialogue on educating Blacks. In 1868 federal legislation mandated the establishment of the Freedman's Bureau to facilitate the transition of the newly freed slaves into the social life of the country. The YMCA, philanthropies, and an assortment of missionary societies soon joined Freedman's Bureau schools in establishing rudimentary education for Blacks.

Fortunately for northern industrialists and power wielders, missionary society-sponsored Black education was not inimical to their interests. Church-sponsored missionary societies had always been interested in spiritual humanitarianism. By the time of Reconstruction their views on education were well articulated and firm. In general, missionary education drew on the tradition of humanism. Notions of altruism, free expression, salvation, and the unfettered development of the individual undergirded missionary views.

Leaders in the missionary movement such as Thomas Morgan, Henry Morehouse, and Malcolm MacVicar wanted civil and political rights for Blacks, but envisioned social progress within the emerging industrial order. Such leaders would help frame a discourse for Black education. Booker T. Washington, who supported industrial capitalism, held out hope for its potential eventually to include Blacks.

Missionary societies were uniquely situated to provide the foundation for a system of Black education. They were part of the cultural and religious evolution of the South, they accepted an evolutionary view of societal change, they espoused the paternal social and racial relations of the South, they accepted the emergent corporate-industrial economic arrangements as modernization, and they were willing and eager participants in educating minorities. Although accepting of America's economic order, the missionary leaders were fervent believers in education as a tool for racial advancement.

The formative years of Black education would witness an all-out effort to build a united nation with seemingly irreconcilable forces. As the industrialists involved themselves in educating minorities, they inherited safe ideological antecedents on which to build. That framework came not only from the missionary societies, but also from other civic-minded groups. The reform and charity movements contributed to this body of safe reform, that is, reform without revolt.

## REFORM AND CHARITY IN RACE PHILANTHROPY

While emerging corporate philanthropies represented the most deliberate and well-funded agencies of race philanthropy and race curriculum ideation, assorted individuals, movements, and agencies also contributed to views and outlooks both on race and education, and on race education. Although not directly involved in policy making, these forces helped shape reform ideology for twentieth-century America. Effective reform outlooks were needed to provide a framework with which to address the vexing problems of race and economic class disparities plaguing the fragile country.

Again, the newly empowered corporate industrialists understood that the post–Civil War period would be of immense consequence in forging the new order. Prominent historian Henry Steele Commanger (1957) identified the "problems of agriculture, urban life, slums, trusts, business, political corruption and the maldistribution of wealth" (p. 245) as the country's glaring maladies following the Civil War.

Thus, political, civic, charity, and reform organizations concerned with the democratic shaping of society thrust themselves into social issues. While these organizations did not reach full maturity until the turn of the twentieth century, their scattered views took shape following Reconstruction. Although not always directly focused on education, these groups understood its growing importance. Within such groups, individuals interacted with, or influenced, educators. Organizations such as the National Municipal League, along with various charity groups, advocated concepts for civic education, which became connected to minority education.

## Municipal Reform Movements

The post–Civil War industrial period found a population shifting to large urban areas. The burgeoning municipalities were hotbeds of graft, corruption, and ethnic discrimination. Large-scale corruption and favoritism, combined with the proletarianization of the new masses, produced schisms unattractive to many. Indignation grew into protest. The populist, Progressive, and labor movements represented the crystallization of mass movements for government action, civil service reform, tax fairness, wealth redistribution, labor rights, and an end to graft and corruption (Meyers, Cawelti, & Kern, 1969). Underlying these movements was a fear of big wealth and its power to corrupt.

The mass movement of the disempowered emerged alongside a movement of civic-minded reformers who understood that the new industrial democracy had to have broad-based support. It could be argued that this stratum of middle-class and professional reformers, totally sympathetic to the corporate ordering of society, helped democratize a system in which avarice ruled over compassion. A view of some social theorists, such as Dr. Thomas Jesse Jones, White sociologist and educator of minorities, discussed later, was that the profit system could be reconciled to social welfare. Jones and like-minded thinkers held that America could and must avoid establishing a self-absorbed and self-consumed aristocracy such as found in many European countries.

Michael Lybarger (1981) discusses how the municipal reform movement affected the school curriculum, especially social education. He notes that prior to the turn of the twentieth century, "over sixty organizations devoted to the reform of city government appeared" (p. 198). These organizations, typically named city club, civic federation, municipal league, reform league, and good government club, often considered education, especially civic education, an important concern. These civic reformers were both connected to and captured the attention of the social scientists and educators who would greatly shape the social science components of the school curriculum. Discussions of school curriculum, particularly civic education, were taking place before the turn of the twentieth century. Howerth's "A Programme for Social Study" (1897), which would influence the Hampton curriculum of vocational training for minorities, was widely discussed in civic clubs (Lybarger, 1981).

The themes of these early proposals for civic education focused more on good citizenship than on good government. The accompanying concepts were good character, health, sanitation, and the benefits of labor. The popularity and advocacy of civic education were evidenced in municipal clubs, scholarly journals, and academic organizations such as the American Social Science Association. Through overlapping memberships and outlooks, civic associations greatly affected the important Committee on Social Studies (U.S. Department of the Interior, 1916). Civic education was an important building block in the evolution of social studies education, which in turn was a building block for minority education.

## The Charity Movement

The municipal reform movement was not alone in its desire to create an efficient society in which broad masses would not feel alienated. Industrialization had created an economic polarization of monumental proportions. The new urban indigents could threaten the fragile industrial democracy.

Like the civic movement, the charity people had a definite political ideology. They were believers in America's corporate industrialism who feared that traditional charity created dependence. Lybarger (1981) summarizes their views:

> First, indiscriminate and ill-thought-out almsgiving had attracted beggars, drunks, and criminals to the cities in order to secure money. Second, with so many charitable agencies providing aid, it was possible for cheats to secure help from two or more. This, according to one scandalized observer, tempted workers to a life of idleness, thus siding with labor against employers. Finally, there existed no effective means to help philanthropists distinguish between the deserving and undeserving poor; or deal with . . . forces of experienced and crafty pauperism. (p. 265)

The charity movement had its ideological roots in both long-standing missionary outlooks and the populist discontent following Reconstruction. While many in the charity movement were socialists or otherwise situated left of center, they did not challenge American industrialism at the root.

Among the most prominent individuals associated with the charity movement was Jane Addams. Her work at Hull House, preparing immigrants for life in America, is well known. Other prominent charity movement actors included Josephine Lowell, James Barnard, and Clarence Kingsley.

It can be argued that the charity movement arose in part because of government inaction during economic downturns. In addition, the charities were concerned about government corruption. The charity movement held a kind of Social Darwinist view of the poor, attributing poverty to inadequate self-esteem, ambition, and character. Again, there was little criticism of the social and economic system in the charity movement.

Key individuals in the charity movement who embraced the charity ideology strongly influenced both social studies education and the Hampton curriculum of vocational training, discussed in Chapter 3. Educators and social theorists such as William Arey, James Barnard, and Clarence Kingsley were important members of the Committee on Social Studies. This Committee, which published its seminal report in 1916, generally is credited with launching the modern social studies curriculum in America. All three men were associated with the charity movement. Barnard actually was employed by the New York Charity Organization Society. Additionally, Thomas Jesse Jones, author of the *Hampton Social Studies* (1906–08) and leading figure in Black education, was employed in the New York settlement houses that were rooted in the charity mentality. Themes found in early civics/social studies education, such as health, sanitation, and Americanizing the "other," soon would be noted in the curriculum of Black education.

Chicago and New York were sites of extensive settlement house activity at the end of the nineteenth and beginning of the twentieth century. Cloaked behind a veil of altruism, the settlement house movement in many ways epitomized the ideology of corporate-industrial charity. Settlement people heartily endorsed a laissez-faire role for the government. They believed that the less fortunate in society were idlers and/or feebleminded. Charity should be only temporary because to help such people would strain society's resources.

Leaders in the settlement houses in New York around Columbia University often articulated colonial views. Many graduate students and professors worked in and studied the houses. A regularly published periodical, the *University Settlement Bulletin*, voiced the views of professional workers. Perusal of the bulletins indicates that pejorative language such as "vagrant," "delinquent," "feebleminded," and "defective" was used regularly to describe clients of the settlement houses. One sample read:

> Incompetency in dealing with the tramp problem has thus far only fostered its growth. While vagrancy is as old as savagery, it would seem as if some uniform system would be adopted for limiting and ultimately extinguishing this evil. (1902, p. 289)

## CORPORATE PHILANTHROPY: MAKING PUBLIC POLICY

A closer look at the origins of the corporate philanthropies reveals early intentions to use them as political and ideological agencies. Edward H. Berman, who has done exhaustive research on foundation ideology, argues that influential philanthropies conform to and reinforce the values of the dominant order.

In *The Influence of the Carnegie, Ford, and Rockefeller Foundations on American Foreign Policy: The Ideology of Philanthropy* (1983), Berman writes:

> The major American foundations were established to accomplish certain ends in the heyday of capitalist accumulation. These included the stabilization of the rapidly evolving corporate and political order and its legitimation and acceptance by the majority of the American population; the institutionalization of certain reforms, which would serve to preclude the call for more radical structural change; and the creation through educational institutions of a worldwide network of elites whose approach to

governance and change would be efficient, professional, moderate, incremental, and nonthreatening to the class interests of those who, like Messrs. Carnegie, Ford, and Rockefeller, had established the foundations. The subsequent support by the foundations for various educational configurations both at home and abroad cannot be separated from their attempts to evolve a stable domestic polity and a world order amenable to their interests and the strengthening of international capitalism. (pp. 15–16)

Beyond utilization of the conventional electoral, legislative, and administrative avenues, the industrialists discovered they could give life to their ideas through grants-in-aid. Policy making through charity was certainly not a new idea. The church-affiliated missionary societies for years had utilized grants to fund programs they believed in. Partisanship and ideology were never far from those activities.

## Development of Race Philanthropy

The possibilities of using philanthropy for social engineering were inviting. The "Negro problem" was among the most vexing and urgent of the time. Politics would be at the heart of using the philanthropies to guarantee an orderly South and a compliant Black population. Race philanthropy now became an important vehicle.

Race philanthropy emerged by the 1880s as a major approach to policy making. It was quick, avoided the slow deliberative processes of law making, and could be expeditiously and unilaterally started and/or halted at will. Race philanthropy was ideally suited to educating Blacks as well as other minorities. The building and support of schools, the training of teachers, and, very important, the construction of curriculum could be accomplished handily by corporate philanthropies.

Anderson's "Philanthropic Control over Private Black Higher Education" (1980) describes the growing involvement of private corporate financial influence in Black education. He argues that industrial philanthropies entertained questions of educating Blacks "for participation in the political economy of the New South" (in Arnove, 1980, p. 147).

Anderson describes the division of labor between the missionary societies and industrial philanthropies in the post–Civil War period and then follows the ascendance of industrialists as the leading funding source. He notes that from the 1860s to 1915 the missionary societies, best represented by the American Missionary Association, Methodist Episcopal Freedman's Aid Society, Presbyterian Board of Missions for the Freedman, and American Baptist Home Mission Society, established more than 30 colleges that enrolled over 60% of the Black students attending colleges. Among the better known of these schools are Talladega, Atlanta University, Clark, Spelman, Morehouse, and Fisk.

While the missionary societies exercised ownership of such colleges, corporate philanthropies such as the Slater Fund, Rosenwald Fund, Jeannes Foundation, Peabody Education Fund, Carnegie Corporation, and others provided financial support. As the power and wealth of these foundations grew, so did their influence. By World War 1 the industrial philanthropies had supplanted missionary societies as the leading influence in Black education.

Throughout this inquiry, evidence supports the argument that corporate philanthropies did not simply provide dollars but indeed offered a political and ideological platform. Their program was one of classic colonialism adapted to the southern United States. This adaptation, accommodationism, would dominate education, the curriculum, and social policy for decades.

## Looking Back at the New Philanthropy: Position and Opposition

Examining nineteenth-century foundations, such as Rockefeller and Phelps Stokes, offers a chance for reflection on the twentieth-century philanthropic movement in general. Situating the new philanthropies within American society is important because of their tremendous impact. Elected by no one, these agencies wielded government-like power. Accountable only to themselves, they were private entities making sweeping educational and public policy. Because they could totally finance and administer projects, their actions had the effect of law. No twentieth-century para-statal or nongovernment organization has enjoyed such influence.

The new foundations achieved their objectives. They became idea brokers and culture makers in a world where ideology is constructed. Their promoted views on capitalism, education, race, labor, and social change became a permanent fixture in the nation's social and political culture. They successfully "objectified" partisan outlooks so as to make them appear natural, ordained, and organic. No societal force since has had the resources or will to challenge corporate-philanthropic ideology.

The foundations have intervened in the most sensitive areas of American life. Sharp criticism has come from academics and the left alike. Critics have examined the motives, activities, and personalities of the philanthropists. Some scholarship, for example, Berman (1983), has shown extraordinary connections between the largest foundations and the highest levels of government. Berman (1983) chronicles how Cold Warriors such as Dean Rusk, Robert Strange McNamara, McGeorge Bundy, and many others came directly from the corporate-philanthropic community to government.

We need to ask, why education? An important issue for students and critics of twentieth-century foundations has been the choice of education for their gifts. Foundations became active at a time when government extended very little assistance to human services. Overcrowded cities cried out for sanitation facilities, roads, hospitals, and the like. The issue of where foundations positioned themselves took on great social consequence.

Lindeman's early study, *Wealth and Culture* (1936), concludes that the foundations had jointly committed to focus their activities on education. He found that between 1921 and 1930, 43% of all foundation gifts went to education, followed by 30% to health issues. Of the money earmarked for education, a significant amount went to higher education.

Critics, particularly on the left, have argued that philanthropists consciously identified schools as sensitive arenas where social ideology was transmitted. The objective was to support a social ideology that would be popularized. The philanthropists needed to propagate and reinforce a social ideology favorable to the corporate capitalist economy and culture. Arnove (1980) points to the Italian cultural Marxist Antonio Gramsci, as summarized by Michael Apple's explanation:

> For Gramsci symbolic and cultural control—hegemony—is as critical as overt political and economic interest and manipulation in enhancing the power of dominant groups; thus, the ideological structures and meanings that organize our everyday lives in schools and elsewhere become prime elements in any explanation of how an unequal society maintains itself.
>
> The cultural hegemony exercised by dominant groups in a society defines in the words of Thompson, "the limits of what is possible" and "inhibits the growth of alternative horizons and expectations." . . . intellectuals and schools were crucial to the development of consensus in society, to the rationalization and legitimation of a given social order. Cultural hegemony mitigated the necessity for the State to use its coercive apparatus to control groups which might otherwise be disaffected. This concept serves as a useful tool for examining the centrality, for foundations, of educational investments. Education—and higher education, in particular—has been the primary target of foundation funding activities. (pp. 2–3)

Early philanthropists could be viewed as power brokers who were driven to intervene in the state's marketplace of ideas (Arnove, 1980). Absent their influence, alternative ideas might have gained in popularity. Ideologically, foundations sought to justify the corporate ordering of society with its colossal divisions of wealth. Capitalism and colonial education had to be presented as though they were natural, inevitable, rational, and optimal. The existing social order need only be touched up and refined around the edges.

Inextricably connected to the new corporate order were the interrelated critical questions of Blacks and the labor market. Resolving the "Negro question" meant Blacks could not be totally frozen out of social participation. They would have to be politically socialized, given hope, and given at least minimal access to survival. A compradore or middle class, as advocated by Booker T. Washington, of Black entrepreneurs, clergy, clerks, and teachers was indispensable to the new formula. The Black American population would have their preachers, morticians, insurance agents, postal employees, and beauticians in the segregated society. Simultaneously, capitalist labor economics required an abundance of semifeudal sharecropper labor alongside cheap semiskilled and skilled industrial labor. American industrialism would be built on the backs of Black labor.

Opposition to foundation activities quickly surfaced. Organized labor led by Samuel Gompers, socialist Morris Hillquit, assorted populists, and the congressionally created Commission on Industrial Relations, or Walsh Commission as it was known (Howe, 1980), led the early twentieth-century public opposition. Their claims were that unregulated foundations wielded too much power by virtue of their funding abilities.

Persistent criticism of foundations has pointed to their ideological bias. Arnove (1980) argues that the philanthropic foundations serve to maintain the social power of economic elites:

> Foundations like Carnegie, Rockefeller, and Ford have a corrosive influence on a democratic society; they represent relatively unregulated and unaccountable concentrations of power and wealth which buy talent, promote causes, and, in effect, establish an agenda of what merits society's attention. They serve as "cooling-out" agencies, delaying and preventing more radical, structural change. They help maintain an economic and political order, international in scope, which benefits the ruling-class interests of philanthropists and philanthropoids—a system which . . . has worked against the interests of minorities, the working class, and Third World peoples. (p. 16)

At the beginning of the twenty-first century, corporate foundations have become firmly entrenched in the nation's political and ideological processes. Their power has spread far beyond America's shores as they have exported their outlooks all over the globe. In many instances, their financial resources supersede the national wealth of the countries in which they are involved. They have refined an ideology on market economics, race, education, and social change. They represent power and wealth and the continuation of the status quo.

## EDUCATING BLACKS: POWER, POLITICS, AND REALITY

Politics was the noteworthy feature of educating Blacks after the Civil War. While Blacks had the desire to uplift themselves, join the social mainstream of American life (Tyack, 1974), and break forever with the bondage of the past, they lacked the resources to achieve either education or their larger freedom.

The industrialization and simultaneous reunification of the United States overshadowed and shaped all other events. The new corporate hegemonists needed to work toward their political and policy objectives. Among those objectives was a stable and orderly South where subservient wage labor and debt farming or sharecropping would provide the livelihood for Black Americans.

The potentially volatile issue of race relations was of primary concern to the industrialists. The practical decision not to interfere in long-standing racial relations served the North well. The conquering of the South could be mollified with the continuation of racial and social privilege. Accommodationism best described post–Civil War race relations in the South. Blacks must learn their "place" in the new industrial order.

Accommodationism dictated that Blacks accept the world the way it was. Existing race relations were simply part of the natural order. Associated with this brand of accommodationism was the notion of evolution. Race relations would gradually change, presumably for the better, if Blacks were willing to remain within the boundaries of "acceptable" behavior.

The politics and ideology of accommodationism shaped the sponsored education of Blacks in the United States. Hampton Institute, Virginia, with its founder and leader General Samuel Armstrong, would become the testing ground and prototype for accommodationist education. Hampton, in many ways, represented the transition from charity-oriented liberalism to hard-edged, corporate-driven philanthropy.

While missionary education prior to the Civil War often aimed at Christianizing and civilizing, corporate philanthropic education had political objectives. The Black population had to be prepared ideologically and practically for their role in a new America.

# 2

# *"Scientific" Racism*

BEFORE WE BEGIN the story of America's architects of Black education, it may be useful to explore the body of "race theory" that preceded and evolved alongside Black education. Many colonial educators in America embraced the tenets of biological determinism as legitimate explanations for societal development.

The naked and brutal exploitation of people of color provided context for "color coding" and classifying. "Scientifically" rendering dark people as inferior helped justify and rationalize colonial plunder. If "proof" could demonstrate that nature rendered Whites superior, a ready-made explanation for social hierarchy could be established.

As world hegemony and power shifted from Europe across the Atlantic during the nineteenth century, America became the main locus of White supremacy. Its virulent brand of slavery outlasted all others. Long after most European countries abandoned slavery and the slave trade, the United States continued building both its economy and social order on the foundations of slave labor, exploited labor, and subservience. This economic base could not help but shape social ideology. By Reconstruction, a modern "sociology of race" was firmly embedded. Race influenced every aspect of America's social order. Moreover, it made its presence felt in both culture making and the culture makers (Takaki, 1990, 1994).

## AN OVERVIEW OF "SCIENTIFIC" RACISM

Scientism was an important theme in eighteenth-century intellectual life. Social scientists looked to quantification as they attempted to construct law-like assumptions about societal and human development. Issues surrounding race began to receive great attention.

Stephen Jay Gould's celebrated work *The Mismeasure of Man* (1981) offers a thorough discussion of the pre- and post-Darwinian movement to measure intelligence, classify races, and critically examine the genetic arguments that have influenced the social sciences for over 200 years.

He illustrates how the early "scientific" racists held two contrasting views on the origins of humankind. The monogenists believed in a single species of people originating from a single source. Locating the creationist story of Adam and Eve at the center of their theory, the monogenists believed human races had degenerated since earliest humankind. This degeneration led to differences in people that likely were caused by climate and environment. The polygenists, on the other hand, argued that human races were separate species. The polygenists believed that Blacks, for example, were simply a different species. By the early 1800s both monogenists and polygenists had developed views of racial inferiority. The then-emerging field of anthropology drew from the race literature of the period.

Notions of difference in the social order have long been a part of the Western intellectual tradition. These views can be found as early as in the writings of ancient Greeks, including Aristotle (trans. 1970). While space does not permit a complete historical examination, a look at important theories and theorists since the eighteenth century is useful in understanding "racial naturalism" and the emergence of "scientific" racism.

## The Father of "Scientific" Racism

The earliest significant intellectual racist was Arthur de Gobineau of France, although far too little public knowledge circulates about this seminal racist historical figure. Born on the outskirts of Paris in 1816, Gobineau was brought up in prosperous circumstances, which included extensive travel in Europe, exposure to the arts, and book learning. When he was in his early 20s, family connections and activities brought him in touch with discussions and individuals involved in politics and the arts. In 1840 he helped form a small society of young intellectuals called Les Scelti, or the elect. They discussed art, history, and literature, and were proponents of aristocracy.

In the mid-1840s Gobineau worked as a journalist and frequent contributor of political articles to a variety of journals. Soon he moved beyond French politics and wrote on issues of German regionalism and nationality. He favored the Prussian aristocracy in its expanding conflicts with the lower classes.

For the next several years, Gobineau wrote widely on a variety of topics, such as Christianity, the Renaissance, and philosophy. He struck up a relationship with Alexis de Tocqueville and both found their discussions intellectually rewarding. Support for aristocracy and for nationalism were common themes in Gobineau's writings. Soon he turned to an exploration of race theory.

The source of virtue was of interest to Gobineau. Christian doctrine had always linked virtue with faith. Questioning this notion, Gobineau began to associate virtue with bloodlines (Biddiss, 1970). He looked at the Aryans, northern Europeans, as he asserted that blood purity was responsible for their heroism and intellect. He asserted that racial integrity had to be maintained.

Gobineau's theoretical racism was articulated in his magnum opus, entitled *Essai sur l'inegalite des races humaines*, completed in 1854. In it, he wrote that the racial question overshadowed all other issues in history. The inequality of races explained all destinies. Of most significance to Gobineau was social decay, or social decline. He rejected social decline as the product of excesses or misgovernment. Rather, he insisted that it was the product of miscegenation between the races. He argued that tribes were unable to remain pure and virile when the mixture of blood has been introduced. He wrote:

> The human race in all its branches has a secret repulsion from the crossing of blood, a repulsion which in many branches is invincible, and in others is only conquered to a slight extent. Even those who most completely shake off the yoke of this idea cannot get rid of the few last traces of it; yet such peoples are the only members of our species who can be civilised at all. . . . Mankind lives in obedience to two laws, one of repulsion, the other of attraction; these act with different force on different peoples. The first is fully respected only by those races which can never raise themselves above the elementary completeness of the tribal life, while the power of the second, on the contrary, is the more absolute, as the racial units on which it is exercised are more capable of development. (in Biddiss, 1970, p. 116)

He further argued that all civilizations derive from the White race, especially the superior Aryan stock. Mankind is thus divided into races of unequal worth. Superior races are in a fight to maintain their position. Racial relationships then become the driving force in history.

He offered a hierarchy of race that influenced the next century and a half. At the top were the Caucasian, Semitic, and Japhetic peoples. The second, or Yellow, group consisted of the Altaic, Mongol, Finnish, and Tartar peoples. The lowest group was composed of the Hamites, or Blacks. He set out descriptions of each group.

White people were characterized by "energetic intelligence," great physical power, stability, inclinations to self-preservation, and a love of life and liberty. Their great weakness, according to Gobineau, was a susceptibility to cross-breeding. Asians were mediocre, lacked physical strength, and wished to live undisturbed. They could never create a viable civilization. Black people, the lowest of all, possessed energy and willpower but were unstable, unconcerned about the preservation of life, given to absolutes, and easily enslaved.

Theoretically, Gobineau developed a notion of racial determinism. He insisted racial determinism was objective and could be reduced to scientific law. His racial view of history meant that race had driven all events since the beginning of time. Race theory was more scientific than politics, morality, or state organization.

In *Essai* (1854/1967), Gobineau wrote about race and social order. He believed that civilization defined itself in the process of war, conquest, and migration. It was, however, these interactions that allowed miscegenation to occur. If unchecked, miscegenation would undo civilization.

For Gobineau, advanced status and civilization, such as possessed by Aryans, could survive only in a rigidly hierarchical order. An elite must totally dedicate itself to the maintenance of racial and social hierarchy, and use force and domination to maintain that social, racial, and economic organization. Society must not be disrupted by the popular classes or lower racial groups.

Gobineau, the "racial prophet" (Biddiss, 1970), was among the first to articulate a political sociology of race and racism forecasting social decline. His ideology helped frame a generation of "scientism" on questions of race and social development.

## Eighteenth-Century European and American Influences

In 1735, Carolus Linnaeus, the acclaimed biological taxonomist, was among the first (Ehrlich & Feldman, 1977; Gould, 1981; Tucker, 1994) to classify human beings by race. He used both skin color and personal characteristics for his typology. His essay *Systema Naturae* divided people into White, Black, Red, and Yellow. He found Whites to be innovative and of keen mind, while Blacks were lazy and careless. The notion that races exhibited different mental and moral traits became a central part of a new discourse.

German zoologist Ernst Haeckel, an early advocate of Darwinism, authored *Anthropogenie* in 1874. In this book he situated Blacks on an evolutionary tree below gorillas and chimpanzees. He hypothesized that individuals, in the course of development, relive their evolutionary history, that is, ontogeny recapitulates phylogeny. Building on this theme, race theorists such as D. G. Brinton (1890) argued that some races retained infantile traits rendering them inferior to others (Ehrlich & Feldman, 1977).

In 1781, Johann Friedrich Blumenbach, physiologist and founder of modern anthropology, added aesthetic judgments to race. He introduced the term *Caucasian*, as he considered White people as beautiful as the southern slopes of Mount Caucasus. For Blacks the pejorative term "oran-outangs" became popular, as it placed them in the realm of chimpanzees and monkeys. Thomas Jefferson used the term "oranootan" in his writings to describe Black men and even himself when he surrendered to his own passions (Takaki, 1990). Perhaps his dalliance with his slave Sally Hemmings was an example of such surrender.

In 1799, British surgeon Charles White added a new dimension to the race dialogue. He asserted that Blacks were a separate species, intermediate between Whites and apes (Tucker, 1994). His book, *An Account of the Regular Gradation in Man and in Different Animals and Vegetables and from the Former to the Latter*, argued that the feet, fingers, toes, legs, hair, cheekbones, skin, arm length, skull size, size of sex organs, and body odor placed Blacks closer to the animal kingdom, most notably apes.

Undergirding the writings of the natural scientists was the philosophical embrace of natural inequality, an Aristotelian idea that inequality was the foundation of the natural order (Tucker, 1994). Natural difference came to be viewed as hierarchical. Organisms and races could be rank-ordered. A central task of science came to be the ranking of living organisms. Colonialism, eighteenth-century slavery, and the exploitation of fertile and mineral-rich foreign lands provided economic and political context for the new pseudo-science to take hold.

These early "scientific" racists wrapped themselves in the robe of science. Charles White repeatedly declared his lack of enmity toward the Black race, claiming he sought only insight into nature.

## Expanding the Discourse: Medicine and Science

"Scientific" racism was reinforced and expanded when the established medical profession entered the field. Notions of anatomical, physiological, and psychological difference framed the medical inquiry.

Benjamin Rush, founding father, signer of the Declaration of Independence, and medical doctor, contributed to views of race and racial inferiority in the early period of the nation. As surgeon general in the Revolutionary Army and professor of medicine at the University of Pennsylvania, Rush had a national podium. Concerned with the survival of the young republic, he spoke out on questions of politics, morality, education, and race.

Rush examined the "savage" American Indians, claiming they were given to "uncleanness," "nastiness," "idleness," intemperance, stupidity, and indecency. By the early 1770s he was writing about Black Americans, slavery, and race relations. Intellectually and politically opposed to slavery, he nevertheless advocated a segregated society (Takaki, 1990).

He believed Blacks to be pathologically infected. Their coloration was disease-driven. In a paper delivered to the American Philosophical Society entitled "Observations Intended to Favor a Supposition That the Black Color of the Negroes Is Derived from the Leprosy" (1799), he presented views on Black "pathology." He argued that the big lip, flat nose, woolly hair, and Black skin were the characteristics of lepers. He also wrote about insensitive nerves, uncommon strength, and venereal desires. Blacks needed to be civilized and restored to morality and virtuosity through righteous living. As a political figure and doctor, Rush helped shape the culture of racism characterizing early America and evolving over the next 2 centuries.

Much of his medical practice involved work with the mentally ill, as he turned his attention to "diseases of the mind." His preoccupation with morality and virtue came to be joined with his exploration of mental disease. He began to insist that idleness, intemperance, masturbation, and sexual excess were associated with mental diseases (Takaki, 1990). His book, *Diseases of the Mind* (1812), presented "remedies" for these problems.

In the mid-nineteenth century, physicians such as Dr. John H. van Evrie (1853) offered a "scientific" justification of slavery. He wrote that dark-skinned people were diseased and unnatural and that Blacks possessed impeded locomotion, weakened vocal organs, coarse hands, hypersensitive skin, narrow longitudinal heads, narrow foreheads, and underdeveloped brains and nervous systems. van Evrie concluded that the aggregation of these traits translated into human inferiority. He asserted that even the animal kingdom recognized Negro inferiority and said that a hungry tiger was more likely to prey on Blacks than Whites.

Also writing on this topic in the 1850s was Dr. Samuel Cartwright, who chaired a committee to inform the Medical Association of Louisiana about the Black race. His *Report on the Diseases and Physical Peculiarities of the Negro Race* (1851) gained attention for its "scholarly" approach. It spoke of the insufficient supply of red blood, smaller brain, and excessive nervous matter found in the Negro. This combination of problems, wrote Cartwright, led to the "debasement of minds" in Blacks. The physical exercise provided by slavery would help increase lung and blood functions, according to Cartwright. Slaves, he argued, sometimes were afflicted with "drapetomania," a disease of the mind, making them want to run away. The prescription for "drapetomania," he argued, was care and kindness, but the whip should not be spared should kindness fail.

Dr. Edward Jarvis, a specialist in mental disorders and president of the American Statistical Association, wrote in 1844 that insanity for Blacks in the North was 10 times greater than in the South. He concluded that slavery had a salutary effect on Blacks, sparing them the problems that free self-acting individuals faced.

## Jefferson's *Notes*

President Thomas Jefferson again fits into the story on "scientific" racism. By 1822, this author of the Declaration of Independence and theorist on democracy and human liberty was the proud owner of 267 slaves. Although opposing slavery in his writings, Jefferson profited greatly from the labor he expropriated.

Jefferson accepted White superiority as gospel. His *Notes on the State of Virginia* (1781/1955) reveal his racial views. He wrote that the differences in the races were fixed and could be found in nature. He also wrote that Blacks were inferior in faculties of reason and imagination. Their intelligence was also at issue, as it was a consequence of their biological status. He dismissed slavery as a reason for impeded development, arguing that the Roman slaves made intellectual contributions. It could not be slavery; hence, Blacks were simply a "distinct" race:

> In general, their existence appears to participate more of sensation than reflection. To this must be ascribed their disposition to sleep when abstracted from their diversions, and unemployed in labor. An animal whose body is at rest, and who does not

reflect, must be disposed to sleep of course. Comparing them by their faculties of memory, reason, and imagination, it appears to me that in memory they are equal to whites; in reason much inferior, as I think one could scarcely be found capable of tracing and comprehending the investigations of Euclid; and that in imagination they are dull, tasteless, and anomalous. (Jefferson, 1781/1955, p. 139)

Jefferson accepted the discourse on morals and passions then popularized by Puritan dogma. The inferior Blacks were unable to control their libido and other passions. With this disposition, they could not be allowed participation in the new American society. Jefferson went beyond segregation, advocating removal of Blacks from the American landscape and their return to Africa.

The race literature of the 1830s–1850s was politically inspired and statistically questionable, as there was a great need to defend slavery in the course of establishing the racial politics of the country (Tucker, 1994). Two things became clear by 1850: First, widely respected scientists had joined the investigation on race and nature, and second, the geographical and ideological flavor of the discourse was becoming more American (Tucker, 1994).

Fueled by a fervor from public figures, an American identity and chauvinism emerged. Ralph Waldo Emerson, for example, pleaded that the United States free itself intellectually from European, old-world influences. Nationalism increasingly influenced theorizing on scientific racism. What was emerging was an American school of anthropology (Gould, 1981) or perhaps an American school of ethnology (Tucker, 1994). The new scientists argued that Blacks represented an inferior species, not just a lesser-developed people.

## Onward Polygeny: Agassiz and Morton

Louis Agassiz (1801–1893) was a respected natural biologist in Switzerland. In the 1840s he moved to the United States where he assumed a professorship at Harvard. His wife, Elizabeth Cary Agassiz, was the founder and first president of Radcliffe College. Upon relocating, he founded the Museum of Comparative Zoology. Additionally, he became fascinated with questions of race. Having never met or seen a Black person in Europe, he now encountered Blacks and, more important, the system of slavery.

Much has been written about Agassiz (Gould, 1981; Tucker, 1994). He initially opposed slavery but later rethought his views as he was drawn into the dialogue on race, public policy, and Black education. His first encounter with a Black person, often cited in race literature, was noted in a letter to his mother:

It was in Philadelphia that I first found myself in prolonged contact with Negroes; all the domestics in my hotel were men of color. I can scarcely express to you the painful impression that I received, especially since the feeling that they inspired in me is contrary to all our ideas about the confraternity of the human type (genre) and the unique origin of our species. But truth before all. Nevertheless, I experienced pity at the sight of this degraded and degenerate race, and their lot inspired compassion in me in thinking that they are really men. Nonetheless, it is impossible for me to repress the feeling that they are not of the same blood as us. In seeing their black faces with their thick lips and grimacing teeth, the wool on their head, their bent knees, their elongated hands, their large curved nails, and especially the livid color of the palm of their hands, I could not take my eyes off their face in order to tell them to stay far away. And when they advanced that hideous hand towards my plate in order to serve me, I wished I were able to depart in order to eat a piece of bread elsewhere, rather than dine with such service. What unhappiness for the white race—to have tied their existence so closely with that of Negroes in certain countries! God preserve us from such a contact! (in Gould, 1981, p. 45)

As Agassiz's research unfolded at Harvard, he developed a notion of "centers of creation" (Gould, 1981). This hypothesis suggests that plants and animals were created in certain places and mostly did not immigrate far from those places or centers. Counterviews of widespread species scattered in different places posed problems for his argument. This and related questions of the origins and development of genes were at the root of his inquiry into human races as separate creations. As a creationist and believer in scriptural text, Agassiz had his roots in monogenism. To claim, as he eventually did, that Blacks were a separate species, meant breaking with the view that all humankind descended from Adam and Eve.

Agassiz's views were expressed in a paper written for the *Christian Examiner* in 1850. Entitled "The Diversity of Origin of the Human Races," the paper argued that while all men shared some commonalities, the races were created as separate species. He wrote that different races occupied various parts of the earth. Those different races had diverse characteristics. The notion of "difference" is once again key to his subsequent sociocultural discussion. The differences were manifested in culture, habit, intelligence, and ability.

Agassiz transformed his investigations of biology and natural history into social and political pronouncements (Gould, 1981). He embraced Caucasian intellectual and cultural supremacy. He now added charged adjectives and adverbs to his discussion of various racial groups. Submissive, cunning, tricky, cowardly, and apathetic were some of the descriptors that flavored his writings. African people were placed at the bottom level of his race classification. He offered the now time-worn argument that Africa never contributed to the building of civilized society.

The Civil War and surrounding activity brought the "Negro question" to the center of social and political debate. The question of what to do with the newly freed slave evoked a multitude of responses. Agassiz would come to acknowledge that the Negro's presence in America was permanent. He also acknowledged that the American political democracy would and should sanction legal equality for all its people. Beyond that, his racial views hardened.

His writings and statements continued the themes of difference and inequality. He argued for restricting the activities of Blacks in American society. For him, Blacks could only ruin the prospects of building a new civilization, and a strictly segregated society must be maintained.

Intermarriage evoked a passionate response from Agassiz. He believed mixed-race children were an offense and a sin against nature and that every effort must be made to maintain a pure civilization. The libidinous Blacks, he believed, would lure the White race to degradation. White people must maintain their natural inhibitions, which were absent in Blacks. Intermarriage, he argued, would create feebleminded offspring with physical disabilities.

Beyond social policy, Agassiz commented on the education of Black people. His views preceded, but were consistent with, the Hampton philosophy later expressed by Samuel Armstrong (Anderson, 1988), discussed in Chapter 3. Agassiz believed that Blacks should be trained for manual labor as opposed to intellectual cultivation.

While Agassiz brought his considerable reputation to bear on the new "scientific" racism, his proven expertise lay in other areas. His theorizing lacked the hard data required by the scientific community. Although his work was popular, it had to be coupled with the empiricism of others, such as Samuel George Morton of Philadelphia. Morton was a highly respected physician and scientist. He held two medical degrees, one granted from prestigious Edinburgh University.

Like Agassiz, Morton argued that there were separately created human species. He posited that the different human species had their origins in primordial organization. Differences in primordial organization, or early organized form, led to differentiated races as well as differentiated species in other animal life. Human races, he claimed, were separate from the start. He too attempted to rank the various human species, placing Africans at the lowest levels.

Morton rose to notoriety for his studies of cranial capacity. He believed that the bigger the skull, the bigger the brain. He began his study by measuring the cranial capacity of 800 skulls from around the world. His method was to fill the skull cavity with white pepper seeds that were then transferred to a tin cylinder from which the volume of the cranium was measured in cubic inches (Tucker, 1994). Unhappy with pepper seeds, he soon switched to using lead shot one-eighth inch in diameter.

Morton's work was highly acclaimed for its quantification of data and especially its attention to detail. Colleagues and supporters in the scientific community argued that his work would have more meaning if he broadened the interpretation of his findings. One such colleague, George Combes, suggested prior to the publication of Morton's first book, *Crania Americana* (1839), that Morton try to read mental and moral worth from brain size (Gould, 1981). For *Crania Americana*, Morton measured 144 Indian skulls, finding a mean volume of 82 cubic inches. Gould's (1981) studies of *Crania Americana* reveal comprehensive efforts by Morton to prove Indians' intellectual inferiority. Assorted passages speak of the deficiency of higher mental powers among Indian Americans, their inaptitude for civilization, aversion to the restraints of education, barbarous skills, and so on. Additionally, Gould (1981) sampled conclusions from Morton's work about other people of color.

Morton then hypothesized that the discrepancy between the skulls of Blacks and Whites would be significant. His friend and colleague George Gliddon, then United States Consul to Cairo, sent him more than 100 skulls from the tombs of ancient Egypt (Gould, 1981). His second major essay, "Crania Aegyptiaca" (1844), held that the cranial capacity for the Africans he measured was 83.44 cubic inches on average. Throughout the 1840s Morton adjusted and refined his measurement procedures. On some occasions when measurements conducted by his assistants did not calculate to his liking, he would dismiss them and remeasure himself (Gould, 1981). By the time of his final tabulations, hundreds more skulls had been collected. Final figures, reported in 1849, found the average volume for Caucasian skulls at 87 cubic inches, Chinese and Mongolian at 82 cubic inches, Native American at 79 cubic inches, and Black at around the aforementioned 83 cubic inches. It should be reiterated here that Gould (1981) argues convincingly that Morton "cooked" his measurements or simply omitted data he did not like.

Together, Agassiz and Morton represent an important thrust in the development of "scientific" racism. First, they Americanized the discourse and, in so doing, provided a powerful rationalization for slavery and the subsequent apartheid system in the southern United States. Second, they gave "scientific" and medical legitimization to their quackery. Medical journals, conferences, and lecturers embraced their themes.

They opened the floodgates for every White supremacist and amateur researcher. Samples include Peter Browne's hair "study" in which he found "canals" in White people's hair that did not exist in the hair of Blacks. He declared that White people had "perfect hair" (Tucker, 1994). Others developed the "cephalic index," a ratio found by measuring the skull shape and multiplying by 100. Skulls that measured 75 cubic inches or less were called "dolichocephalic," those between 75 and 80 were called "mesocephalic," and those above 80 were called "brachycephalic." The progression went from less round to more rounded heads, as beauty and intellect were associated with less rounded heads. In an equally ridiculous study of sex organs, French anatomist Etienne Serres (1860) "found" the distance between the navel and penis shorter in Blacks. He concluded that belly button height variance, penis or hymen size differences, and flattened labia in Black women were all signs of inferiority and close kinship to apes. These studies were followed by those of internationally renowned Paul Broca. Broca, a professor of clinical surgery and founder of the Anthropological Society of Paris in 1859, continued to defend the cranial capacity thesis against a variety of European theorists and scientists who disagreed (Gould, 1981).

Such studies became a fixture in research and public policy. Agassiz and Morton established the foundation for a century and a half of "scientific" racism. Shockley (1972), Jensen (1995), and Herrnstein and Murray (1994) continue the tradition, as America's brand of racism influences every aspect of social and political life.

It can be asserted that "scientific" racism was an important component in American social theory. It explained racial difference. It provided justification for twentieth-century segregation. Equally important, it provided the rationale for the shaping of colonial Black education. The architects of Black education, with few exceptions, embraced the general precepts of "scientific" racism.

Conservative social theorists wedded explanations of racial differences to explanations of human differences. By the end of the eighteenth century, Social Darwinism was widely embraced within the new sociology. The White architects of Black education were consistent in their support of Social Darwinism.

## Darwinian Revolution: Changing the Discourse

Charles Darwin, the English naturalist, questioned whether the distinctive biological populations of each locality were created separately. He also wondered whether there were cycles of creation and extinction as he observed significant rates of birth and death among plants and animals. Finding that organisms change over time, he searched for explanations. Building on the preceding work of naturalist Jean Lamarck and economist Thomas Malthus (Garrity & Gay, 1972), Darwin found that as organisms evolve, some are selected by nature to survive and bear offspring while others become extinct. Darwin's *On the Origin of Species by Means of Natural Selection or the Preservation of the Favored Races in the Struggle for Life* (1859) persuasively argues that, among other things, organisms evolve, there is a seemingly endless variety of species, species can be classified into natural groups, organisms are geographically distributed, and useless vestigial organs are present.

Early in his work, Darwin was confused about the origins of variability and how it was transferred through the generations. Initially believing that randomness and spontaneity accounted for hereditary differences, he later came to believe in the influence of environment. Darwin's work suggested a struggle for existence among biological organisms. Those better suited survive, because some organisms are superior, others inferior.

The Darwinian thesis struck a significant blow to creationism but did little to deter the "scientific" racists. Many simply placed less emphasis on the origins of humankind, while maintaining their advocacy of polygeny. Few would question that the Darwinian revolution established a new paradigm in science.

Soon Social Darwinist themes evolved from an extrapolation of Darwin's notions of biological life to societal life. The emerging urban industrial state replaced the old agrarian democracy. New means of production, property relations, and divisions of wealth allowed for a new political sociology. Conservative sociologists, social theorists, and "scientific" racists adapted Darwinian themes to the ordering of society. Survival of the fittest came to be viewed in terms of business, the economy, and race relations. Darwin's notion of inheritance of variations served as a reaffirmation of inequality and difference. Adaptation to the surrounding condition was seen as success in a competitive environment.

## Social Darwinism and Colonial Conquest

The thought and scientific work of Charles Darwin do not underlie the rationale of Social Darwinism or modern "scientific" racism. Racism in its different manifestations, such as Anglo-Saxonism or Aryanism, is a socially and politically constructed phenomenon. Such racism is more appropriately associated with modern nationalism (Hofstadter, 1944), conquest, and the labor market than with biological science. The exploitation of people of color needed justification on the basis of their inferiority. Racial subjugation often masked political subjugation.

As colonialism spread throughout Asia, Africa, the Caribbean, and Latin America, the theoretical base of "scientific" racism continued to expand. Views and theories of heredity, popular in the late nineteenth century, gave credibility to the emerging eugenics movement.

## THE EUGENICS MOVEMENT

The eugenics movement began in Europe in the mid-nineteenth century with the theorizing of Sir Francis Galton. The concepts quickly caught hold in the United States. Haller (1984) divides the American eugenics movement into stages. During the first stage, 1870–1905, hereditarian explanations took root. This was a period of labeling and discerning the dependent, insane, ill, and criminal as genetically inferior. Nascent eugenicists began to think in terms of restricting propagation.

An organized movement emerged between 1905 and 1930. Its theorists directly associated feeblemindedness, insanity, pauperism, and crime with heredity. Reform, correction, and charity organizations advocated custodial care and sterilization as solutions for "defective" types. European and other immigrants became targets of eugenics discourse, influencing notions of human intelligence, IQ, and development.

The research and writing of naturalists, physicians, anthropologists, Darwinists, and others opened a Pandora's box of intellectual, sociological, and scientific interest in genetics, heredity, race, and evolution. The study of heredity, in particular, came to receive great attention. As more scientists accepted Darwin's thesis as the biological explanation of the path of human development, questions arose: If nature selected the fit, what then could be concluded about the unfit? What was to be their plight? Were the unfit a threat to the advancement of civilization?

Eugenics became another building block in the platform of "scientific" racism. Once again the ideological voices of imperial thinking, national chauvinism, and White supremacy exerted their influence. The eugenic explanation was used to describe many phenomena. Right-wing eugenicists came to attribute poverty, ignorance, infirmities, intemperance, incompetence, feeblemindedness, and criminality to genetics. The opportunity to include race in this discourse was not missed.

## Galton: The "Scientific" Dimension of Eugenics

Sir Francis Galton (1822–1911) was the undeniable founder of eugenics ideology. A cousin of Charles Darwin, Galton dabbled in psychological testing, statistics, geography, and fingerprint identification. He soon became consumed with the study of heredity.

His work focused on an examination of the pedigrees of famous men. Several assumptions undergirded his work. He discounted social class and family advantage. He also ignored political and sociological variables. He believed in the absolute inequality of humans as supported by what we now call the bell-shaped-curve distribution. He evolved a thesis of hereditary mental ability. Interestingly, the most outstanding flaw in his data was that he relied on reputation and totally subjective secondhand descriptions of his subjects.

In 1865 he published an article, "Hereditary Talent and Character," followed 4 years later by his well-known book *Hereditary Genius*. The core of his outlook asserts that human character and capacities are shaped primarily by heredity and that the current generation can shape the future by how they breed (Haller, 1984).

For Galton, human abilities differed, and inheritance was the cause. Not only did people differ, races differed. While conducting research with the Royal Anthropological Institute in Britain, Galton advanced his commentary on race. He utilized ranking systems that placed the ancient Greeks at the top followed by Anglo-Saxons and other Europeans, followed by Africans, with Australian aborigines at the bottom.

Determined to elevate his thesis to natural and mathematical law, Galton collected data on family pedigrees. He sought correlations and deviations on height, eye color, temperament, artistic ability, disease, and so on. In an influential book, *Natural Inheritance* (1889), Galton argued that he had found significant correlations and consistent distributions approaching the mean.

Galton's efforts to establish statistical correlations attracted supporters, among the most formidable of whom was Karl Pearson (1857–1936). The brilliant Pearson was a mathematician, lawyer, philosopher, historian, and one-time socialist. Pearson studied under Galton and became a fervent supporter. His interest was in applying statistical methodology to biological problems. He believed the story of evolution could be told through statistics and mathematics (Haller, 1984).

Known to modern-day researchers as the originator of the Pearson Product Moment Correlation and other formulas, he argued, as a eugenicist, that personality and intelligence were predetermined in the germ plasma before birth. Using his pet formulas, he calculated that one-fourth of married couples were producing one-half of the children for the next generation. His concern was that this sector was populated by the poor, the lazy, and the feeble. This group's influence would then expand.

Throughout the 1890s Galton and Pearson worked as partners and became central figures in the eugenics movement. They shared a vision of making this movement scientific by establishing laws and theorems backed by mathematical truth. Galton and Pearson were the key figures in the Francis Galton Laboratory for the Study of National Eugenics, associated with similar work at universities in London and other places.

Pearson was among the first to use the term "biometrics," by which he meant the application of statistics to biological problems. Galton and Pearson were considered the important figures in the biometric school. Racial heredity became a central focus of study for the Laboratory in particular, and the biometrics movement in general. Galton defined this movement as follows: "Eugenics is the science which deals with all influences that improve the inborn qualities of a race; also with those that develop them to the utmost advantage" (in Farrall, 1985, p. 55).

Ultimately, eugenics, like Black education, never implied a backward or fascistic movement. Ostensibly, it promoted human betterment and forward-looking reform. Eugenics helped forge a twisted notion of what counts as social reform. Purifying society had a permanent place in the long-term view of refining civilization.

## Eugenics and Race in America

Nativism, racism, and anti-immigrant sentiment provided fertile soil for eugenicist outlooks in America around the turn of the twentieth century (Selden, 1999). A central premise of the eugenicists was that American institutions were incapable of molding or assimilating the "inferior" races (Haller, 1984). The eugenicists perceived an America under threat.

Eugenics literature became widespread in the early twentieth century. Sociologist Edward A. Ross wrote *The Old World in the New* (1914), attacking the character and physical features of Mediterranean Europeans. Ross wrote of people with "low foreheads," "open mouths," "weak chins," "skew faces," "knobby crania," who were "servile," "wife beaters," "criminals," "alcoholics," given to crimes of sex and violence. Another sociologist, Henry Pratt Fairchild, advocated the exclusion of southern Europeans, fearing they might mix with Nordics, thus causing "reversions" or throwbacks. Gregor Mendel's work in genetics often was utilized in eugenic arguments. One researcher, Edward M. East, who worked on a breeding project at Harvard, argued that hybridized people were inferior. He wrote:

> The Negro is a happy-go-lucky child, naturally expansive under simple conditions, oppressed by the restrictions of civilization, and unable to assume the white man's burden. He accepts his limitations, indeed, he is rather glad to have them. Only when there is white blood in his veins does he cry out against the supposed injustice of his position. (in Hasian, 1996, p. 54)

Popular books, such as Madison Grant's *The Passing of the Great Race* (1916), Lothrop Stoddard's *The Rising Tide of Color Against White-World Supremacy* (1920), and others, cautioned against European decline, colored people domination, "mongrelization," and the eventual end of Western civilization.

The specter loomed of people of color overrunning America and, ultimately, the world. Drawing from the existing traditions of racism dating back to early slavery, the eugenicists embraced and further developed such racial attitudes.

## Eugenics and the American Black

Popular belief held that Blacks were biologically moribund. The "Negro question" thus would solve itself as the race died out. "Race crossing" then became even more problematic because hard-line eugenicists believed it would prolong the life of the Black race. Eugenicists commented frequently about the races of color, particularly the Negro. A sampling of this commentary is revealing.

The respected Galton, in *Hereditary Genius* (1869), wrote, "The average intellectual standard of the Negro race is some two grades below our own" (in Hasian, p. 53). Frederick Hoffman, archenemy of Black intellectuals and educators such as Howard University's Kelly Miller, wrote a widely circulated book in 1896 entitled *Race Traits and Tendencies of the American Negro*. In it he argued that poverty, tuberculosis, venereal disease, and other ailments would always plague Blacks because of their inherent immorality. Hoffman argued that no social or political reform could alter these hard scientific facts.

Hard-line eugenicists took up views that suggested that education and/or social reforms could not change the historical status of Blacks. Attorney Madison Grant, a point man for the hardliners, argued throughout his works, such as *The Passing of the Great Race* (1916), that no environmental force could overcome heredity.

Eugenicists argued that the use of large data bases validated their conclusions. They frequently pointed to the massive samplings in the army alpha and beta tests, "intelligence" tests given soldiers in the early 1920s. Princeton psychologist Carl C. Brigham in his work *A Study in American Intelligence* (1923) utilized those data. He concluded that Blacks were deficient in native or inborn intelligence and that their lack of intelligence would likely lead to a decline in the nation's collective intelligence.

Perhaps the most damaging aspect of the eugenic views on Blacks was its application to segregation. So-called scientific data provided a rationale for containment and segregation. The notion of human difference undergirded the segregationist argument. The differences were beyond skin color; they were about mental characteristics.

Many in the political and legal establishment, especially in the South, accepted the "scientific" racist and eugenics arguments, as segregation was codified and practiced everywhere. It actually was not until *Brown v. Board of Education* (1954) that "scientific" racism was officially debunked. For the first time in a school desegregation case, the Supreme Court agreed with testimony and amicus curiae briefs that presented sociological evidence of the debilitating impact of American apartheid. The testimony of Columbia's Otto Klineberg, Harvard's Jerome Bruner, Berkeley's David Krech, City College of New York's Kenneth Clark, and many others represented a long-awaited counterattack on "scientific" racism and segregation. Despite this legal coup, hereditarian views of intelligence have continued throughout the twentieth century and beyond. Herrnstein and Murray's *The Bell Curve* (1994) represents a recent effort in that direction.

## SCIENTIFIC RACISM AND BLACK EDUCATION: RETROSPECTS AND PROSPECTS

"Scientific" racism cannot be separated from the economic and political order. It cannot be separated from the historical dynamics of power and oppression. The connection of "scientific" racism to Black education and the new social sciences is far from coincidental. It can be understood as an ideological and political issue.

In 1860, no body of thought existed to explain how an agrarian, rural, and somewhat communalistic society could rapidly give way to a centralized, bureaucratized, obscenely unequal corporate juggernaut. Twentieth-century capitalism became difficult to explain. What was clear was that slavery and racism had demonstrated the benefits of social and economic privilege. Post–Civil War corporate industrial America required theory and explanation.

"Scientific" racism was indeed the centerpiece of the new social science, which presented human difference as the rationale for inequality. "Scientific" racism also could explain the capitalist exploitation of labor, the factory system, and the usurpation of power by northern industrialists. Most important, "scientific" racism justified the hierarchical order of races as historically evolved, divinely ordained, and socially expeditious.

"Scientific" racism was a fundamental precept in the architecture of Black education. It was felt that the naturally inferior Black must always occupy a socially subservient position. Industrial education, therefore, was right for the Blacks, and they for it. More significant, industrial education was presented as progressive reform. After all, wasn't it a step up from slavery? It could be marketed as democracy and a way to increase Black participation in the society and economic community.

"Scientific" racism provided legitimization for colonial policies. Blacks got all they could intellectually manage. Destiny ordained their place.

"Scientific" racism provided a lasting framework around which to rationalize all forms of social privilege in the twentieth century. It suggests that Whites are better because of their inheritance and that White rule came about because of natural forces. "Scientific" racism has undergirded the imperial mentality that holds that Whites should utilize their wealth in the interest of "justice" and "progress."

Most important, "scientific" racism provided a foundation for both institutional and attitudinal racism in America. The race issue saturates every aspect of our social, economic, political, educational, and personal life. Notions of racial "difference" affected the architects of Black education, as evidenced in both their thought and their actions.

# PART II

*Architects of Accommodation*

# 3

## *General Samuel Chapman Armstrong*

OF OUR ARCHITECTS of Black education, none is more important than Samuel Chapman Armstrong (1839–1893). Moving from missionary to soldier to educator to college president, Armstrong was both ideologist and organizer for the education of Blacks in the South. Additionally, Armstrong was an effective and farsighted social, political, and economic theorist working for the cause of a segregated and orderly South. As theorist, curricularist, founder of Hampton Institute, and mentor of Booker T. Washington, Armstrong is at the center of our story.

Hampton Institute, in Virginia, catapulted Armstrong into the history of America and the world. Neither the United States nor the rest of the world would ever be the same. The Hampton idea was about much more than education. It was about nation building. It was about carefully situating the newly freed Black in a new sociopolitical and economic order. It was about (re)shaping delicate race relations. Finally and most important, it was about forging a social order rooted in apartheid, economic exploitation, oppression, and inequality. The Hampton model of education and societal development dramatically influenced 100 years of Black schooling.

Ideologically, situating Armstrong is important. Neither a great scholar nor a diabolical genius, Armstrong was above all else a patriot. In a country wracked by Civil War, regionalism, racial antagonism, and uncertainty, Armstrong envisioned the possibility for reconciliation and rebuilding. He knew that myopic and extreme solutions should be avoided if an orderly, prosperous, and unified nation was to come about.

Armstrong's canonization by the established order was certainly justified. The questions of the new South, the new nation, the new economy, and the new positioning of Blacks were most complex. Armstrong's tact, insight, and pragmatism helped chart a previously uncharted course. Biographer Francis G. Peabody (1927), in his sainting of Armstrong, wrote: "In all parts of the world—in India, in Greece, in Southern Africa, this 'Hampton idea' has been welcomed and imitated, and the pedagogical genius of Armstrong has made him the recognized prophet of education for life" (p. 198).

In the missionary and corporate philanthropic community, Armstrong was widely respected as a pioneer in Negro education. Its leaders looked to Hampton as a model for subsequent projects that they funded. Beyond his support from the business, political, and "charity" communities, Armstrong had a most fervent advocate in Booker T. Washington. Washington's praise and recommendation of Armstrong's ideas guaranteed widespread support from the Black population desperate for education and uplift. Washington (1901) said of Armstrong:

> But I have not spoken of that which made the greatest and most lasting impression upon me and that was a great man—the noblest, rarest human being that it has ever been my privilege to meet. I refer to the late General Samuel C. Armstrong. (p. 37)

Further explorations reveal Armstrong as an astute and effective political theorist and economist. Hampton was not set up to provide total freedom nor was it established to extend slavery. Hampton was neither a school nor a church nor a factory nor a prison nor a barracks, yet it was simultaneously all those things. Hampton was an ideological and practical training ground for the Negro in the new industrial order.

Hampton education came to exemplify colonial education for Blacks both in America and in the rest of the world. The various missionary societies would export the Hampton model, especially to Sub-Saharan Africa. It thus became an international movement (Berman, 1980; King, 1971; Watkins, 1989).

Armstrong went to Hampton with the same outlooks he took into the military. He neither hated nor loved Blacks. He believed in White superiority. Most important, he believed in a unified nation and its cause. That cause was to peacefully and profitably rebuild and function.

Like others in the emerging American republic, Armstrong rejected the rigid feudal traditions of European social class and caste. He felt no need for insurmountable social barriers in American democracy. He believed the political state and structures of power could support both the accumulation of great wealth by the few and programs of social welfare for the masses. Such were his politics of reconciliation and social accord.

It is important to examine Armstrong's writings firsthand, as he was a maker of history. His outlooks and programs were efforts at reconciliation. He hoped to demonstrate that through well-considered and timely insights, disparate forces could be brought together. Theoretically, Armstrong brought together the powerful with the powerless. He brought racial supremacists together with those seeking equality. He brought together the lion and the lamb. It was always clear, however, that he was working for the powerful, the supremacists, and the lion.

Armstrong marketed his racial accommodationism as progress. He sold evolution as revolution. He promised that his politics of gradualism would forge a new society. He proffered a rhetoric and language of possibility and hope. Armstrong's commitment to the existing economic and racial order was masked by his language of human uplift. However, his version of human uplift was absolutely compatible with the most despotic and oppressive political apparatus. He mastered the art of crafting social change without changing society. Armstrong advanced the practice of promoting social reform without disturbing existing economic and racial arrangements. He showed the path to reform-without-revolt.

Although untrained in sophisticated market theory, Armstrong understood labor economics. He understood that efficient production, depressed wages, and massive profits were the building blocks of the new corporate capitalist state. He also understood the historical role Blacks had and would continue to play in that process. Because of the relevance of his parents' backgrounds, especially his father's, a glimpse of his early life is useful.

## EARLY LIFE

Samuel Chapman Armstrong was born January 30, 1839 on the island of Maui, Hawaiian Islands. His parents, Richard and Clarissa Armstrong, were missionaries deeply involved in the religious, social, and educational life of the island.

Richard and Clarissa's daughter Edith Talbot's (1904) biography holds that this was an important period for both Hawaii and Richard. She argues that the "heathens" of Hawaii were finally embracing the teachings of Christianity after decades of missionary efforts. This new "enlightenment" coincided with the years of her father's ministry.

Armstrong family members were major figures in Hawaii's, especially Maui's, social, educational, political, religious, and economic life. Richard wondered why the indigenous people did not exploit their natural resources and join the movement toward industrialization occurring in the Western world. He became a strong advocate for industrial and agricultural vocation on the islands. He became instrumental in establishing the islands' first sawmills and sugar plantations (Talbot, 1904).

### The Formative Years

Samuel received his early education at the Royal School at Punahou. His schoolmates were other missionary children and upper-class, even royal, Hawaiian children. From there, he transferred to Williams College in New England.

He enlisted in the military in 1862, and the great Civil War awaited. Passionate patriotism guided his actions, including his evolved dislike for slavery. He wrote to a friend during the war: "Chum, I am a sort of abolitionist, but I haven't learned to love the Negro" (in Talbot, 1904, p. 86).

Advancing in rank and experience, Armstrong was assigned assorted leadership responsibilities over Black soldiers. Correspondence indicates that during military service, he sometimes reflected on the role of Blacks in history, in society, and especially in the immediate war effort. Consistently reaffirming his beliefs in White superiority, he believed it was time for Blacks to step up and command respect: "The African race is before the world, unexpectedly to all, and all mankind are looking to see whether the African will show himself equal to the opportunity before him" (Talbot, 1904, p. 101).

Superiors considered Armstrong effective in working with Negro soldiers and offered him several career military leadership positions that he turned down. Upon discharge, he also rejected offers to enter the world of business and commerce, then very popular among discharged officers. Instead, he embarked on a new path that would influence the plight of millions.

He believed that his mission in life was to be a humanitarian, to do God's work. Humanitarianism, for Armstrong, did not mean egalitarianism but rather the work of patriotism. In one of his final letters as a soldier, he wrote: "I shall seek some chance of usefulness where I can use my talents to the most advantage and for the cause of humanity. . . . My purpose is to serve the Great Master" (in Talbot, 1904, p. 131). He saw a way to that end by accepting a position at the newly formed Freedman's Bureau.

## The Freedman's Bureau

Following the end of the Civil War in 1865, the uncertainties of northern hegemony, Black emancipation, southern agriculture, and race relations loomed large. The cotton, tobacco, and sugar plantations cried out for harvest. How would the transition from slave labor to free labor come about? How would the South peacefully re-annex to the North? How would a new social and political status for Blacks play out? How would the United States unite?

The Freedman's Bureau provided part of the answer to these questions. It would help with the transition of newly freed slaves into a life without slavery. It would provide rudimentary education and social services. Established as a government department by an 1865 act of Congress, this agency came under the leadership of General Oliver O. Howard. He defined the job as he went along.

The savvy General Howard decided that owing to great uncertainties, he would place former officers of the regular army in the most sensitive and responsible positions. Armstrong sought and received a Bureau appointment in Virginia. He was one of eight men who administered various counties. The Bureau urged him to use the title General as he supervised other staff army officers as well as the educational and social life of thousands of newly freed slaves.

Armstrong's overall task was to reorganize a society in which working-class Whites were rowdy and uncertain, and Blacks had scattered throughout the countryside, barely surviving in roving bands. Martial law would guarantee peace and order. Government provisions and teachers from the American Missionary Association would help stabilize both Black and White populations. He wrote to his mother in June 1866:

> The work is very difficult; there are here, congregated in little villages, some 5,000 colored people, crowded, squalid, poor, and idle. It is my work to scatter and renovate them. (in Talbot, 1904, p. 139)

Armstrong developed a reputation for "handling" Negroes well. He acknowledged the great interest demonstrated by ex-slaves in learning. He also acknowledged the existence of humble, yet thriving, schools scattered throughout the piney woods. Armstrong believed in the inferiority of the Negro. However, he did not deny that the Negro would occupy a permanent place in the socioeconomic life of the nation. He foresaw no re-enslavement, no mass deportations, and no genocide. For Armstrong, his version of education would train and civilize the ex-slave. He wrote: "Freedmen as a class are destitute of ambition; their complacency in poverty and filth is a curse" (in Talbot, 1904, p. 148).

In his view, the Negro, was, above all else, immoral. Schooling would provide training in common morality as well as the habits of industry. He wrote: "The North generally thinks that the great thing is to free the Negro from his former owners; the real thing is to save him from himself" (in Talbot, 1904, p. 150).

As Reconstruction came to an end, so too did the Freedman's Bureau. The crushing of Reconstruction (Peery, 1975) signaled a great reaction from the South. People resorted to the terror of the Ku Klux Klan and the lynch mob. Northerners had successfully re-annexed the South, and their support of Negro civil and political rights was withdrawn. By 1870, the Bureau dissolved and another chapter in Armstrong's life came to an end.

Armstrong supported the work of the Bureau. He believed that providing accommodationist-style education to the Negro was key to resolving the larger racial, social, and political problems of the time. Beyond his commitment to the work, he had grown fond of the Piedmont region. Moreover, he recognized that the large numbers of Black people living there made it an important area. He chose to continue his work in the area by founding the Hampton Institute.

## THE HAMPTON INSTITUTE

The property known as Little Scotland, comprising 159 acres along the Hampton River in Virginia, captured Armstrong's attention. He wrote to the American Missionary Association in 1867 asking for $19,000, the purchase price for the estate. An arrangement was worked out whereby the Association paid $9,000, and philanthropist Josiah King of Pittsburgh paid most of the remaining $10,000. An important vision statement written to the Missionary Society in 1868 read:

> The thing to be done . . . is clear: to train selected Negro youths who shall go out and teach and lead their people . . . to teach respect for labor; to replace stupid drudgery

with skilled hands; and in this way to build up an industrial system for the sake, not only of self-support and intelligent labor, but also for the sake of character. (in Peabody, 1927, p. 189)

On April 1, 1868, Hampton opened its doors with 15 pupils, alongside one teacher and a matron, both employed by the American Missionary Association. Within a month, the student population, drawn from "colored refugees" or "contrabands," doubled.

Students engaged in manual labor in the morning and studied in the afternoon and evening. Young men did farm work, while young women did domestic tasks. A wage of 8 cents per hour was applied to the $10 per month boarding fee. Tuition of $70 per annum was most often waived or paid by the Missionary Association.

Within a few years, the agricultural operations were profitable. Armstrong wrote in 1878: "It is now spring harvest, and we shall gather $2,000 worth of vegetables which the students have raised. They will be sold in New York and Baltimore. Just sold a pea crop for $900—half of it clear profit" (in Talbot, 1904, p. 169).

## Establishing a Sociopolitical and Educational Ideology

The Hampton experiment was important for various reasons. It helped address the dilemma of what to do with the Blacks in the conquered South. In so doing, it addressed both the political questions of the South and the "Negro question." In addition to these broad political concerns, the Hampton project would hammer out a model for colonial education of Blacks, with profound implications for the next century and more.

Armstrong's vision for Hampton was multidimensional. It would be a manual labor school. It would provide badly needed teachers for a mostly illiterate, alienated, and displaced Black population. It would provide training in character building, morality, and religion to "civilize" the "childlike" and "impetuous" Negro. Eventually, Armstrong favored educating poor southern Whites. His sister wrote:

> It was an early dream of his, never realized except in the case of one struggling family of poor whites to whom he gave shelter and a job, that he could directly help the whites of the South by giving them industrial education at Hampton. He foresaw the coming lack among them of skilled labor, saying mournfully, "The whites have no apprentices!" and sincerely wished to aid them in their economic distress. (Talbot, 1904, pp. 177–178)

Despite his larger vision, he recognized that addressing Black Americans' issues was most immediate. It was the Blacks who were key to socioeconomic progress in a segregated and hoped-for stable South. Northern industrialists believed racial segregation must be made to work in this fragile new undertaking.

Armstrong understood that Hampton could be a training center. Thousands could be trained at Hampton who in turn would go out and teach thousands more. Hampton could influence Black life as few other institutions could. However, Samuel Armstrong's educational ideology was a product of his views on race, politics, religion, and morality. A few days after Hampton opened for its first fall term, he wrote:

> This is no easy machine to run wisely, rightly. The darkies are so full of human nature and have to be most carefully watched over. They are apt to be possessed with strange notions. To simply control them is one thing, but to educate, to draw them out, to develop the germ of good possibilities into firm fruition, requires the utmost care. Eternal vigilance will be the price of success. (in Talbot, 1904, p. 171)

Anderson (1988), who writes extensively on Armstrong and Hampton, holds that teacher training was Armstrong's central objective for Hampton:

> The Hampton–Tuskegee curriculum was not centered on trade or agricultural training; it was centered on the training of teachers. A condition for admission to Hampton was the "intention to remain through the whole course and become a teacher." This goal was achieved because approximately 84 percent of 723 graduates from Hampton's first twenty classes became teachers. Moreover, Hampton did not offer any trade certificates until 1895, twenty-seven years after the school's founding. (p. 34)

Anderson goes on to assert that the manual labor component was part of a "self-help" ideology aimed at building character and moral foundation. He says:

> The primary aim was to work the prospective teachers long and hard so that they would embody, accept, and preach an ethic of hard toil or the "dignity of labor." Then, and only then, believed Armstrong, could his normal school graduates develop the appropriate values and character to teach the children of the South's distinctive black laboring class. (Anderson, 1988, p. 34)

Hampton offered no bachelor's degree, nor did it offer the standard 4-year unified curriculum. Hampton students arrived with mostly a sketchy elementary school education. Armstrong embraced industrial education because it would accommodate Blacks in the new South.

## Creating a Hampton Culture

Hampton was not just a school. It was a concept. As such, it created and fostered a culture and spirit to which both its students and the larger community could relate. It sponsored a number of activities such as choral groups, fairs, and various celebrations. Among its better-known celebrations was the annual commencement.

Armstrong invited dignitaries from far and wide so that he could show off the school, its curriculum, and, most important, its graduates. Politicians, clergymen, journalists, and philanthropists came to this celebration. Guest J. C. Kinney observed Hampton's seventh commencement in 1875 and sent his account to the *Hartford Courant*:

> The design of the school is to fit its graduates to do helpful work among the ignorant and degraded colored masses of the south. For such an object Latin, Greek, and the higher mathematics are useless, and they are wisely omitted from the course. A practical English education is given, sufficient to make good teachers, and with it there seems to have been imparted some comprehension of the needs of the race and a genuine missionary spirit. (in Harlan et al., 1972, p. 49)

Kinney observed that during the morning, visiting guests first toured the campus and then quizzed the students on what they had learned. After a noon meal, the guests listened to choral "old songs." The ceremony itself was Armstrong's opportunity to display his finished products. It was orchestrated to impress and extol the benefits of the Hampton experience. Beyond that, he engineered it to present a political claim about the future of race relations. Black people could indeed be cleaned up and made polite and useful. Here is how Kinney observed the event:

> The exercises were notable for the good taste of all who participated. The girls were dressed plainly and neatly with no attempt at display, and they, in common with the young men, conducted themselves with unassuming dignity. Alice and Maria Ferribee are two sisters of full African blood and features. . . . The other rhetorical exercises are worthy of mention, but I will only specify the valedictory, which showed a comprehension of the ignorance and superstition of the black race. The native whites he said must convince the blacks that they are their best friends, and this can only be done by action, for the blacks have learned that words are cheap. (in Harlan et al., 1972, pp. 50–51)

Armstrong was trying to show the world that his Blacks could look and act respectable by White standards. They were quiescent and conforming. They demonstrated a level of intelligence that justified Hampton's attracting additional funding. They could not appear uppity or threatening to the social order or their own subservient position in the South.

Another guest at the 1875 commencement, Charles Brace, recorded:

> The girls looked like respectable working-girls, and the boys much as young country teachers would anywhere. All had remarkably good heads, and many showed large frontal development of the brain; some few were so white that at the North no one would have dreamed of their being of the negro race. (in Harlan et al., 1972, p. 55)

An important part of Armstrong-authored Hampton culture was promotion of a Black retrospective on slavery. The cultivated view was aimed at defusing anger. Slavery, which only recently had ended, was to be observed as an unfortunate episode or an aberration. Black students were to celebrate freedom in song. The Old Testament concept of "jubilee" or joy at emancipation was fostered. Several choral and jubilee singing groups formed then continue to tour the country to the present day. After attending the event in 1875, Charles Brace wrote:

> Many of the students alluded to their former condition of slavery, but without any tone of reproach or of desire for vengeance, and yet there was an expression on their faces, which showed that all had felt the "iron in the soul." One was pointed out to me, nearly white, who, while a teacher, had been driven from his school into the woods by the Ku Klux—his two assistants being murdered, and he himself barely escaping with his life. (in Harlan et al., 1972, p. 58)

He continued:

> Not an expression of hostility or ill-feeling appeared in any address. Each speaker seemed to feel that the fortunes of his race depended on the self-control, virtue, and intelligence of each individual, and that their future was in their own hands. They all, apparently, deprecated any intruding of themselves socially, or of pressing their social rights beyond what was proper and convenient. . . . The most interesting speech of the occasion was made by Joseph Towe, a full-blooded negro from North Carolina. . . . The speaker described with what eagerness the slaves would work to some of these cheerful melodies. . . . A peculiar feature of all the addresses was that they closed with a fervent and sincere religious sentiment—for the college is peculiarly a religious seminary. (in Harlan et al., 1972, pp. 58–59)

## Black and Native Americans Together

Often understated in Hampton memory is the education of significant numbers of Native Americans, especially from the tribes indigenous to the surrounding area of Virginia. In the most general terms, Armstrong and Hampton displayed the same colonial mentality toward American Indians as toward Blacks. The American Indians were viewed as barbaric and immoral. Even Hampton's Blacks were convinced that the Native Americans were lower on the social ladder than themselves.

Booker T. Washington offered many vignettes on what it was like for the "colored" students to interact with the Indians at Hampton. He wrote: "Many of them are a good while learning that their under garments must be kept clean and frequently changed. I have noticed recently that some of them are beginning to shave—a strange thing for an Indian" (in Harlan et al., 1972, p. 87).

In the course of studying with Native Americans, Washington changed his views. He, along with fellow students and teachers, soon realized they were human beings with feelings, aspirations, and compassion. The American Indians were not unlike themselves. Washington noted that they showed up for Christmas dinner nicely dressed, worked hard on improving their manners, and courted women. A Hampton teacher of mechanics, J. H. McDowell, noted this about them:

> My views have been radically changed in my brief intercourse with the Hampton Indian students, for instead of finding them indolent, indifferent, intractable and without interest in acquiring mechanical knowledge, as I was led to believe would be the case, I find the reverse to be the fact . . . of boys, I have not found any, who, as a class, have learned more rapidly, been more eager to learn or more obedient to rules and regulations of the shops, than those at present under my charge. (in Harlan et al., 1972, p. 105)

Just as they had for the Blacks, Armstrong and Hampton were purporting to solve the "Indian question." Hampton education would transform the inferior American Indians and ready them for a place in the new order.

## ARMSTRONG ON POLITICS, RACE, AND EDUCATION

Beyond his role as missionary educator, Armstrong's voice would occupy a central role in shaping the new South and establishing the new social order. Despite wide coverage and exposure in the existing newspapers and journals of the time, Armstrong wanted his own platform from which to discuss the pressing issues of the day.

### *The Southern Workman*: Ideological Pulpit

In 1872, Armstrong, with assistant Hollis Frissell, founded *The Southern Workman* (*SW*), a school newspaper. Beyond printing school news, Armstrong intended the paper as a forum. Although stating that the paper would be a nonpolitical "instructive monthly" (Anderson, 1988), Armstrong, from the outset, took up issues such as Reconstruction, the Black vote, and self-government.

Politics, race, and education were central among the themes Armstrong addressed. All of these themes were inextricably connected. His writings in *SW* made it clear that Black education was joined to the political economy of the South and, ultimately, the whole country. Armstrong's writings on race, race relations, and politics profoundly influenced the social theory and culture of the time.

Few White men were situated as was Armstrong. His status, socioracial views, and politics made him welcome among industrialists, governors, high political officials, educators, and other influential people of the time. He interacted and exchanged views with northern hegemonists and southerners alike. On the other hand, his background and work in Virginia made him very knowledgeable about and connected to Black life.

During the crucial postslavery and post-Reconstruction periods, Armstrong addressed the nation's most sensitive problems. The uncertainties were great and the stakes were high. His 20 years of essays in *SW* supported Black subservience and a sociopolitical inequality that characterized the next 100 years.

## On Politics and the Political Economy of the South

Armstrong intimately understood that the "Negro problem" was the key to the country's future. Failure to properly solve the problem and situate the newly freed slave could mean the undoing of the delicate new relationship between the agricultural South and the emergent industrial North. Solving the problem created the possibility for social stability and economic prosperity.

Powerful voices held conflicting views. Reactionary southern sentiment turned violent after the slavocracy was defeated. Southern moderates and northern industrialists wanted social order without disturbing traditional race relations. The northern industrial working class wanted a labor and wage system unthreatened by peonage. Such voices aired their views within the nation's major political parties. Early on, Armstrong began to comment on the political uncertainties of the time.

The tricky new politics of northern industrialization and southern labor needed to be charted. The period was right for Armstrong, and he was right for it. He understood the political economy of peonage and where Blacks "fit." They would be semicitizens with semifreedom. Their place would be midway between slavery and freedom. Their cheap labor would continue its role in the new order. He wrote:

> There is no source whatever of a suitable supply in lieu of Negro labor. The large, low swampy, malarial, but highly productive area of the South would become almost a desert without it. The successful Southern farmer knows that he has the best labor in the world. The Negro is important to the country's prosperity. (*SW*, January 1878, p. 4)

The class structure of the South, always important, would become more significant as it would have to change, but not too much. New elements had to be absorbed without antagonizing the old. Armstrong addressed the changing class status of groups in the South when he wrote:

> In the old regime in the South there were three classes, whose fortunes have somewhat changed. The aristocracy or gentry being generally bankrupt, and without adaptation to the new order of things, are struggling against a tide of troubles. But some of this class have met the change with wisdom and energy, and by making the best of things are improving their fortunes and have become rallying points of new efforts and hopes. The poor whites and the Negroes were the other two classes. (*SW*, April 1876, p. 26)

The Negro would be the key to the new South. Blacks must be free, but not too free. Negro freedom had to be reconciled with traditional racial relations.

Anything other than continued racial subservience could prove disruptive, as volatile White southerners might rebel. Armstrong believed the situation provided circumstances that could be built upon.

Armstrong most often spoke to the South. He exhorted southerners to support his conciliatory program in their own interests. Prosperity depended on stability:

> Prejudice, persecution and bull-dozing lead to scarcity of capital, demoralized labor, bad crops, burnt barns, and end in ruin. . . . Southerners must make the best of Negro labor; they cannot afford to do otherwise; with them it is that or none. Their enlightened leaders are aware of this; they see that there is a direct ratio between race feeling and comfortable living, that the interests of both classes are identical, and that all members of the body politic must prosper or suffer together. (*SW*, May 1877, p. 34)

## Blacks and Politics

The extent of political participation for Blacks was of utmost interest to Armstrong. Reconstruction had created a fervor for the franchise. Black sentiment regarded voting as crucial for social progress. Armstrong initially counterposed voting to education. He argued that education would lead to social uplift, whereas voting would not:

> Those who regard the welfare of the ex-slaves as dependent directly on the use of their political power may well weep, for the ballot is nearly useless in their hands; those who see that the ballot is secondary to the improvement of the race in mind, morals, and condition, may be joyful, for this work is flourishing better than ever. (*SW*, December 1877, p. 90)

Merit, industry, thrift, and sobriety were far more important than engaging the political process, Armstrong believed. He later changed his position and argued that universal suffrage would serve the nation well, but Blacks must still place their focus on work.

Demographics, movement, and the possibility of exodus were of great political concern to Armstrong. The possibility of a significant movement of Blacks captured his attention. He fully understood the sentiments of those wanting to move westward following the Civil War. However, he believed Blacks should remain in the South where, he insisted, they had both roots and resources. He referred to the South as a "friendly" region for Blacks. In describing the so-called "Exodus to Kansas," Armstrong cautioned Blacks about venturing into uncertainty. He argued that their economic base was the Black Belt South.

By the early 1880s, Armstrong was convinced that the politics of the new South was succeeding. He believed prosperity, national unity, class peace, and workable race relations were realities. Armstrong wrote in *SW* (February 1881) that a prosperous South meant a prosperous North. The South had a solid and productive agricultural base with great possibility for further industrialization and investment. The guarantee of cheap labor made the South attractive for manufacturers. He summed up his view of Negro life in the South:

> Some of the Negroes are leaving the South, not because they are oppressed or outraged, but because they are anxious to better their condition. He is told that he can do better in the North, or East, or West than at home; and, being of a trusting, confiding nature, easily led and easily influenced, he believes the representations that are made to him. But, except in some rare instances, there is no oppression of the black man in the South today. He is paid fair wages, and he has all the work he cares to do. His work, however, is altogether in the field. He is not a success—at least the recent generation is not a success—in the factory. He has not the steady application that is needed around machinery. If a circus passes, he rushes to the window to see it. If a stranger goes into a factory where colored men are employed, the chances are ten to one that every one of them will forget all about what he is doing and stare at him until he leaves the place. The next generation may be better in this respect, but I have no hope for the present one. (*SW*, February 1881, pp. 16–17)

Armstrong believed that the South ultimately belonged to Whites. Blacks should be allowed limited social and economic participation, but the uplift and economic betterment of the poor White must always be kept in focus.

## On the Black Race

Among the many complex issues Armstrong addressed was the continued genetic existence of the Negro. "Scientific" racists insisted that high infant mortality and lower life expectancy signaled a moribund race. Armstrong understood that such extreme views would not serve racial détente. In what would become a consistent line of the defense of Black humanity, he wrote:

> Is the colored race dying out? According to the census of 1870 it had, during the previous ten years, increased a little over ten percent, in spite of war, want, suffering and wide-spread ruin throughout the South. . . . Learned Southerners have, from time to time, solemnly asserted the decrease of the race from the neglect of infants and of the sick, and from other causes, chiefly Negro improvidence. . . . The negro is prolific. The phenomena of a dying race, such as one sees among the decaying Polynesian tribes, are not seen among them. Children are abundant and healthy in city and country. The pickaninnies do not seem destined to die young. They are a numerous, frisky, healthy class of unfailing humor and appetite as unlike as anything can be, the sore-spotted scarce Hawaiian child whose race is doomed. (*SW*, January 1878, p. 4)

Armstrong appeared as a moderate racist in his utterances. He staked out a position between citizenship and chattel property. Political expediency seems an important factor in his racial views.

He ultimately supported the thirteenth, fourteenth, and fifteenth amendments, and other similar legislation, in principle. He accepted that basic civil rights should protect all citizens. With great insight, he observed that civil rights legislation was not so much a facilitator of Black progress as it was a control mechanism. He believed such laws bonded Blacks to gradualism and social obedience. They established peaceful parliamentary change as the only legitimate vehicle for change. He wrote:

> We are glad to observe but few indications in the South that the colored people are being unduly elated by the congressional guarantee of civil rights. On the contrary, there is every reason to hope that the avowed enemies and the unwise friends of the race, will, in this respect, be signally disappointed. Up to this time a peaceable demeanor has been the political salvation of the ex-slave. By it, he has inspired faith in his capacity to become a useful citizen. No other course of action on his part would have induced such warmth of sympathy at the North, and such efforts for his relief and enlightenment. His moderation has extorted the praise of all but rash and wild counselors. Thrift is blessing his industry and teaching him that for him, too, it was written that the meek shall inherit the earth. When he stands upon a basis of substantial prosperity he will command the attention of the powerful class who ask only "will it pay?" (*SW*, July 1876, p. 26)

Consistent with his views on the politics of Blacks was his assessment of their intellectual and social nature. For him, the Black could learn, but would always be held back because of a lack of character. His writings in 1876 are among the most revealing on his racial philosophy:

> But capacity for knowledge is not necessarily capacity for progress. Lack of brains is not the greatest difficulty with tropical or oriental races. The Hindoos and the Zulus have poets and orators. . . . We cannot reason from intelligent negroes, necessarily, to a civilized progressive race. The question with them is not one of special proficiency, of success in one direction—the pursuit of knowledge—but of success all around. It is one of morale, industry, self-restraint, of power to organize society, to draw a racial line between the decent and indecent, to form public sentiment that shall support morals and to allow common sense in the relations of life. (*SW*, July 1876, p. 50)

Armstrong felt that, for the most part, the Negro was lost. Blacks had the capacity to become civilized, but civilization was not likely to happen any time soon. A few could be saved if they were educated and Christianized. He wrote: "This race presents many discouraging aspects, but it is saved and continually improved by a leaven of good and true men whom schools and seminaries of learning yearly supply" (*SW*, July 1878, p. 50).

In 1877 Armstrong delivered what might have been his most comprehensive statement on the Negro race at the anniversary meeting of the American

Missionary Association in Syracuse, New York. He gave a kind of state of the race address. He expressed great ambivalence about the future of the Negro and the race. Without undergoing the Christianizing and civilizing process that a place like Hampton could provide, he held little hope for the race. Like a creature of the wild, the Black had to be tamed. He wrote:

> His worst master is still over him—his passions. This he does not realize. He does not see "the point" of life clearly; he lacks foresight, judgment, and hard sense. His main trouble is not ignorance, but deficiency of character; his grievances occupy him more than his deepest needs. There is no lack of those who have mental capacity. The question with him is not one of brains, but of right instincts, of morals and of hard work. (*SW*, December 1877, p. 94)

Blacks belonged to the "savage races" who, argued Armstrong, were "mentally sluggish" and "indolent." Only with character training could they be salvaged. Hampton-style education then took on new significance. It was not mere schooling; it was the saving of a race from itself.

In many ways, Armstrong was a kind of White supremacist pluralist. While other White supremacists suggested draconian measures that would have led ultimately to fractured, dysfunctional, and unstable race and societal relations, Armstrong called for "unity in diversity." Sounding like a 1990s cultural pluralist, Armstrong understood that racial subservience could be reconciled to the new democratic order. The rhetoric of equality easily could be wedded to the practice of racism. Armstrong discovered, as Jefferson and others before him, that one need not subsume the other. In a far-reaching statement that summarized his outlooks, he wrote:

> Unity in diversity is the problem of our country; not only in the variety of its interests, but in the diversity of its people. . . . From across the water have come many branches of one race, and from Africa an entirely distinct race; each with its peculiar ideas and instincts; each with more or less strong contripetal tendencies the African having decidedly the strongest. . . . Commercially and politically, the movement is, and must be, concentric; for there can be but one system of trade and of government. Socially, the movement is eccentric; the play of social preference of instinct is free. The various branches of the white race have their own separate centres, but with no decided barriers to a commingling, which, though frequent, is not general, but, so far as it goes, invigorates the population. . . . The Negro, a distinct race, is by its inherent qualities let into close relations with the whites, chiefly by way of service but by its instincts, into a social and religious life of its own. . . . This is fortunate, because not only practical men, from long experience, believe, but Professor Agassiz, as the result of close observation, especially in Brazil was satisfied that the races are better in their purity and that the mixture tends generally to a weaker rather than to a stronger and more valuable product. (*SW*, January 1879, p. 4)

In that same essay, he wrote:

> Prejudice is one thing; race instincts or tendencies are another; the former will be, or ought to be, transient; the latter are of their nature permanent. . . . Among the sensible of both races there is a decided movement toward the "unity in diversity" that on the side of the colored race has long been a vexed question. (p. 4)

## On Educating Blacks

Armstrong's educational views joined his sociopolitical platform. Educating Blacks was for the good of the South and the whole nation. A stable society, for Armstrong, was a civilized society. Regional and national progress connected to social order. Armstrong spoke often about the qualities and divisiveness of ignorance at the societal level. Ignorance accompanied jealousy, instability, and uncertainty. Education, for Armstrong, was key to the reconstruction effort, which represented the first step in building the new industrial democracy with its requisite social and economic order.

Armstrong repeatedly reaffirmed his view that Blacks had the intellectual capacity to learn. It was not book knowledge, however, that they required. Rather it was the knowledge required for a people in the "ruts of barbarism." Blacks, he felt, needed character, morality, and socialization. They needed the knowledge of industry, self-restraint, and decency. Such were the qualities that would allow the building of community and societal participation.

He viewed Negro life as backward and restraining. The culture of Blacks was retrograde. One must become educated to rise above such circumstances. He wrote:

> Colored youth, to escape the terrible associations of negro life, the temptations of which are inconceivable to those in good circumstances, and to become better than their fathers, need the training and the refuge of Christian homes. Are they springing up as the result of negro education? (*SW*, July 1876, p. 50)

Character education and hard work were the key. Like his Puritan and missionary ancestors, Armstrong believed in the connectedness of work and character. One resided in the other. Work and productivity are measures of education. He wrote: "The black man can learn. Deficiency of character and not lack of brains is his difficulty. The negro question is one of morals and hard work" (*SW*, March 1876, p. 18). Referring to his major address at Syracuse, he wrote:

> Drill, training, toning up, is the important feature in the Association's work; it is making men and women; it is, I believe, a well-balanced, thorough-going system of culture, aiming directly at the mark, mingling mental with moral and physical training; satisfied to send out graduate teachers as Christians, no matter what denominational flag they may fly. (*SW*, December 1877, p. 94)

In the true spirit of the missionary, he believed teachers were key to the Hampton ideal. Being backward, Negroes could not improve themselves by themselves. The credo of morality and human betterment had to be brought in from more enlightened individuals. The teacher thus became the major actor in civilization building. Armstrong wrote:

> The negro teacher is the hope of his race; he is looked up to; his influence for good or evil is vast; when well-fitted for his work he has not been found wanting. What the colored race needs most, and needs now, is teachers of the right sort, as well as preachers fitted for the pulpit by some stern discipline. Let us make the teachers and we will make the people. (*SW*, December 1877, p. 94)

The embodiment of the Hampton ideal came in the person of Booker T. Washington. He emerged as Hampton's prize student, Armstrong's protégé, and a major educator and leader of the Black population for several decades.

## Booker T. and the General

When Booker T. Washington arrived at Hampton Institute, Armstrong was an energetic 33-year-old with a wealth of missionary and soldiering experiences already behind him. The two were tailor-made for each other. Armstrong was looking for students who would quickly and enthusiastically embrace his views on Negro socialization and education. Washington was looking for decent Whites not committed to the slaver's whip.

Washington found Armstrong compassionate yet demanding. He believed that Armstrong's views on discipline, orderliness, and character building for Negroes were desirable. Bontemps (1972) describes young Washington at Hampton:

> Booker absorbed the philosophy of the program as readily and as eagerly as he adopted the ritual of a daily bath, clean shirts and socks (washed nightly for wearing the next day), the enchantment of a toothbrush, sleeping between sheets, eating on a tablecloth at regular hours, and using a napkin—all of which were startlingly new to him. Almost instantly he detected a relationship between cleanliness of the body and self-respect, between physical and mental health, and he liked what he discerned. Splashing gleefully in his tub, he knew he had plopped into a way of life suited to his nature. (p. 11)

By his own account (1901), Washington enjoyed the regimentation at Hampton. Armstrong conducted daily military-style dormitory inspections. Clothing, rooms, and personal possessions had to be in order. Additionally, Washington acknowledged that the emphasis on personal hygiene and habits was welcome. He brushed his teeth daily, sewed tattered clothing, and learned to sleep between sheets.

He viewed Armstrong as a good White man committed to Negro education and advancement. Washington and others were fond of telling the story of how the dormitory rooms at Hampton became overcrowded with newly admitted students. As the overcrowding reached the crisis point, all were puzzled about what to do. The calm and resourceful Armstrong expeditiously pitched tents on the grounds, alleviating the problem. All was well.

Washington thoroughly embraced the Hampton ideal. It was at Hampton that he developed a philosophy of racial uplift that accommodated existing racial or economic relations. Washington's concepts of self-help, hard work, and character building were all Hampton ideas.

Finally, it was General Armstrong who brokered the deal for Washington to go to Tuskegee and head that school. Washington was thus a loyal and lifelong disciple of Armstrong and the Hampton ideal. He would be among its most enthusiastic advocates within the Black race.

## ARMSTRONG'S LEGACY

Much has been said here about Armstrong. He was at once a teacher, preacher, social engineer, political theorist, racist, amateur anthropologist, cultural pluralist, and social economist. Armstrong might be described most accurately as a colonizer for the twentieth century. He represents a departure from the primitive barbaric colonizer for whom rape, plunder, and pillage were the order of the day. Armstrong understood that domination and subjugation of a people must take on new forms. Force, cruelty, and the denial of human dignity would not succeed in the new industrial democracy.

Like others, Armstrong discovered that domination and democracy were not incompatible. A semiliterate peon could be just as profitable as a chattel slave. The new corporate industrial economy required skilled individuals. Apprentices of both the Black and White races were desirable. He understood that the Black, productive under slavery, could be equally productive in the new order. The old forms of labor and social organization had to be supplanted by new labor, markets, techniques, and social organization. In this regard, Armstrong was a visionary.

Beyond his understanding of how to socially reorganize the South in the interests of industrial capitalism, Armstrong had profound knowledge of race, race relations, and racial attitudes. He knew the Blacks and he knew the Whites. He understood their respective desires, fears, and limitations.

He knew that Negroes wanted to be a part of the system. They were desperate to abandon pariah status. Such intimate knowledge helped Armstrong conceptualize and plan around Hampton and think through issues in the larger environment.

Interestingly, Armstrong developed great insight into the evolved culture of Blacks. A complex quality of that culture is a kind of conservatism that has eluded even contemporary sociologists. It is a conservatism rooted in religion, tradition, and family socialization. In many ways, it acts as a restraint on historical anger and righteous indignation. The notion of divine retribution against the oppressor race is popular among Black Americans. Armstrong perceptively wrote:

> God had been very near to them, and has ever been ready to return to them whenever they would return to Him. They remind us, in many ways, of the children of Israel. The strong religious nature of the negro race makes it with its peculiar experience seem like one that has been led by a pillar of cloud. They appear to be better fitted for a theocracy than for a republic. (*SW*, December 1877, p. 94)

Armstrong's programs of gradualism and incrementalism could thus work with a people governed by such self-restraint. While racial theorists, including Armstrong, often talked of the possibility of mass Black violence, he seemed to understand that it could be averted with minimal measures. Armstrong thus gives us his dialectical view of Negroes. They are at once given to wild passion, yet simultaneously are near God. Armstrong, the colonizer, demonstrated much colonial insight in this area.

The Hampton notion of education and social organization was above all else successful in achieving its objectives. It trained thousands of teachers in accommodationist social, political, and religious outlooks. It became the model for the ideological training for the Black South. It fostered a politics of gradualism and moderation. Most important, it helped ready a labor force for its position in the new industrial era.

Finally, Armstrong and Hampton played no small role in creating a Black compradore class for the twentieth century. Black compradores have anchored the Black South. They have been pious, conservative, obedient, and loyal to the sociopolitical order. They have supported gradualism, incrementalism, and non-violence over revolution. They have provided a sometimes prosperous middle class without which the capitalist economy could not have stabilized. They have acted as a buffer in the South, providing business services, education, religion, fraternal orders, and hope to a people battered by slavery, sharecropping, violence, and four centuries of oppression.

# 4

## The Social, Racial, and Educational Ideas of Professor Franklin H. Giddings

FRANKLIN H. GIDDINGS (1855–1931) should require no introduction. His considerable theorizing, mentoring, and ideas have made a permanent impact on the social, intellectual, political, and racial life of the country. The passage of time, however, has seen his name slip from prominence. He was an influential leader in the new field of study to be called sociology, but he was no ordinary sociologist. Unlike today's academic specialists, he wrote widely on matters of history, economics, politics, race, education, culture, and morality.

Giddings's interests in societal development, race relations, education, and the role of the individual in nation building led him to explore what he considered the ingredients of the good society. He found America's racial demographics troubling. He viewed the heterogeneous society as inherently weak. Although never an educator in the narrow sense, his deep involvement with social scientists concerned with social studies curriculum and citizenship training connected him to the field of education.

Unlike other architects of Black education who engaged directly in funding and shaping policy, Giddings operated in the arena of social theory. His pronouncements on society and "civilization" helped frame a colonial model of segregation fitted for America.

His discourses on race and society were substantial. He became the major influence on and Ph.D. dissertation advisor to Thomas Jesse Jones, discussed in Chapter 6. Additionally, he mentored more than 50 Ph.D. candidates during his career. Giddings undoubtedly influenced the intellectual climate of the time. He warrants recognition as an important racial sociologist, colonial educator, and architect of Black education.

### EARLY YEARS

Giddings was born in 1855 in Sherman, Connecticut. His father was a Congregational minister who traced his lineage to Puritan ancestors (Hankins, 1968). During his intellectually formative years, he was said to be influenced by the writings of Charles Darwin, T. H. Huxley, John Tyndall, Herbert Spencer, Adam Smith, Auguste Comte, and John Stuart Mill. Biographer Hankins (1968) says the young Giddings cultivated a devotion to individualism.

He was graduated from Union College in 1877. Originally pursuing civil engineering, he switched his major to the social sciences. Economics first captured his attention before he moved to sociology. For the next 10 years he worked for the *Springfield Republican* and *Springfield Union* newspapers. In 1888, he made the transition into academia, accepting a professorship in political science and sociology at Bryn Mawr College. He stayed at Bryn Mawr until 1894, when he became the first full-time professor of sociology in the United States, at Columbia University.

Drawn early to the themes of Herbert Spencer, Giddings embraced notions of social development that relied on natural evolutionary forces. Evolution governed everything in the cosmos. In his view, opportunities for individual and social action were conditioned by natural forces. He was committed to Spencerian outlooks.

By the 1880s, Columbia was a hotbed of activity in the social sciences. Giddings soon would be influenced by Professor Richard Mayo Smith and other scholars who were advocating statistical research. As a young sociology professor, Giddings viewed himself as a strong proponent of "scientific" sociology, which he believed could stand separate from the more eclectic and broader social sciences. He soon would become a crusader for the cause of independent sociology.

## INFLUENCE OF HERBERT SPENCER

Herbert Spencer was the towering figure within the emerging field of sociology during the post-Darwinian period. Just as Darwin shook the world of biology and science, Spencer's "applied" Darwinian notions equally influenced the social sciences. Here is how Lybarger (1981) observed Spencer's impact:

> It is probably impossible to overstate the influence of Spencer upon the development of American sociology. American sociologists very early acknowledged the debt. Charles Horton Cooley asserted: "I imagine that nearly all of us who took up sociology between 1870 and 1890 did so at the instigation of Spencer." Cooley wrote in the 1920's but as early as 1890, the founder of American Sociology, Lester Frank Ward commented that American sociologists were ". . . virtually the disciples of Herbert Spencer." Hofstadter has argued that "almost every American philosophical thinker of first or second rank—notably James, Royce, Dewey, Harris . . . had to reckon with Spencer at some time. (p. 127)

Spencer's Social Darwinism fit nicely into the nation-building outlooks of conservative business tycoons, hegemonists, culture makers (Takaki, 1990, 1994), and other brokers of ideas. It provided a much-needed "rationale" to explain the unexplained economic order of the mid-nineteenth century. It was nature that chose those who would captain industry. He claimed it was nature that sought out the most capable and fit. It was God and nature that entrusted those who would manage the organization of government, wealth, and the social order. Humankind could provide no higher explanation or formula than that which was divinely ordained.

Spencer's ideas became widely embraced by the corporate and intellectual world. His work became the ideological glue around which the incipient sociology community was organized. That community, led by Albion Small, Lester Frank Ward, and Franklin Giddings, was politically and economically conservative. It embraced a tradition quite apart from the emerging populist critique of the day. Anticommunism and Christianity were among the pillars of its philosophical outlook. Giddings emerged as a potent intellectual force within that community. His views on social development provided context for his outlooks on the capabilities of Black Americans.

## ON THE SOCIAL ORDER

Within the American Social Science Association (ASSA), Giddings, among others, lobbied vigorously for an independent sociology. At ASSA's 1894 annual meeting, he proclaimed, "Social science is dead and its heir is scientific sociology" (in Lybarger, 1981, p. 154). The heart of his critique asserted that social science was "unscientific." At that same convocation he went on to argue that his sociology "is not a study of some one special group of social facts; it examines the relations of all groups (of facts) to each other and to the whole" (in Lybarger, 1981, p. 155).

Sociology, according to Giddings, must embrace quantification and the special explanatory power of numerical expression. It must move away from moral philosophy into inductive research. To make sociology scientific, Giddings demanded "men not afraid of work, who will get along with the adding machine and logarithms and give us exact studies, such as we get from the psychological and physical laboratories" (in Lybarger, 1981, p. 156).

### Classifying People and Groups

For Giddings, quantification served the interests of classification. He believed natural evolution had rendered distinct classes. Those classes were of people, behaviors, abilities, intelligence, and so on. Sociology must be able to understand the distinct nature of people. The most important distinctions for Giddings were physical, mental, and social. An understanding of these distinctions would allow us richer explanations of societal development. Classification then became a focus of his work.

Giddings believed people and races were divided physically into three vitality classes: high, medium, and low. The high group was characterized by bodily vigor, high mental power, a high birth rate, and a low death rate. The medium group experienced adequate bodily vigor, high mental power, a low birth rate, and an equally low death rate. The lowest group experienced low bodily vigor, low mental power, extremely high birth rates, and high death rates. The higher groups described European people, while people of color, especially Blacks, belonged in the low-vitality group.

Giddings's classification of mental or personality types also offered three categories. The high group was called the "inventive." This was the genius group, who made disproportionate contributions to the world in business, law, government, art, literature, music, and so on. He calculated that this group numbered approximately 250 out of every 1,000,000 people. The second personality or mental group was called "imitative." This was the middle group and was led by the high group. The lowest mental group for Giddings was the "defective." They were the incompetents, cripples, insane, and imbecilic. This helpless group had few grounds to justify its existence.

Regarding social class, Giddings constructed four groups: the "social," "non-social," "pseudo-social," and "anti-social." Similar to his other categorizations, this one was hierarchical and full of implicit ethnic references.

Members of the highest social group were identifiable by their consciousness. Those in this group were aware of their surroundings and their legacy, and were guided by a higher calling. They were dedicated to the betterment of the social order. They were the leaders and pillars of the community. The second group, the "non-social," represented for Giddings the majority of society. This was the in-between group capable of moving in either direction. The "pseudo-social" group contained the "congenital and habitual paupers." Giddings believed that this group pretended to be the victims of misfortune but were really shirkers and loafers who leeched from the public trough.

The final "anti-social" grouping had no redeeming value. Its members existed totally without virtue. This was the class of criminals who carried out aggression against the other classes. This group grew with the expanding affluence of society, living off its surplus.

These social classes, for Giddings, were difficult to escape. They were the products of lengthy evolutionary development; thus it was extremely difficult to abandon one's class moorings. An individual's social class was manifested by his/her "consciousness of kind" or "social mind," both of which were allegedly indicators of an individual's level of civilization.

Giddings's writings on sociology were saturated with these classification schemes. He believed that "differences" were the essential dynamic within humankind. We could never truly understand society and its various ability and racial groups unless we could explain differences.

## Civilization Building

Using his theories on difference and classification, Giddings offered an investigation on the organization of society, in which natural processes shaped the social order. Everything and everyone had their place in this order. Hierarchy was natural and normal. White people were to rule in this order. Civilized society was naturally forged.

Evolution was at the heart of Giddings's views on the historical development of organized society. The aggregation of people into communities was a natural process resulting in "fit" and order. The evolutionary process, for Giddings, created homogeneity, which was synonymous with community. To understand his views on racial groups, socialization, and ultimately education, it is important to deconstruct Giddings's views on the evolution of organized society.

Unlike many of his contemporaries, Giddings challenged the conventional evidence of the geographical origins of civilization. Surveying the commonly accepted anthropological views, he reaffirmed notions of separate racial and regional development, as they were important to his homogeneity argument. The Nordic and colored peoples were forever to be divided. Because "higher civilization" was demonstrated by the White race, Giddings could not accept Africa as the cradle of civilization. He wrote:

> It is highly probable that civilization was a product of the region now known as France rather than what is now Egypt or the Valley of the Euphrates. We will probably have to reverse our theories on that point but we do not need to get excited. (Giddings, 1932, p. 87)

Beyond the origins of humankind, Giddings saw civilization as the extension of homogeneous, atomistic, "family" groups. Biological aggregation and like-mindedness was the core of social organization. Biological aggregation led first to psychological kindredness, then to sociopolitical functioning. He wrote:

> A society, then is a relatively large number of human beings that are disposed in family groups and these family groups maintain a relatively approximately permanent association generation after generation. (Giddings, 1932, p. 32)

The progression, for Giddings, was quite neat and logical. Civilization began with the "gens" family structure, progressed to clans, then developed into tribes and finally into sociopolitical units such as city-states. In the course of this progression, the bonds of homogeneity grew ever stronger. Proximal and biological kindredness became the basis for political unity. Giddings argued that patriotism and social cohesion were the products of this sociogenerational inbreeding.

As a result of like-mindedness, law was able to emerge. With law as its scaffolding, sovereign society was able to engage in commerce, technological advancement, and regeneration.

## The History of Social Groups and Civilization

Giddings viewed all human history in terms of struggles that existed between groups, classes, and races. His analysis borrowed from Darwin and Marx, among others. Groups struggled within nature for survival, simultaneously battling for position, for "domination and subsistence," in his words. Some groups were ascendant, while others could not compete. Groups were to be seen as the components of civilization. Their viability and behavior shaped civilization. Groups were in constant motion as they battled for position. The challenges of nature forced both geographical and political movement.

Ancient societies, argued Giddings, were forged by the interactions of military force, religion, property, and privilege. He saw the origins of modern society rooted in primitive societies. Group survival must be sustained by power.

Giddings surveyed the different discipline-based explanations of history and the evolutionary development of people and groups. He wrote of the "geographical theory of history," which held that civilization developed in regions "that could sustain and energize dense populations" (Giddings, 1922, p. 89). The Mediterranean Basin exemplified such a region. The biological theory of history insisted that vital organisms able to adapt were selected by nature for survival. Psychological theories, which Giddings said were weak, argued that people developed through their dreams, vision, imagination, and self-determination. Anthropological explanations turned to a culture of dominance, will, and achievement for their understanding. Outdated sociology had fixed its explanations around the collective actions of human groups to account for development.

Giddings found elements of validity in all these explanations, but rejected any one as comprehensive. He found notions of collective behavior missing in most of these discourses. He argued that collective behavior was important to historical development, because it shaped survival and progress.

For Giddings, not all civilizations were viable. Quality was the key variable. Only those groups that established and maintained ethnic and social solidarity would survive (Giddings, 1922). He pointed to the Egyptian, Roman, and Greek societies as early exemplars of this kind of quality. Those societies, he believed, possessed the physical and human prerequisites for viability. Additionally, they understood the role of militarism and force in history.

All civilizations must have certain ingredients to advance. Among those were favorable physical context, ethnic cohesion, leadership, and recourse to force and collective will. The implications for America were profound. America possessed most of these qualities except ethnic cohesion. It would provide an Achilles heel. Giddings (1992) wrote of America:

> The resources of a new continent have drawn to America a population as variegated as that which crowded the Euphrates valley and more miscellaneous than that by the

Tiber. . . . The American population has been working out an experiment largely new
. . . it has created a more than imperial political solidarity with relatively little restraint until now of local or personal liberty. It has created, too, an individual enterprise without parallel, but it has yet to achieve the diversified and finer results of
collective efficiency. (p. 59)

In Giddings's view, America had many positive physical and historical features;
however, its ethnic diversity would be problematic. His writings went further
to explain the symbiosis between human interactions and the physical environment. His outlooks on the prospects for racial groups were framed in this
context.

## The Physical Environment and Social Formation

Nature and natural selection were at the heart of Giddings's interpretation of the
structure of society. Communities functioned well because nature forged them.
Once again homogeneity was the key. Organisms, whether animal or human,
evolved together in like fashion over long periods.

Giddings held that the physical environment played no small role in the natural
formation of a society. Communities could evolve only where the physical features of land and climate were favorable. He believed that the environment provided both primary and secondary resources. Primary resources included good
soil, fruits, grains, roots, fish, and game enough to sustain life. Secondary resources
included, for example, precious metals and spices, along with the possibilities for
commerce and property.

An important factor in Giddings's views of the environmental shaping of
society was climate. His discussion of the "heat belt" (Giddings, 1906) helped fuel
twentieth-century racial folklore. The heat belt exists between 30 degrees north
latitude and 30 degrees south latitude. It is 3,600 miles across and has a mean
temperature of 68 degrees Fahrenheit. In this belt lie Mexico, Central America,
the West Indies, much of Africa, Indo-China, India, Burma, Polynesia, the Malay
Archipelago, the Philippine Islands, and other countries.

The notion was that civilization within the heat belt had remained stationary
for thousands of years. Paraphrasing *The Far Eastern Tropics* written by Alleyne
Ireland (1905), Giddings (1906) wrote:

During the past five hundred years . . . the people of the heat belt have added nothing
whatever to what we understand by human advancement. Those natives of the
tropics and subtropics who have not been under direct European influence have
not during that time made a single contribution of the first importance to art, literature, science, manufactures, or inventions, they have not produced an engineer, or
a chemist, or a biologist, or a historian, or a painter, or a musician of the first rank.
(pp. 69–70)

Attempting to raise the heat belt notion to the level of natural law and science, he endorsed the claim that body functions were facilitated by atmospheric conditions, which made evaporation from the skin and lungs rapid. People in humid climates could not be as strong and energetic as those in dry areas. The rate of water evaporation then became crucial: "Hence in the torrid zone, we may expect constitutional differences between the inhabitants of low steaming tracts and the inhabitants of tracts parched with heat" (Giddings, 1906, p. 92).

Giddings accepted Herbert Spencer's view that energy was a central force in building and maintaining a thriving civilization. For him the "proof" was that the relatively dry areas of Mesopotamia supported early civilization. Again relying on the work of Herbert Spencer, Giddings (1906) paraphrased:

> Speaking of the varieties of negroes, Livingstone says: "Heat alone does not produce blackness of skin, but heat with moisture seems to insure the deepest hue"; and Schweinfurth remarks on the relative blackness of the Denka and other tribes living on the alluvial plains, and contrasts them with the "less swarthy and more robust races who inhabit the rocky hills of the interior," differences with which there go differences of energy. But I note this fact for the purpose of suggesting its probable connection with the fact that the lighter-skinned races are habitually the dominant races. (p. 94)

Dismissing effective precolonial societal formation, Giddings constructed models of civilization based exclusively on post-Renaissance European development. From this model he offered his hypothesis of "aggregation" as an explanation for societal formation. This notion suggested that development and modernization were the products of homogeneous population aggregation.

This aggregation about which Giddings spoke began as both natural and genetic, and emerged as functional and social. Disturbances to aggregation or the natural evolutionary processes were cause for contamination and distortion. For Giddings, a central problem of social progress in the past 2 centuries had been migration and mass movements of people.

In addition to establishing his version of social and physical prerequisites for viable civilization, Giddings launched a discussion on civil government. He defended both capitalism and democracy. He believed they could be joined amicably in the modern liberal state. He lived to see the development of the aggressive corporate state in search of foreign resources and markets. He reflected on new alignments of force in the unfolding twentieth century. His sociophysical and political views were inextricably connected to his outlooks on race and education.

## JOINING THE PHYSICAL WORLD TO POLITICAL SOCIOLOGY

Giddings spent considerable time trying to understand and rationalize the world as he saw it. He lived during a time of monumental changes. Slavery had ended, industrial corporate capitalism was reordering the socioeconomic landscape, massive immigration and migrations were altering world demographics, and the United States was stepping into its new role as a world power.

Prophetically, he envisioned the unfolding of a bipolar world where the United States and Soviet Union would emerge as preeminent superpowers. He foresaw the formation of two great world empires in the twentieth century. Simultaneously, he recognized the democratic impulse sweeping the world as people increasingly demanded participation in political processes.

He was thoroughly dedicated to market economics. He believed that a competitive business environment helped provide the scaffolding for nation building and societal development.

## ON CAPITALISM AND COMPETITION

As mentioned earlier, Giddings wrote widely on political economy. He believed that capitalism was nature's purest form of economy. Competition, for him, was consistent with evolutionary struggle. Competitive capitalism represented highly evolved civilization. For Giddings, all other economic systems were either "uncivilized" or "semicivilized." His views on the optimum economy were indicative of a belief that everyone had his/her place in the social order. The natural competitive environment ultimately would dispatch everyone to that place.

His economic views illuminated his outlooks on race and society. He believed the economy was natural. It gave everyone the same opportunities. In a little-known work entitled *Big Business: Economic Power in a Free Society* (1888/1973), Giddings collaborated with faculty colleague and anticommunist John Bates Clark to explain his economic views.

Writing at a time when populist critics were beginning to call attention to corporate price fixing, monopoly, collusion, and unfair business practices, Giddings insisted that free and fair competition would always assert itself. Competition, for him, represented stasis. Acknowledging that imbalances would occur periodically, he, like many market economists, believed that corrections were inherent. He wrote: "That competition in some form is a permanent economic process, is an implication of the conservation of energy" (Clark & Giddings, 1888/1973, p. 22).

Industrial production obeyed the laws of the market. Giddings commented on how the division of labor and competition for jobs affected society. Certain people were better suited for certain jobs. There were "natural demarcations" of labor. The innate differences in people qualified them differently for the job market. That phenomenon should not be tinkered with. He reminded the economic community that there were differences in the "moral qualities," "psychological gradations," and "mental mass" of people.

As a political economist and social theorist interested in the march of civilization, Giddings believed that the new order would link democracy to domination. Giddings was in the company of other social scientists, educators, and intellectuals who also believed that America, unlike Europe, could establish a social order where plutocracy could accommodate citizen participation. One of his central works, *Democracy and Empire* (1901), offered an exhaustive exposition of his views. Several propositions emerged from that book offering suggestions on how to manage and educate subject and "uncivilized" peoples.

Giddings was the quintessential imperialist. His belief in homogeneity was matched by his belief in order. Order was a prerequisite for the advancement of empire. Empire, for him, was the social and political manifestation of natural hierarchy. Empire, for Giddings, offered stasis in a struggling and uncertain world. He wrote:

> My studies of theoretical sociology long ago led me to believe that the combination of small states into larger political aggregates must continue until all the semi-civilized, barbarian, and savage communities of the world are brought under the protection of the larger civilized nations. (Giddings, 1901, p. v)

His notion of homogeneity was of special importance. He asserted that only people of the same tribe, the same "mother," the same class, and the same community could get along. Nature evolved, like people, in like ways. The problem for civilization was that in the modern era these homogeneous populations were brought together with other groups, ultimately leading to discord. By necessity people of different qualities would have to coexist lest there be permanent warfare. Such coexistence required both order and hierarchy, since the mixing of groups seldom resulted in equality. Giddings (1901) described what he viewed as the historical coalescence of a new body politic:

> The first step was an effort to bring under one central administration all adjoining regions which, together with the dominant city state, formed a natural geographic unity, and those populations which spoke allied languages and could easily be assimilated to the common type. Thus was created the enlarged or national state, in contrast to the small city state which had been its nucleus. Through this policy a strong military power was developed, and minute military regulation was extended throughout society. (p. 6)

Social history, for Giddings, was best described as the coming together and flying apart of heterogeneous peoples. He saw cycles of amalgamation followed by disintegration. Modern society simply represented advanced variation on the same theme. He viewed the Civil War and other dramatic world events as examples of this thesis.

Giddings offered a "rationale" for empire. It was the optimum way to structure order among unequal and heterogeneous peoples and territories. Empire was a vehicle for administration. The modern empire would differ from the feudal empire. It would honor citizen participation. Here is how Giddings (1901) viewed this construction:

> We have now the principle by which to explain the wonderful phenomenon of the democratic empire. It is a corollary of the principle that, when a nation makes itself the nucleus of an empire, step by step extending its sway over distant lands and peoples successively annexed, it can continue to be democratic; it can become, decade after decade, more democratic; it can even permit its colonies or dependencies to be democratic, while at the same time maintaining a strong imperial government for purposes of a common defense. (p. 11)

Although an imperialist, Giddings was also a democrat. The citizenry must enjoy a modicum of participation as investment in the system. Giddings went on to articulate the oxymoronic and hyphenated relationship between plutocracy and participation.

## ON RACE, SOCIETY, AND PUBLIC POLICY

Giddings applied his theories on social stability in his writings and conclusions on the complexities and problems of diverse society. With his protégé and doctoral student, Thomas Jesse Jones, Giddings studied social homogeneity among the teeming immigrant and slum areas of upper and lower Manhattan. From this work came Jones's dissertation, discussed later. Relying on notions of aggregation and migration, they concluded that "demotic composition," the blending of different qualities in human societal development, was problematic in social development.

Demotic development occurred by migrations, invasions, and other activities that caused people to move and create compound societies. Undesirable, demotic societies were inevitable. Giddings believed that there ultimately evolved a "demotic unity."

Some ethnic groups developed the American qualities of loyalty, piety, honesty, and so on, while others could not shake the habits of their inheritance. Little doubt was left that the African peoples of North America, the Caribbean, and Central America constituted a disproportionate percentage of the lowest group. Spanish-speaking Caribbean people drawn to New York City likewise would be classified here.

### Race and Societal Development

Giddings's racial views were inextricably connected to his outlooks on social evolutionism, homogeneity, and the democratic empire. Race, for him, was an illustration of nature at work. He viewed race issues as both sociocultural and political in nature.

Once again, the underpinning of his analysis turned to evolution and the struggle for existence. This struggle framed all human history and all societal relationships. He wrote:

> The struggle for existence in its collective form today affects entire races. It affects nations and has become associated with economic affairs in the new struggle of nations and of races. (Giddings, 1932, p. 187)

For Giddings, race conflict was associated with the struggle for survival. In the modern era, races were expressed in the form of nations. Nations vied for economic advantage, disagreed over boundaries, argued law, disputed immigration, and frequently went to war. All this was intertwined with the race struggle. He wrote:

> There are many conflicts among modern nations, not all of them wars, by any means. For instance, there are trade conflicts, legislation forbidding certain trade rights to certain nations. . . . Besides trade conflicts, there are cultural conflicts, and these are sometimes possible sources of a serious antagonism. (Giddings, 1932, pp. 195–196)

Questions of racial homogeneity were compelling for Giddings. They served to problematize issues of social development. America was particularly crucial because of its heterogeneous population. He noted that in colonial America, "different stocks," such as French Huguenots, German Mennonites, and assorted Dutch and Swedish groups, anchored the population.

He believed that heterogeneity was among the greatest threats to democracy. Immigration created great peril. Immigration led to incongruence. A mixed people offered the greatest threat to the democratic order. Social disorder, fracturing, and class conflict certainly would result. He cautioned:

> If you want to have all peoples of the earth come to America with equal freedom and no restriction, you can make that choice, but you will have to pay a certain price for it, and you will have to consider whether you want to pay that price or not. The price you will have to pay will be a complete breakdown and disappearance of those so-called free institutions which America has been supposed to have as her great aim in the life of the world. In other words, you cannot have freedom, liberty, democratic representative government, or anything of that kind, if you have a highly heterogeneous population. (Giddings, 1932, p. 339)

Giddings believed that the differences in people were too great to overcome. He observed several categories of differences. There were differences in appearance, attitudinal differences in beliefs, and finally socioeconomic and political differences in class and power. He summed up that outlook as follows:

It may seem from what I have been saying that I am assuming that some classes of people are a great deal better than others. I have no doubt that this is true but that is not the real contention. The real contention is that what makes the mischief is not inequality even of brains, but different attitudes, different points of view, different beliefs, different purposes, and, if you get too many of those differences in a population, you cannot bring about smooth and orderly working of government such as you have in popular government. If you are going to have popular government you are going to have people that can get together and who have similar ideas, who do not spend most of their time in trying to pull each other down. (Giddings, 1932, p. 341)

Giddings offered contrasting scenarios for how future societies might look. The homogeneous societies, perhaps many in Asia, had good prospects for efficacy, survival, and democratic regimes. The heterogeneous nations inevitably would lapse into anarchy followed by the corrective, fascism. He pointed to Italy as a case in point. Declaring himself in opposition to fascism, he nevertheless pointed to its efficiency in restoring and maintaining the integrity of law and order.

He expressed curiosity about the "experimental" societies, Australia and America. Both were settled by far-away Britons who displaced indigenous peoples and later were joined by many others. He applauded both countries' attention to their idiosyncratic arrangements. He believed both were experimenting with a variety of "solutions," but in the final analysis he felt that both might experience insurmountable problems.

From the standpoint of politics and public policy, Giddings felt that heterogeneous peoples would never be able to act together. Democratic and representative institutions required the collective action of people.

To elaborate his thesis on race and homogeneity, Giddings delineated four historically evolved dimensions of associations in nature. The zoogenic, anthropogenic, ethnogenic, and demogenic associations were Giddings's explanations for socioracial, biological, and genetic development.

*Zoogenic Association.* For Giddings, zoogenic association described early forms of life, that is, animals, which evolved social habits and relationships. The notion of animal association advanced in the course of evolution. Hence, sociability was susceptible to evolutionary law and change. Giddings hypothesized that certain levels of consciousness evolved in the process. Among them was the consciousness of choice. Thus, even early animals displayed preference in association. He viewed preferencing as fundamentally natural.

*Anthropogenic Association.* Anthropogenic association explained the social characteristics of primitive people. Giddings believed that there were parallels between characteristics of peoples in primitive society and those of contemporary "savages." His argument held that some peoples evolved poorly and remained in a state of arrested development. Those that experienced this retardation were the "lowest" of societies. Giddings (1911) wrote:

> There are many reasons for assuming the parallelism. One is found in the fact that the beliefs and customs of civilized peoples contain many survivals of beliefs and practices that still exist in full force in savage communities. These indicate not only that civilized nations have developed from savagery, but that existing savage hordes are in a stage of arrested development, and therefore approximately in the condition of primitive men. Another reason for the assumption is afforded by the fact that the oldest remains of human workmanship show that paleolithic and neolithic men had the same arts that savage men have at the present time. (p. 208)

While he held that there were no totally anthropogenic societies in his day, he did believe that anthropogenic groups existed within larger societies. He wrote:

> Modern savages are doubtless to some degree degenerate, enfeebled and on the way to extinction. Primitive men had no greater intelligence than modern savages have, and they had substantially the same ideas that savages have, although they were possibly in many ways more distinctly animal than savages are; but it is probable that primitive men were relatively well nourished, and that they lived in relatively large bands and evolved a relatively large total of energy for expenditure in the life struggle. (Giddings, 1911, p. 210)

It was in his writing on anthropogenic association that Giddings expanded his critique on the prevailing explanations of humankind's origins. Thoroughly reaffirming the evolutionary thesis, he again challenged the findings that Africa was the earliest venue of human evolution. He found Africa's environment favorable to physical evolution but not mental. He wrote:

> The scientific objections to the conclusion that man's development from a lower type was accomplished wholly in Africa are many and serious.
>
> An intensely hot and humid climate might have helped man to shed his hair, but it would have been extremely unfavorable to the physical and mental activity essential to a high cerebral development; while a genial, sub-tropical, lowland climate, passing into a cool and temperate climate in mountainous regions, would have been favorable in a high degree.
>
> The distribution of the black races is apparently irreconcilable with any theory that would limit the primitive home of man to an area west of the Indian ocean and south of the Sahara. The dwarf blacks of the far East, which are best represented by the Mincopis of the Andaman islands, are in all probability a remnant of one of the earliest human stocks, and it seems to have been demonstrated that the black races moved from southeastern Asia westward, and not from Africa eastward. (Giddings, 1911, p. 213)

Continuing his critique, he pointed to a polemical body of work that argued that Europe was the venue of humankind's evolution.

His discussion concluded that mental and moral development was inextricably tied to anthropogenic association. Thus, for him, intellectual development was an evolved phenomenon. Likewise, behavior such as intimacy and "festivity" were evolved.

**Ethnogenic Association.** True civilization, for Giddings, began when subjective associations occurred. It was not enough to have people physically proximal. There must be thoughts and feelings of association and kindredness. Groups, thus, after a while became "cooperating bodies" and "self-perpetuating" social groups. They ultimately displayed the all-important "social mind" that bound them together.

For Giddings, the classic and most efficacious example of association was the family structure. The problem existed at the next level up, the clan. Owing to expanded sexual contact, clans did not maintain the purity of the family. Clans, which developed into "tribes" and "hordes," represented the initial break in homogeneity.

As societies developed from the clan structure outward, human problems intensified. The sexual division of labor, inheritance of property, divorce, warfare, slavery, and "woman-stealing" were but some of the problems Giddings identified.

Over a long period of time, tribes mediated but never fully resolved political and cultural problems. Giddings suggested that the divisions of wealth, military matters, and ancestor worship were among the most contentious issues. At some point, tribes recognized a leadership structure and joined in confederation. This concluded the ethnogenic era, as a "gentile folk" or "ethnos" evolved. Human groups then moved forward to demogenic association.

**Demogenic Association.** In Giddings's framework, this was the most complex and developed form of civic association. It represented modern civilization where humankind moved beyond ethnogenic association. This was the modern political state with vast populations, industry, and citizen participation. This was the "modern commonwealth."

Giddings asserted that not every developed civilization reached demogenic association. To reach this status, a society would have to break through the fetters of militaristic dominance so that its citizens could pursue intellectual and personal freedom. Societal advancement had to be associated with liberty. "Barbarism" and "savagery" had to be eradicated.

The highly developed political state, for Giddings, forever abandoned primitiveness. It was committed to science, spiritual consciousness, economic advancement, and human liberty. It would always be plagued with the divisiveness of race and ethnic conflict, but it could function.

## Prospects for Modernity

Giddings believed that his brand of sociology and evolutionism explained social development. The "laws" of social causation and evolutionism had created heterogeneous populations. Despite the appearance of stability and stasis, there would always be fissures under the surface.

On the other hand, Giddings was encouraged by the prospects of human liberty and economic advancement. He saw those two phenomena in a symbiotic relationship. Liberty, prosperity, and progress were inextricably connected.

He compared society to a high-level organism that could and would evolve. Unlike lower forms of organisms, it had consciousness. Humans could create and legislate. They could problem solve. In the final analysis, society could influence its destiny within the context of powerful evolutionary forces.

Education would become an important force in the conscious society. Education could unleash the intellect for some, and train others. Education could serve the purposes of both enlightenment and control. Both would be necessary in the democratic empire.

## ON EDUCATION

As a social evolutionist and a democrat, Giddings had to philosophically resolve certain educational issues. His belief in natural difference directed him to embrace many Aristotelian viewpoints. Society should be intellectually led by the self-reliant, the calm, the wise, the virtuous, and the prudent. Those given to passion, illogic, and "unreason" must never become the guiding force. Every group would be identified in the evolutionary shake-out.

Beyond identifying an intellectual aristocracy, Giddings understood and supported the popular impulses. The masses increasingly were demanding voice and participation. Mass education thus needed to protect the privileged position of the learned and simultaneously facilitate popular sovereignty. He explained:

> We are beginning to perceive how important have been other means of education, particularly the family, the church, the public meeting, the lyceum, and the library. In every large city at the present time and, to some extent, in most of the towns and villages, attempts are being made to stimulate these educational agencies to greater activity and to supplement them by courses of definite popular instruction, through university extension lectures, through the clubs and classes that are maintained at university and other social settlements, and through numerous other means. (Giddings, 1901, p. 233)

In keeping with his view on the desirability of homogeneous society, Giddings also believed that education must be aimed at maintaining order and civilization.

More than cognitive and intellectual development, education was to serve a societal function. It should ideologically police threats to the natural, evolutionary,
and homogeneous development of society. He noted:

> At first education is not distinct from, nor, as we say in scientific jargon, is it differ-
> entiated from social control in its broader and more general aspects. The great pur-
> pose of social control, including education, is the protection and well being of the
> community. . . . That is a very recent achievement in education. It will be remem-
> bered that the primary purpose of all social control, including all social education is
> to protect the community against all sorts of baleful influences, against all disorder
> that might break up the community, and against economic burdens the community
> is unable to bear. (Giddings, 1932, p. 305)

Education, for Giddings, thus had differing functions, among them, control
and socialization. Children, he believed, came into this world with their nature
determined by inheritance. Many would be "defective," criminally minded, or
ne'er-do-wells. For those, education should be geared toward forging and altering their character as well as subduing their passions. He feared that the well-being
of the community was perpetually under assault.

While Giddings wrote about popular sovereignty, his notion of popular education was distinct from the emergent populist, progressivist, and experientialist
views. John Dewey (1916, 1938), noted Progressive educator, wrote of child
centeredness, the recreation of experiences, and democratic participation. Dewey
and other Progressive educators wanted learning to proceed from the child's needs
and agency. Giddings, on the other hand, wanted citizenship training.

For Giddings, popular will was not as important as the "virtuous" society.
Cloaking himself in Aristotle's *Politics*, Giddings noted: "A city can be virtuous
only when the citizens who have a share in the government are virtuous, and in
our state all the citizens share in the government; let us then inquire how a man
becomes virtuous" (Giddings, 1901, p. 234). Giddings wanted to instruct. He
wanted an educational system that molded children. Education, for him, was requisite for the efficacious civilization. He wrote:

> The business of education then is so to instruct that nature shall be kept vigorous,
> alert, and brave, while appetite is subjected to the control of reason. Since nature is
> modified by both habit and reason, it is important to inquire whether the training of
> early life should be chiefly that of reason or chiefly that of habit. (Giddings, 1901,
> pp. 234–235)

Giddings identified a cluster of interrelated objectives for public education
in the twentieth century. The most important was maintaining order. He envisioned
an America under siege from disgruntled and undisciplined minorities, laggards,
"criminals," and other pariahs. The educational system must attempt to socialize

these groups toward conformity, acceptance, and consensus. If possible, they should be trained in reason and intellect.

Giddings believed that the White race must guarantee its integrity and continued existence through the vehicle of education. In an ever-evolving world, the more feeble colored races would experience decline. They would drink themselves into oblivion. The White race must hold firm the principles responsible for their "superiority." He remarked:

> We read to-day of the superiority of the Anglo-Saxon, and of the decadence of the Latin race; and the handwriting of fate is again revealed, as in Babylon of old, not at sunrise in Belshazzar's camp, but at midnight at his feast. A people that idly sips its cognac on the boulevards as it lightly takes a trifling part in the comedie humaine, can only go down in the struggle for existence with men who have learned that happiness, in distinction from idle pleasure, is the satisfaction that comes only with the tingling of the blood, when we surmount the physical and the moral obstacles of life. (Giddings, 1901, p. 243)

Rationality must be the companion of restraint. Giddings argued that non-Anglo-Saxons, especially people of color, had only emotion, belief, and impulse as intellectual underpinnings. Those factors would not serve their advancement. The Europeans in America must embrace rationality.

Giddings wrote that ideas, opinions, public discourse, and argumentation must be rooted in clear, scientific, and rational thinking. In the course of its political life, society would encounter many problems. The propositions of cynics, malcontents, and charlatans must be countered by rational intellectual thought lest the social order fracture. Popular education must be rooted in calm, rational thinking, and reasoning.

## GIDDINGS'S IMPACT

Giddings's views on evolutionism, racial hierarchy, the social order, and citizenship training helped construct the ideological undergirding of Black education. His evolutionist views proclaimed and celebrated human difference. God made us different. Nature provided historical drama beyond our will. It rendered the segregating of people, and any violation would not be salutary. Such were the immutable laws of the universe.

For Giddings, racial hierarchy was part of those laws. Equatorial people would never reach the intellectual level of Nordic and European people. Their role would be that of laborers in the industrial society. They would have to be trained for their vocational and political roles.

The social order, for Giddings, must observe the laws of cohesion; otherwise it surely would fracture. The heterogeneous society required special attention. Racial, ethnic, cultural, and societal interaction had to be checked.

Finally, social development required direction. Citizens and citizenship had to be cultivated. Democracy could not be allowed to drift into anarchy.

As ideologist and social engineer, Giddings offered a blueprint for the social order. America needed planned racial segregation alongside citizen participation and economic development. The successful joining of hierarchy to democracy would be America's destiny.

# 5

## The Phelps Stokes Family, Friends, and Fund: Adventures in Philanthropy

THE PHELPS STOKES FAMILY embraced a body of ideas that profoundly shaped not only the education of Blacks in America for decades, but also the evolution of public policy and social welfare ideology at the turn of the twentieth century. The Phelps Stokes family was part of a much larger story of how America's influential people came to express their views on the poor, the Black, the dispossessed, and the outcast. This powerful family was instrumental in the development of the missionary charity of the mid-nineteenth century as well as the corporate philanthropy of the later nineteenth and early twentieth century. Both provided guideposts for minority education, immigrant education, and important public policy issues.

Deconstructing the views of this family and their close associates offers a study in how partisan ideology, politics, and big money shaped corporate-funded Black education. The Phelps Stokes corporate philanthropic view became important after the Civil War when the industrialists were confronted with the issue of reuniting a fractured country, including addressing vexing racial and political issues. Philanthropic foundations emerged center stage in the late nineteenth and early twentieth century as the country forged modern institutions and outlooks.

The views of the Phelps Stokes family contributed greatly to the evolution of a new corporate outlook. Members of the family were both missionaries and industrialists. As such they helped establish a bridge between the earlier missionary-oriented charity movement and the corporate foundation model employed in the twentieth century. The Phelps Stokes Fund represented the quintessential early corporate charity voice. Anson Phelps Stokes, Jr., emerged as the Fund's leader and guiding force. He became a major architect of Black education.

Translating ideas into action were key family members Anson Sr., James G., Caroline, Olivia, and especially Anson Jr. Of special interest is the close and telling relationship Anson Jr. had with Thomas Jesse Jones, discussed in Chapter 6. Together, they supported their version of human social justice while fundamentally embracing the precepts of human inequality.

Anson Jr. and the rest of the family represent an important viewpoint. Neither devils nor angels, they were part of a successful ideological and political effort to reconcile corporate avarice with social welfare. This is an essential notion underlying not only Black education but also nearly every aspect of America's public policy in the twentieth century. It bears repeating that, during this period, America hoped to avoid the pitfalls plaguing many European countries, namely, the politics of confrontation, class struggle, and long-term ethnic warfare. Private philanthropy became an important concept in the social and political life of the United States.

Josephine Lowell Shaw, well-known charity matriarch, should be mentioned as part of this inquiry. Her tireless charity work, close friendship with the Phelps Stokes family, and conceptual essays contributed to the shaping and joining of the charity movement to Black education.

In the last quarter of the nineteenth century, a new philanthropy was born. Inheriting ideas and practices from the past, this philanthropy was more partisan and goal-oriented. It fit into the new industrial and social order.

## TOWARD A NEW PHILANTHROPY

The Christian charity movement had deep roots in pre–Civil War America. As discussed throughout this book, missionary societies were actively involved in Black education, almsgiving, and comforting those in need. The robber baron oligarchy advanced a new, politicized conception of charity and gift giving. While Christian charity continued, corporate foundations possessed tremendous resources to influence public life. Howe (1980) has referred to this time as the emergence of "scientific" philanthropy. She argues that the new corporate philanthropy became distanced from public charity. The new foundations possessed large endowments, conducted research, and articulated an "appeal to science" in their efforts. Science implied organized study. Proponents declared that a scientific approach prevented haphazard and unsystematic gift giving. This new scientific philanthropy argued that social problems could be examined, isolated, and remediated.

These beliefs were drawn from the new social science outlooks, especially structural functionalism. The structural functionalists, confident in their beliefs, influenced sociology, education, anthropology, and political science (deMarrais & LeCompte, 1995). Additionally, this scientism turned increasingly to the propositions of behaviorism for societal remedies. Behaviorism posited that behavior could be shaped and, thus, influenced. Structural functionalist outlooks rejected notions of class struggle, conflict theories, or any hint that there were irreconcilable problems. All problems could be solved within the system.

Rationality became an important watchword of the new philanthropy. Rationality and "science-in-giving" were promoted by attention to the new social theory and the increasingly popular social science outlooks. The new social scientists talked in terms of planning and the amelioration of social ills through institutional problem solving.

Foundation philanthropy soon defended itself as benevolent, altruistic, and instrumental in social reform. Linking its objectives to the new social sciences, the corporate philanthropic community possessed "theory" and rationale. Many of America's wealthiest families began chartering large foundations that quickly became active.

Slaughter and Silva (1980) argue that the post–Civil War foundations were interested in ideology. The authors state that the new America was a confusing and somewhat anarchic place. The advent of monopoly corporations, industrialization, agricultural displacement, massive immigration, labor unrest, and a wildly gyrating economy created societal and cultural uncertainty. No adequate intellectual, legal, rational, or scientific explanations were available by which to understand this uncharted and rapidly developing new order. They posit that the corporations funded explanations and justifications by theorists who rationalized the new, dramatically unequal distributions of wealth and power.

New foundation ideology presented capitalism as the only viable economic system. Social problems were inevitable growing pains to be remedied within the capitalist framework. The new corporate charity movement was presented as a key vehicle for social reform.

With new theories, new money, new views on Black education, new objectives, a new industrial order, and a new century, the corporate philanthropies were ready for action. The Phelps Stokes family was well placed to apply the new philanthropy to Black education.

## CHARITY IDEOLOGY: A FAMILY PORTRAIT

The Phelps Stokes family was both a product of its times and simultaneously a shaper of those times. Its story begins with A. G. Phelps of Connecticut at the beginning of the nineteenth century. He was a trader in precious metals who was joined in business by his two sons-in-law, William Dodge and Daniel James. From that association came the well-known and prosperous Phelps Dodge and Company, which engaged in mining precious metals. Phelps was active in the New York State branch of the American Colonization Society, which favored Blacks returning to Africa to recolonize settlements there. The establishment of Liberia eventually resulted from this effort. A. G. was also an active member of several missionary societies during his lifetime.

On the other side of the family, Thomas Stokes (1765–1832), a New York City merchant, also had been a leader and activist in missionary society work. Friends, A. G. Phelps and Thomas Stokes enjoyed joining the two families. Stokes's son James married Phelps's daughter Caroline in 1837. Their four children were instrumental in creating corporate charity and in influencing the direction of Black education in the United States.

Anson Phelps Stokes, Sr., the first child of this union, expanded the family's business interests into banking. As both he and the businesses grew in prominence, he began to insert himself into national political matters. Anson Jr. described his father as aristocratic but possessing deep interests in public affairs. Anson Sr. extended his interest in civic affairs to the international scene. Concerned about America's involvement in overseas adventure, he declared himself an anti-imperialist. He founded, incorporated, and became the first president of the National Association of Anti-Imperialistic Clubs. Through these activities, he caught the attention of President Grover Cleveland, who offered him the ambassadorship to Austria in 1888.

He turned down that offer, instead cultivating an interest in Black Africa and her plight. It should be noted that Africa had been a venue for both European and American missionary activity, and such interest remains today as Africa's plight worsens. Missionary romanticism often sees Africa as central to its efforts.

Within national politics, Anson Sr. represented the missionary charity outlook. He was founder and first president of his local civic-minded Reform Club. The missionary charity movement is of particular interest because of its early ideological influence on Black education.

### The Evolution of Missionary Charity

Missionary charity has its roots in Christianity. Notions of support to the poor and altruism have long been associated with Christian charity. The political culture of the United States exalts the individual and his/her ability to achieve. Hence, morality, sobriety, piety, thrift, and labor have provided the formula for success. The Puritan and Social Darwinist contributions to the American culture dictated that the fit survive and prosper, while the idlers, feebleminded, and ne'er-do-wells struggle and suffer. Corporate philanthropy embraced the legacy of missionary charity; however, it was discernibly political.

As upper-middle-class and often wealthy reformers, such as the Phelps Stokes family, adopted corporate philanthropy, the charity movement changed. Committed to concern for the downtrodden, their close associates were bankers and industrialists who profited greatly from those whose labor they expropriated yet whose causes they celebrated. An efficient society always provided the rationale for their charitable actions. Economic, class, and racial peace and order were their central objectives. These people were, above all, nation builders committed to the industrial reordering and reunification of America. Anson Sr. and Anson Jr. were essentially political missionaries of charity. Many who have studied both the missionary and corporate charity movement agree that their views and activities were motivated as much by patriotism as by any other factor (Lybarger, 1983).

A sociopolitical analysis of this period and its outlooks is important because the ideology that influenced reform politics, the poor, and minority education were all forged during this time. That ideology represented an effort to reconcile the profit system with social welfare. Participants in the corporate philanthropic movement such as Thomas Jesse Jones and others were fearful of what they saw in parts of Europe. There, it seemed, callousness and an old aristocratic mentality contributed to conflict between the classes. Widespread worker unrest led to protest, anarchy, and eventually Bolshevism. Corporate philanthropists hoped that America could short-circuit such a predicament.

It was this charity ideology that made the Phelps Stokes family important in public policy. An argument can be made that the corporate philanthropic outlook, with its conflictual and conciliatory themes, has been a building block for minority and "antipoverty" policy as well as education for nearly 150 years.

## Caroline Phelps Stokes: Charity Matriarch

Caroline Phelps Stokes, second child of James and Caroline, was born in New York on December 4, 1854. Her sister and biographer, Olivia Eggleston, believed the environment of New York City profoundly affected both of them. Olivia writes that their Puritan and Christian background compelled her to take note of the unfolding plight of Blacks and the poor (Phelps Stokes, n.d.).

In describing other influences on Caroline, Olivia writes of family members in the preceding generation who gave their time to colored orphanages, the abolition of slavery, and temperance. Olivia recounts that family homilies and themes regularly spoke of "relieving suffering," "turning many from wrong doing to Christ," and "overcoming evil with good" (Phelps Stokes, n.d., p. 2).

Caroline, during her formative years, lived in New York and summered in Ansonia, Connecticut, a town named after her grandfather. Interestingly, she spent considerable time with her cousin Grace Dodge, a member of the Dodge family who was soon to be associated with the colorful, left-wing, libertine, counterculture, New York coffeehouse crowd. On her sixteenth birthday, Caroline rededicated herself to the Christian mission. She wrote in her diary/journal: "O Blessed Jesus, I wish to give myself away, body and soul, to the Blessed Savior who has died for me" (Phelps Stokes, n.d.). An entry on her eighteenth birthday read: "With God's help I will endeavor to live the years that still remain with a fixed and determined purpose to do my duty, no matter how hard or disagreeable that duty may be" (Phelps Stokes, n.d., p. 3).

That same journal showed a young woman greatly concerned about the urban poor. She wrote on December 2, 1873:

I do not think I like living in a city; there is so much sorrow sin and distress on every side that the little one can do seems to make little or no impression, and it makes me unhappy to see all the trouble and not do anything to relieve it. (p. 4)

Olivia says that Caroline was "naturally interested in the Negro race," because of the family's extensive background in the African colonization and charity movement (Phelps Stokes, n.d., p. 4). That interest expanded as Caroline began a life of extensive travel. On visits to London and continental Europe, Caroline met with assorted Africans, especially those connected to Liberia. During these times, she made financial contributions, particularly to education in Black Africa. Additionally, she made long trips throughout India and Palestine and other parts of the Middle East.

Within the United States, Caroline visited Hampton Institute, Tuskegee, the Calhoun Colored School in Alabama, and other Black schools and institutes scattered over North Carolina. On a visit to Hampton she encountered American Indian students, thus sparking her continuing interest in Native Americans and their education. Caroline made financial gifts to many of the schools she visited. Additionally, she arranged to have Bibles and religious tracts donated to these schools.

Although she witnessed great suffering throughout the world, Caroline's attention was always drawn to New York City. Over the years as her philanthropic activities expanded, she became deeply involved with housing for the poor. One project that gained her attention and money was the creation of tenement housing for the Black poor. She contributed to the erection of two buildings for this purpose, which she promptly named Tuskegee. Consistent with charity movement activities, Caroline also developed interests in prison conditions, health care, and the aged.

Olivia writes that Caroline spent considerable time with, and was likely influenced by, Josephine Shaw Lowell, who also worked tirelessly for charity and wrote essays about the charity movement and Black education. The Lowells represented paternalistic and detached corporate charity. Josephine's altruism was embedded in a conservative economic and political context. She viewed people in need as ignorant, shiftless, and irresponsible. Charity or relief, she believed, could transform idlers into productive citizens as it eliminated poverty from our midst.

Josephine became enamored with Booker T. Washington and his model of industrial training. On at least one occasion in 1903, she gave a speech introducing Washington to an audience of admirers. Throughout her activities, she believed Black people needed moral development and the opportunity to become more noble citizens.

Caroline shared Josephine Lowell's view on industrial education for Black people. Those views are articulated in her famous last will and testament, which established the written and financial directives for her family to fund Black education (see the section "The Phelps Stokes Fund" in this chapter; see also Berman, 1980; King, 1971; and Weber, 1986).

## INTRODUCING JAMES G. PHELPS STOKES: MISSIONARY IDEOLOGIST

Rarely written about, James G. Phelps Stokes was the fourth sibling of Caroline, Olivia, and Anson Sr. James G. offers us a case study in the charity mentality established by late-nineteenth-century missionaries and politicized robber baron industrialists. Corporate foundations in the twentieth century embraced, developed, and institutionalized this outlook. The mentality is rooted in the American colonial and paternalistic mind.

James G. was part of the movement that redefined charity. As mentioned, charity rooted in Christian duty, almsgiving, and altruism gave way to the new corporate philanthropy as public policy. Combining religion, sociology, and humanism, charity people were determined to prove that rugged individualism and bare knuckles capitalism could be compatible with compassion for the less fortunate. James G.'s views on schools, schooling, Black Americans, ethics, and politics were representative of this distinct point of view.

James G. wrote and spoke of his outlooks. Like his sister Caroline, he too was an active Christian, missionary charity proponent, and social activist. James G., however, was more political, commenting on everything from poverty to race relations to overpopulation to the rise of communism. His views offer an incisive sample of the more political emergent ideology within the missionary charity movement.

### James G. on Social Problems and Their Amelioration

In the true spirit of Christianity, James G. was concerned about the "flawed" individual. The human character, he wrote, had "defects" and was "marred" (Phelps Stokes, 1904a, p. 1). Human beings, he believed, were given to selfishness, narrowness, and the "furtherance of their own personal ends":

> The constant encouragement given to personal ambition for personal triumph and personal reward, tends to develop desire of a similar order to that of the criminal offender who, in seeking his personal gratification, gives no proper regard or consideration to the relation of his acts or of his course to the welfare of others or to the welfare of the community. (Phelps Stokes, 1904a, p. 1)

Self-centeredness and ambition were for James G. the ingredients for injustice; injustice was the product of inhumanity. The economic and social systems were all right, but flawed people were causing discord and disorder. The eroding "social nature" of humankind was unleashing negative, even deviant, behavior (Phelps Stokes, 1904a).

The crumbling social nature of individuals was seen as the greatest threat to an otherwise stable civilization. For James G., selfishness was the forerunner of evil. He argued: "Vice and vicious habits are but products of self-centered desires for immediate gratification" (Phelps Stokes, 1904a, p. 2).

One of his discussions, entitled "Ye Have the Poor Always With You" (1904b), published by *The Independent* on September 29, 1904, reveals his outlook on the source of human problems: "Where the fault appears to lie in self, it is perhaps due, more often than not, less to depravity of the individual than to errors of defects in his early training of early associations" (p. 3).

He went on to describe the underdeveloped personality as the root cause of poverty. More specifically, it was the defective personality. Well-developed people, he argued, will rise above the ranks of the unemployed and dispossessed. Beyond the defective personality there also exists poverty caused by drunkenness, vice, crime, cerebral abnormalities, congenital structural defects, and moral weakness.

James G. believed that these problems, although serious, could be overcome. People must seek to redeem themselves. They must seek out the wholesome, develop personal ambition, become better educated, and receive constant encouragement.

Despite the widespread existence of poverty, James G. seemed optimistic for the future. He believed that the environment was having profound effects on individuals. He believed in a kind of Darwinian progress where all was evolving. He also believed that improved work environments would contribute to the quality of life. He wrote:

> Factories and workshops are being better planned, better constructed, better ventilated and better equipped . . . sweatshops are disappearing, hours of labor are being reduced, the purchasing power of the average wage is increasing. (Phelps Stokes, 1904b, pp. 12–13)

James G. did not totally absolve the industrial ordering of society for poverty and other problems. He acknowledged excesses and "industrial evils," but saw the development of the individual as paramount. In the last analysis, James G. believed in altruism and "service." Individuals must see to the welfare of others. He insisted that individual caring will make poverty vanish and that the "social spirit" can coexist with the corporate-mindedness of modern society.

### Expanding the Role of Schooling

As a charity proponent, James G. was also interested in public schooling. Many participants in the charity movement took great interest in public education as well as Black education. James G. wrote about schools and the massive role they would have to play in shaping the new society. In an article entitled "Public Schools as Social Centres" written in 1904, James G. (1904a) argues that schools should teach human cooperation in place of greed, selfishness, and personal advantage.

He firmly believed that schools had a role in this process of individual uplift. Schools should focus on career guidance, personal rewards, and ridding individuals of unsanitary environments. Parenthetically, this notion of sanitation recurs throughout the literature on Black and immigrant education.

Beyond his concern that schools teach helpfulness, he wanted schools to be the geographical centers of community life. He felt it impractical that expensive school buildings were utilized only 5 hours a day when they could be used by clubs, community and recreation organizations, and settlement houses.

Through James G. we gain a clearer picture of missionary charity families. They extended great sympathy to the very people from whom their considerable commercial enterprises expropriated profits. They wanted to help those whose situation as social pariahs they helped to create, but they never took responsibility for their creation.

## On Bolshevism

By the end of the nineteenth century, the charity movement began to identify a new nemesis, Bolshevism. The romantic intellectualizing of Fabians and utopians was giving way to determined political organizing. Karl Marx's exhortations to proletarian revolution were a reality in Eastern Europe. Anticommunism became a core building block of the twentieth-century corporate charity movement.

James G. became very interested in the Bolshevik threat. Observing that the communists had a program of altruism and social egalitarianism that might attract popular support, James G. and like-minded people looked for ways to discredit the new insurgence. He appeared concerned that the idealism of the communists might increasingly attract the support of the dispossessed, including Black Americans. Discrediting their call for land, peace, bread, and national self-determination, James G. denounced the Bolsheviks as despots and charlatans. He proffered that they hid behind high-sounding phrases in order to initiate their true "tyrannical" agenda. He proclaimed the revolution antidemocratic but cloaked within the shield of democracy (Phelps Stokes, 1918).

Philosophically and politically, James G.'s anticommunism was very telling. He demonstrated that he truly favored an economically stratified society in which the deserving industrialists and managers maintained control and economic privilege. Moreover, he revealed little confidence in or respect for the intellect and capabilities of the common people. They were at the bottom where they belonged. Finally, James G. demonstrated that the charity movement was not only about reform, but about maintenance. He wanted to maintain capitalism and property rights. He wanted gradual and manageable change whereby mass upheaval could be short-circuited.

The implications for Black education were far-reaching. The "Negro question" had to be resolved within certain boundaries lest it interfere with commerce. The Blacks would have to be trained in capitalist economics or they might reject the notions of private property, which so affected their lives. James G. believed that the concepts of public property, wealth sharing, and the "workers' state" might sound appealing to a people dispossessed for 300 years.

James G. contributed political vision to the family's charity outlook. Perhaps most important, he expanded the ideological foundation for his nephew Anson Jr., the fund, and ultimately Black education.

## THE PHELPS STOKES FUND

The bequests in Caroline's will created a fund devoted almost exclusively to the education and welfare of Black Americans. The $10,000 gifts to the Burnham Industrial School in New York, the Calhoun Colored School in Alabama, and the Hampton Institute made an important political point, given that other options existed. That is, by 1910 many schools with more liberal or progressive platforms were operating, such as Atlanta University, Howard, and Fisk.

Interpreters and executors of the will decided early that subsequent funds would be targeted to industrial-style programs. Anson Jr. was legal executor of the will, which was estimated to exceed $800,000. The trustees and their designated planning committee, staffed with family members, worked through the politics for over 6 months and on May 10, 1911, officially chartered the fund. The crucial act of incorporation read:

> It shall be within the purpose of said corporation to use any means to such ends (erection of tenements and educating of Africans, American Negroes, American Indians and deserving white students through industrial schools, as well as founding of scholarships and erection or endowment of school buildings or chapels). (in Berman, 1969, p. 61)

Within a short time the trustees further defined and refined their objectives with another policy statement, which read:

1. That in providing for the establishment of the Phelps-Stokes Fund the testator showed a special, although by no means exclusive interest in negro education.
2. That it is wise for the Board to disperse its philanthropy as far as possible through existing institutions of proven experience and of assurance of future stability.
3. That the co-operation of the best white citizens of the South is of prime importance in solving the problem of negro education. (in Berman, 1969, p. 62)

The Fund got up and running. Treasurer Francis L. Slade estimated they would gain $37,000 annually from interest on their total holdings. Anson Jr. joined the powerful education committee through which he would direct policy and funding. The fund became a trailblazer. It commissioned studies on Negro education from prestigious universities such as Georgia and Virginia, thus building an expansive data base in the field. It established links with other foundations such as the Peabody, discussed in Chapter 9, the Slater, and the Jeannes Funds, among others. After the appointment of Dr. Thomas Jesse Jones as educational director in 1912, Phelps Stokes would become a leader, if not the leader, in Black education. The larger and wealthier foundations, such as Rockefeller, Carnegie, and Ford, were profoundly influenced by Phelps Stokes and its activities.

## ANSON PHELPS STOKES, JR.: ARISTOCRAT, "YALIE," REVEREND

Coming from this environment, Anson Phelps Stokes, Jr., in the early twentieth century consolidated the family business and fortune. He devoted his life to the full practice of missionary corporate charity through the Phelps Stokes Fund.

Anson Phelps Stokes, Jr., was born April 13, 1874, at New Brighton, Staten Island, New York. A graduate of St. Paul's School in 1892, Anson Jr. entered Yale where his love affair with the school began. Firmly imbued and accepting of the family's views on Christian charity, philanthropy, and aiding the Negro and the tenement dweller, he took up the study of theology.

Anson Jr. found Yale a wonderful place. He joined the staff of the *Yale Daily News* and soon became its chairman. In 1896, he received his bachelor of arts degree and enrolled in the Episcopal Theological School. In 1900, he was graduated with a bachelor of divinity degree. Anson Jr.'s missionary charity views were exceeded only by his love for Yale. His objective was to combine these two interests.

In 1899, at 25 years old, he accepted appointment as secretary of Yale under its president, Arthur T. Hadley. In that capacity, he established an Alumni Advisory Board and the Yale-in-China organization. Additionally, he was known for obtaining substantial gifts and endowments for the university.

Desirous of fulfilling his Christian mission, he was ordained a deacon in the Protestant Episcopal Church in 1900. He executed that position at St. Paul's Episcopal Church in New Haven for the next 18 years. During those early years in New Haven, Anson Jr. participated in numerous civic, charity, and university committees. As his prominence grew, his activities expanded. He helped found the National Committee on Mental Hygiene and the Lowell House Association. Additionally, he participated in the Institute of Government Research, the Committee on Japanese Peace Plans, and other national committees.

After the death of Caroline and the inception of the fund, Anson Jr. turned his attention increasingly to matters of education. He immediately was made a trustee of the fund and shortly thereafter, in May 1912, became a trustee of the powerful General Education Board, discussed in Chapter 7. Over the next decade, Anson Jr. maintained his broad charity work and interests in tenement housing reform, health issues, Yale, and other issues and organizations. It appears, however, that education matters occupied more of his time. The war years underscore this point.

At the request of the War Work Council of the YMCA, Anson Jr. conducted a study of the educational needs of soldiers. The results were published as "Educational Plans for the American Army Abroad" (1918). Additionally, he helped organize the American University Union in Europe and sat on the boards of the Institute of International Education and of Central China College. Recognized for his educational work in Europe following World War I, he received the Chevalier of the Legion of Honor award from the French government.

His international education activities matched his work within the United States. He helped organize the National Council on Religion in Higher Education and acted as chair of the Special Gifts Committee of both Hampton and Tuskegee Institutes. This work continued into the early 1920s when Anson Jr. reached one of his life's major turning points.

In 1921 the presidency of Yale was vacant. Some accounts argue that he desperately sought this position. While he was considered, he lost out to James Rowland Angell. Anson Jr. resigned as secretary of Yale, and in 1924 became president of the board of directors at the Phelps Stokes Fund. He simultaneously accepted a position as canon of the Cathedral of St. Peter and St. Paul in Washington, DC, better known as the Washington Cathedral.

After his 1925 ordination as a priest in the Protestant Episcopal Church, "Canon" Stokes became nationally prominent in the church. During his time in Washington, DC, he facilitated the church's missionary charity activities. In addition to fund-raising successes, he worked tirelessly on, often chairing, scores of boards and committees. In these capacities, he participated in and directed studies on topics ranging from Negro housing conditions to discrimination in public theaters in Washington, DC.

In association with his work at the Phelps Stokes Fund, Anson Jr. became a trustee of the Brookings Institute and of the Booker T. Washington Institute in Kakata, Liberia. He was to become widely recognized for his work in international education, Black American education, African education, and a wide variety of other charity efforts.

Beyond his life as a missionary-oriented clergyman, fund raiser, and committee worker, Anson Jr. supported an ideology that was to help shape a half-century of Black education and political life in both the United States and Africa. Anson Jr. was instrumental in translating missionary and corporate charity into accommodationism. His life was a testament to the views that were to affect the educational, social, and political landscape of America in general and Black America in particular.

## Anson Jr.'s Views on Race, Education, Politics, and Society

While Anson Jr. was certainly no ideologue, a sense of his views comes through in his writings and speeches and from reminiscences by family members. Perhaps more important than his words are the people and programs he supported and funded. In most instances, the sober and reserved Anson Jr. spoke with the voice of the pious man he was. Seemingly conscious of his image and position, he spoke words that were neither harsh nor polemical.

No doubt a family such as his would be highly concerned about its public face. While many of the idle rich, then and now, engage in conspicuous consumption, build monuments to themselves, and live lives of grandeur and self-indulgence, the Phelps Stokes family image was one of conservatism, sobriety, charity, and humility. It appears that strong religious convictions played a role here.

Although dignified, sober, and "liberal" in his own estimation, Anson Jr. wholeheartedly supported the likes of Thomas Jesse Jones, J. L. M. Curry, William Baldwin, and others who held hardened colonial attitudes on the lives and education of Black Americans. This curious duality provided Anson Jr. wide access to disparate groups and a politically enviable position.

Anson Jr.'s stated views on Black people do not appear overly egalitarian. Ahead of equality, he seemed most concerned with social mistreatment. Anson Jr. wanted an efficient, harmonious society without the extremes of the desperately poor and the totally excluded Black. He believed that great advancements had been made since slavery and was confident that society was moving toward the reconciliation of problems. Anson Jr. expressed himself in his reports on the progress and mission of the fund. His last report was a comprehensive exposition of his views over a half-century. In this book-length, 35-year report of the fund, entitled *Negro Status and Race Relations in the United States 1911–1946* (1948), he wrote:

> The change in attitude in thirty-five years both on the part of the Negro and of the white man in this country has naturally altered. The Negro leader is no longer a weak suppliant for assistance without political influence. He is confident, aggressive, determined and a political factor to be reckoned with. The Negro knows that his group is "on the march." . . . The white man also knows that a Negro slum is a breeder of disease which endangers the health of whites as well as of Negroes, and recognizes that ignorant Negro masses are a menace to the well-being of the nation. He has come to see, whatever be his attitude towards what is called "social equality" a term difficult to define and probably incapable of legal recognition—that no opportunity for development can be denied the man with Negro blood, and that the evidence, as far as it is in, seems to indicate that there is no height to which, under suitable educational, social, and economic conditions, the Negro cannot rise if he will. (p. 33)

Anson Jr.'s discussion of the reasons for Black progress is also of interest in situating his views. Among the general factors, he first acknowledged recent studies debunking "scientific" racism or biological inferiority. This is curious, given his frequent lavish praise of Dr. Jones, who embraced much of the biological argument. Second, he insisted that America's constitutional democracy worked and could refine the imperfect society. Finally, he credited the spreading influence of Christianity and its message of human brotherhood.

Among the special features of Black progress, he listed federal and state governments' extended legal protection of Blacks; the expanded number of Black colleges; increased faculty hiring of Black scholars; increased corporate funding for Black education; expanded church involvement; organized labor's changing attitudes; the formation of the NAACP, National Urban League, Black medical associations, Black Greek letter fraternities, businesses, and professional associations; and finally the "wise and courageous public leadership" of the respected George F. Peabody, James Dillard, Mary McLeod Bethune, Robert Ogden, and J. E. Spingarn (Phelps Stokes, 1948, pp. 43–58).

Throughout this lengthy report, Anson Jr. marveled at the "progress" of Blacks on both sides of the Atlantic. He was especially heartened at the emergence of Black scholars, athletes, and literary figures who were beginning to stand out and receive public renown.

In this document as well as other writings, Anson Jr. never legitimized oppositionist points of view existing within the Black American community. He mentioned Dr. DuBois and Booker T. Washington as examples of Black leadership (Phelps Stokes, 1948), never stating that they were philosophically worlds apart. He seemed surprised that significant sections of the Black intelligentsia and population were disgruntled, often outraged, at accommodationist education, political exclusion, segregation, discrimination, and the continued violence perpetrated against Blacks.

His discussion of what he perceived as Black radicalism was interesting. Throughout his life and writings, Anson Jr. avoided publicly criticizing individual Black "radicals" or opposition thinkers. Occasionally, he made polite remarks about Carter G. Woodson and other scholars, but typically left to Dr. Jones the more strident criticism with which he certainly must have agreed. There is almost no mention of Marcus Garvey or the massive Garveyite movement that swept across Black America during that time. In the 35-year report, Phelps Stokes's (1948) discussion of "extreme racism—white and negro" reveals a view that is telling:

> By racism I mean emphasis on the importance of the racial group to which a person belongs so extreme as to involve the disregard, or relative disregard, of the capacities and rights of other groups. . . . Such racism I believe to be equally serious whether it is white racism or black racism. The former has been in the past much more common than the latter, but the latter has been growing in recent years among the left

wing Negro leadership, and there is danger of its becoming almost as serious an obstacle for mutual understanding between the races as its progenitor. (p. 60)

## Anson Jr. on Thomas Jesse Jones

Anson Jr. and Thomas Jesse Jones, discussed fully in Chapter 6, enjoyed a mutually satisfying working relationship in the 1920s, 1930s, and 1940s. More important, Anson Jr. endorsed Jones's views on nation building, race, and education. He viewed Jones as a man of great intellectual depth and organizational ability. He attributed much of this to Jones's background and preparation:

> This Dr. Jones acquired largely as a result of his training in sociology under the late Professor Giddings of Columbia University. Scholars may differ as to some of Dr. Jones' emphasis and conclusions, but they must acknowledge that in all his reports he lays firm foundations through careful studies of educational and sociological conditions. (Phelps Stokes, 1948, p. 28)

Interestingly, in the 35-year report, he referred to Jones's educational work as affecting "rural," "agricultural," "country," and "undeveloped" populations. He argued that those rural people required a special kind of education. He defended Jones against those who criticized his special kind of education. His defense suggested that Jones was not advocating a curriculum for subservience but rather for an essential education:

> [Jones] has frequently been misunderstood and attacked on the ground that he favored a practical rather than a liberal arts training. The best answer is that he devoted a large amount of his time to the development of institutions of higher education such as Howard University and Fisk University, and that in his writings he frequently pointed out that the white man needed the "four essentials" as much as the Negro. (Phelps Stokes, 1948, p. 28)

Anson Jr. portrayed Jones as a man of great vision who would not yield to the immediate or short-sighted demands of any narrow group. Jones was at work for the greater good of all people. Anson Jr. praised Jones as one who worked for racial peace.

Anson Jr. believed that Jones was organically connected to African Americans. He felt that Jones had special insight into their culture. Anson Jr. insisted that Black Americans experienced shame because of the backwardness of mother Africa. Because Jones, through international missionary associations, had involved himself in improving education and social life in Africa, Black Americans could feel more pride in their homeland.

Anson Jr.'s (1948) concluding remarks on Jones praised his work among the Negroes as the fulfillment of a Christian dutiful life:

Religion has been a vital part of his educational creed. He has appreciated to the full the natural religious instinct of Negroes, has enjoyed their "spirituals," and has taken a deep interest in everything which has had to do with the improvement of their moral and spiritual life. His heroes—General Armstrong, Dr. Booker Washington, Dr. Dillard, Dr. Buttrick, Mr. Aggrey—have all been men of deep religious convictions. (p. 30)

Theirs was a symbiotic relationship, as their respective roles were clear. The relationship between Anson Jr. and Thomas Jesse Jones was critically significant to Black education. Jones was the theoretician, while Anson Jr. gave his blessings and money. Jones developed curriculum and programs that provided safe, measured, gradual, orderly, and minimal improvement for a people with nothing, while Anson Jr. proclaimed monumental social changes in the works. Jones was the social engineer, while Anson Jr. financed the project. Both were men of the cloth and regularly invoked the name of the deity in their activities.

Most important, their relationship was productive. Their support of industrial education and accommodationist politics helped illuminate the path for the corporate philanthropic community. They carefully brought together and refined a program that offered both theory and programs. They were wizards of compromise.

## Situating Anson Jr. and the Shaping of Black Education

The profile of Anson Phelps Stokes, Jr., thus begins to take shape. Behind the rhetoric of Christianity, altruism, and charity, resided a more narrow, although muted, outlook. Anson Jr. viewed the Black experience through his own sociopolitical and philosophical lens. Seldom did he acknowledge views from Black scholars, thinkers, or any that did not conform to his own. Anson Jr.'s view of history is "his-story" not the story. His story of the continued progress, acceptance, and uplift of the Black masses was consistent with the Darwinian, gradualistic views of those he supported. While Anson Jr. saw onward and upward progress, many, such as Dr. DuBois, in the Black American community saw business as usual and the continuation of oppression by other means.

Anson Jr. represented a refinement of the missionary charity philosophy and movement. He upheld "progress," gave generously, and avoided the messy polemics of the national public discourse on race. Seeking to reject the extreme solutions of either side, Anson Jr. saw himself taking the high ground, for he was surely acting in the name of God and all that was holy.

His support of colonial educators must again be noted. Anson Jr., Thomas Jesse Jones, and others worked closely together for nearly 40 years. It could be argued that Anson Jr.'s real, but understated, views were expressed by his nearly unqualified support of the accommodationists.

Any claim that the Phelps Stokes family was simply educating Negroes must be examined. Indeed, its members were social engineers. Anson Jr. funded political, social, and educational views that accepted racial inferiority, Black subservience, and gradual change.

The legacy of gradualism and accommodationism is now known to all. Segregation, discrimination, mistreatment, and exclusion are part of that legacy. Anson Phelps Stokes, Jr., and his missionary charity ideology should be seen as contributing mightily to the shaping of race relations, minority education, political "reform," and social welfare policy in the twentieth century.

# 6

## Thomas Jesse Jones:
## "Evil Genius of the Black Race"

"THIS IS Thomas Jesse Jones, savior of the Negro in America and the redeemer of the heathen in Africa." That statement was made by Anson Phelps Stokes in the *Confidential Memorandum for the Trustees of the Phelps Stokes Fund: Regarding Dr. Carter G. Woodson's Criticisms of Dr. Thomas Jesse Jones* (1924, p. 17). This statement and the critique that prompted it are indicative of the sentiments surrounding the controversial Dr. Jones. Loved by some and reviled by others, he left an imprint on Black education like few people could.

An immigrant to America, he gained an education and, in time, became the central ideologist and architect of Black education in the early twentieth century. Until recently, little was written about him. He was mentioned in writings on colonial education, such as King (1971) and Berman (1969, 1980), but more recent works, such as Correia (1993), Watkins (1989, 1990, 1991, 1993, 1994, 1995), Anderson (1988), and Arnove (1980), have expanded the investigation into Jones's background, ideas, and activities. This most powerful man greatly influenced a century of Black American and African education. Because Jones aligned himself with industrial education, Booker T. Washington, and the accommodationist educational community, he attracted the ire of Dr. Carter G. Woodson and Dr. W. E. B. DuBois, who referred to him in 1919 as the "evil genius of the black race."

### COMES A WELSHMAN: THE EARLY YEARS

Thomas Jesse Jones was born in Llanfachraeth, the Isle of Anglesey, Wales, in August 1873. In 1884 his widowed mother and her children immigrated to the mining community around Middleport, Ohio.

Jones appears to have experienced a typical immigrant life. He established ties in his new community, became acculturated, and developed interest in his education. Exhibiting strong religious beliefs during his teenage years, Jones enrolled in Washington and Lee (Virginia) University in 1891 on a ministerial scholarship. After a year there, he returned to Ohio where he engaged in community and educational activities. He evidenced a growing commitment to Christianity. In 1894 he received another ministerial scholarship to Marietta College in Ohio.

Jones was serious about his studies and came under the influence of the sociology professors interested in applying Christian and religious teachings to current social problems. The advent of industrialization, urbanization, massive immigration, and changing racial demographics had created new problems in urban and national politics. Geographical displacement, labor relations, race relations, and immigrant exclusion were foremost. A variety of reformers, muckrakers, utopian socialists, Bolsheviks, syndicalists, anarchists, Christian patriots, and many others entered the sociopolitical discourse of the day. At stake was the direction of public policy for America's new industrial democracy in the twentieth century.

## Developing an Ideology

Jones was drawn to the emerging Christian social sciences. An important wing of that outlook was the "social gospel" movement. Social gospel adherents held that America was at a significant crossroads. They feared both plutocracy and socialism. They hoped twentieth-century America would forsake both autocracy on the right and the "workers' state" on the left. They wanted this new America to eschew excesses and to attempt an ideological reconciliation of the accumulations of great wealth by the few with social welfare for the many. They proposed Christianity to provide rationale, redemption, rules, salvation, and second chances for all. They advocated Christian democracy based in classical liberalism.

Correia (1993) provides an extensive discussion of the early Christian-academic influences on Jones. Jones's interactions at Marietta with Wilbur Crafts, J. H. W. Stuckenberg, Washington Gladden, and J. A. Smith decidedly shaped his lifelong ideology. Correia represents these professors as Christians with social consciousness connected to the social gospel philosophy.

Social gospel advocacy was only part of a flurry of activities among social scientists. Demands for greater adherence to scientific principles, empiricism, quantification, and specialization also surfaced. This was a social science community reinventing and realigning itself.

## THE EMERGENT SOCIAL SCIENCE MOVEMENT

The nineteenth century in America might be seen as a vast sociological laboratory. Slavery, the opening of the western frontier, economic recessions, and the new immigrant polyglot all contributed to America's complexity. The growing intellectual movements in Europe were defining and redefining politics, economics, sociology, and philosophy in an effort to explain the complexities of society.

The social science movement of the latter half of the nineteenth century brought new interests and approaches to the study of social issues.

The English philosopher John Stuart Mill was the first to use the term "social science" in 1839 (Lybarger, 1981). Soon a three-volume work entitled *The Principles of Social Science* (1858–59), written by Henry C. Carey, appeared. The subsequent founding of the American Social Science Association (ASSA) in Boston in 1865, along with the appearance of its periodical, *The Journal of Social Sciences* (*JSS*), demonstrated growing activity in this field.

The early foci of the ASSA on education, public health, jurisprudence, and social economy indicate the range of interests. Scholars, students, reformers, bureaucrats, and specialists alike were drawn to the new social science movement. Lybarger (1981) suggests that politics and political positions were easily discernible in the early activities of the ASSA. He cites influential members such as *JSS* editor Frank Sanborn, who feared that newly freed Blacks might join economically oppressed working people to form a potentially volatile mix. With Europe as a reference point, the fear of spreading communism, socialism, and anarchism emerged. Similarly situated were other forces opposed to radical political ideology. These groups wished to depoliticize social problems. C. Wright Mills (1940/1952), who studied the ASSA, argued that its leaders consciously avoided politicizing social problems.

Many in the emerging social science movement promoted novel approaches to the study of social problems. Horace Greeley, prominent in the ASSA, favored extensive study of social problems. He wanted these studies published, believing that exposure of such problems would lead to remediation.

Eventually, turn-of-the-century social science emerged in a rapidly changing and complex America. Many, but not all, in the new social science movement came under the influence of anticommunist "objectivity," as they established ideological boundaries for inquiry. This group opposed the "working-class" or Marxian orientation. It accepted, rather, a corrective approach, that is, that social problems could be ameliorated and solved within the existing framework and political structure of society. This alliance adopted gradualism and incrementalism and favored planned social change.

Interestingly, a parallel Black social science emerged. In 1896 the University of Pennsylvania contracted Dr. W. E. B. DuBois to conduct a study on the lives, occupations, education, and social issues of Philadelphia's 40,000 Blacks. Having studied at Harvard and published in White academic journals, DuBois was well acquainted with the social science movement. Marable (1986) recounts how DuBois developed comprehensive questionnaires, interviewed 5,000 people, and presented "exhaustive data . . . on the character and social institutions of the Black community, including statistics on health, marital and family relations, crime, education, vocation status, and literacy" (p. 25).

The final product, *The Philadelphia Negro* (1899), is the first comprehensive study of Black Americans by a Black author, using contemporary social science statistical research methods. Unlike White social science scholarship, which was largely descriptive, DuBois's work offers an indictment of the racial practices of the day. He wrote of social injustice, historical oppression, and the exclusion of Blacks from the mainstream. His is an oppositionist scholarship that helps frame a century of Black social inquiry and a "Black intellectual tradition" (Watkins, 1990).

The ASSA did not survive the century's turn (Lybarger 1981). Its influence waned as generalization gave way to specialization. Subdisciplines within the social science community began to assert themselves, as history, political science, sociology, economics, and social studies developed their own organizations, activities, and advocates.

Despite the decline of the ASSA, a tradition of methodology and ideology took hold in the social sciences. Quantification, classification, verifiability, and predictability became the agreed-upon characteristics of the social sciences, as they were of the natural sciences. Ideologically, mainstream social science had moved to support and accept the free enterprise system, existing labor relations, and racial inequality. Problems had to be addressed through gradual and evolutionary change, while radical or revolutionary social reform had to be rejected.

## FORMING AN IDEOLOGY:
## THE FURTHER EDUCATION OF THOMAS JESSE JONES

The early 1890s found Jones in New York City seeking to further his studies in sociology, religion, race, and ethnicity. He enrolled simultaneously in graduate social science courses at Columbia University and religious studies at the nearby Union Theological Seminary. Columbia's reorganized social science department provided Jones a variety of classes in political science, economics, and sociology. He studied with renowned professors Edwin Seligman, Richmond Mayo-Smith, John Bates Clark, James Harvey Robinson, and Franklin Henry Giddings, discussed in Chapter 4, among others.

While these scholars differed in political orientations, all of them studied societal development (see Correia, 1993). Seligman, an economic evolutionist, believed in a functioning and inclusive capitalist marketplace. Mayo-Smith promoted statistical method, anticommunism, restricted immigration, and the scientific reform of society. Clark, also an economic evolutionist, held that the problems of corruption and labor discontent eventually would resolve. Robinson, known for his "new" history, believed that a vibrant interpretation of history could improve society. It was Franklin Giddings, however, who became Jones's mentor and ideological guidepost. Giddings promoted his views as "scientific sociology." He was a strong advocate of quantification, classification, and sociology as a separate subject area.

## Graduate School Theses

Jones's master's thesis, entitled *Social Education in the Elementary School* (1899), explored education in the promotion of nationalism and the building of civilization. His focus was on Western society. Elementary education, Jones wrote, should cultivate the highest levels of the "social mind" in children. "Sympathetic," or low-level social-mindedness, could not be tolerated, as it is characterized by impulsiveness and behavioral disorder, which is the "dread of society . . . and democracy" (p. 23). "Formal," or high-level social-mindedness, he argued, represented "rational reflection," wise moral judgment and "ethical purpose" (pp. 23, 24). He supported Harvard's Charles Eliot's idea of a "democratic nobility" (p. 25).

The thesis demonstrates a growing familiarity with pedagogy and school policy issues. He assessed teacher training, proposed changes in credential standards, and wrote about the social mandate of education.

Jones was becoming interested in how schooling could and should contribute to social development. More specifically, he showed concern about the potential social role of marginalized and nontraditional groups, such as immigrants and minorities. These groups, he believed, must be carefully situated so as to play a positive role in twentieth-century America.

## The Dissertation

Jones's doctoral dissertation, *The Sociology of a New York City Block* (1904), provides a more developed statement of his intellectual interests, ideology, social philosophy, racial views, and nationalist spirit. In the opening chapter, Jones speaks of his intention to embrace "scientific" sociological methodology to chart the social traits of the ethnic groups he encountered on his Saturday morning visits to his upper east side (New York City) "Block X."

His objective was to study the motor reactions, type of intellect, type of character, and particular character traits of a variety of ethnic people. He classified his subjects as Teutonic, Celtic, Ibero-Latin, Slavic, and Semitic. He then went on to offer his portrayals of the various ethnic and racial groups. He wrote about the "struggle for the streets" (p. 24); the "careless habits" of the Irish (p. 23); that "the Irishman hates the Italian" (p. 27); that "there is scarcely a nationality that does not indulge in this form of gambling, but the Italians are probably the most addicted to it" (p. 46), and so on. While he saw the ethnic groups as squabbling, petty, and yielding to impulses, the native-born were viewed as sober, calm, and intelligent.

"Findings" suggest that immigrants "have an intellectual interest in their environment. Emotion enters so strongly into some apparently intellectual motives" (p. 43). He wrote that these people are intellectually inferior, possess physical appetites, and are given to base instinct. Unable to control their environment, lowly immigrants learn to adapt to their surroundings, while superior Anglo-Saxons conquer new frontiers.

Jones classified the people on Block X in four ways. First, he divided them by emotion: the joyous-sanguine, who could rejoice in spite of hardship; the morose, who were completely discouraged; the choleric, who were quarrelsome as a way of dealing with suffering more reverses than they could endure; and the melancholic, who were broken in health and spirit (p. 76). He found the majority of Block X dwellers to be joyous-sanguine.

Regarding "intellectual" types, Jones believed most of his immigrant subjects were either "credulous," offering unwarranted believability to others; superstitious; or "conjectural," given to guesswork.

As to character, he included the forceful, who were robust and given to physically challenging labor; the convivial, who were slothful pleasure seekers; the austere, who were diligent and self-denying; and the rationally conscientious, who were the brahmins of the immigrant groups and most likely to be intelligent and successful. Finally, he categorized type of mind: the ideo-motor, those capable of responding to stimuli in the passive sense; the ideo-emotional, those capable of some imagination; the dogmatic-emotional, those with limited functioning; and the critically-intellectual, those capable of full functioning and reasoning. Jones concluded: "None of the critically-intellectual were found in Block X" (p. 87).

He concluded that there existed a "consciousness of kind," that is, that ethnic and racial groups hold a "primitive" affinity for their own kind. Societal heterogeneity can bring on "urban chaos." "Lower" classified people cannot participate in a democratic society, as their cultural weaknesses are overwhelming. "A dictator seems to be necessary to every successful organization on the upper East Side" (p. 129).

Jones ended his dissertation demanding that the immigrant population transform and assimilate. "Every possible agency should be used to change the numerous foreign types into the Anglo-Saxon ideal" (p. 133).

Jones accepted notions of racial hierarchy among people. While this study focused on European ethnics, he clustered the Cubans and Negroes in his focus area with the lowest-status Mediterranean groups.

## Settlement House Work: Toward an Ideology of Social Reform

Today's liberals might label Jones a racist, conservative, or even reactionary. He, however, viewed himself as an enlightened progressive and modern social reformer. The brand of sociology Jones embraced was, for him, dynamic. It combined rigorous inquiry, quantification, and action research with the politics of nation building and refining the corporate democracy. It was a sociology aimed toward a new industrial society facing the complex issues of postslavery race relations, massive immigration, urbanization, and the new politics of industrial wealth and poverty.

Jones's concern lay with the viability of early twentieth-century America. The reform community, consisting of scholars, urban social workers, church missions, charity people, and corporate philanthropies, to which he was attracted was refining an ideology. That ideology looked to gradualism and planned social change as guideposts. A working or common ground between wealth and poverty had to be identified. Jones was a future leader in this reform movement, influenced by his work in the settlement house movement in New York City.

While completing his doctoral study, Jones lived and worked with other graduate students and several faculty members at the University Settlement House. His position as assistant headworker, paying around $1,000 annually, thrust him into the practical aspects of what he was learning theoretically at Columbia. He gained valuable experience as an educator, administrator, and social worker.

The settlement house "movement," which began with the (Arnold) Toynbee Hall project in East London, spread to New York. Founded in 1877 by Stanton Coit, the first project was called Neighborhood Guild. Soon relocated to Delancey Street in lower Manhattan, the house had a boys club, girls club, kindergarten, and a variety of other activities aimed at the immigrant and impoverished populations.

The objectives of the settlement house were self-help, uplift, education, citizenship, Christianity, and the imbuing of culture. *Guntons Magazine* (1890) describes the house:

> It acts as an educational center through its classes for study of economics, its free circulating library, its recreation classes, its committees on civic reform, its youth clubs, its kindergarten, its conferences on social questions, its lectures, its penny provident bank, etc. (p. 432)

Settlement house proponents, including Jane Addams, claimed to be expanding social opportunity and elevating the masses in the difficult new industrial society. As leaders of a movement, they hoped to become a force for societal amelioration. Advocates foresaw the houses ultimately as workingmen's clubs where increasingly cultured clienteles would bridge the gap between rich and poor. The houses were to serve a civilizing mission.

Jones's sociopolitical views were influenced by the settlement house movement. The ignorant and character-flawed could be transformed. Jones found an agency with a concept that proposed to shape individuals and society through "safe" reform, that is, it would not disturb the existing economic, political, and racial arrangements. Critics of the settlement houses, such as Thorstein Veblen, viewed them as promoting industrial efficiency. Jones (1902b) saw them as important partners of the school and church in the new America. These views, alongside new personal contacts, would serve Jones well in future pursuits.

Lybarger (1981) argues that the settlement houses had two objectives: societal betterment and the social evolution of the individual. He holds that Jones, in his settlement house work, reinforced his belief that the foreign-born and the "other" must look to the superior Anglo-Saxon for guidance and leadership. Thus, Lybarger believes, settlement house work influenced Jones's lifelong views on racial and social development and especially his major educational writings.

## THE HAMPTON EXPERIENCE

In the autumn of 1902, Jones accepted an appointment as associate chaplain and professor at the Hampton Normal and Agricultural Institute. As mentioned, Hampton had been founded in 1868 amid differing interests. Its founder, General Samuel Armstrong, was committed to accommodationist racial and class relationships and an orderly South. On the other hand, the students, mostly former slaves, wanted a new South and indeed a new world (Anderson, 1988).

Hampton was perfect for Jones, and vice versa. Jones's social science could and would provide an ideological foundation on which to build a curriculum suited to the unique features of America's new industrial, racial, and political order. The Hampton mission was similar to Jones's previous work, that is, citizenship training, "civilizing" non-Anglo populations, teaching America's industrial democratic values, Christianizing, shaping individual evolutionary development, and effecting incremental, gradual societal reform.

Jones explored his social, political, and educational ideas in his essays, sermons, and articles in the *Southern Workman* (*SW*), Hampton's journal, beginning in 1904. His memorable *Hampton Social Studies* was introduced in *SW*.

Correia (1993) assesses Jones's early sermons, arguing that they foreshadow evolved social, political, educational, and religious outlooks. Jones's inaugural sermon, *Courage of Our Convictions* (1902a), talks of the responsibilities of citizenship in a rapidly changing world. He asks Hampton students to go back and lead their people to be responsible. Correia argues that Jones, from the start, imparts a message of subservience to God and Whites. Another sermon, *Fatherhood of God* (1903), exhorts listeners to be cautious in the "age of moneymaking." He encourages students of color to choose simplicity and God's work over materialism. The great irony is Jones's later decision to dedicate most of his adult life to work in the interests of those of great wealth and power.

Christian nationalism for Jones was a combination of democracy, patriotism, education, accommodationism, the evolving of the individual and the refinement of society. Minorities would have a role in this new order so long as they learned to fit in.

Within a short time, Jones was asked to teach social science courses. In addition to his teaching, he began contributing essays to *SW*. As stated in Chapter 3, Armstrong and Frissell established *SW* in 1872. Created as a school news organ, it became a political journal. Anderson (1988) writes:

Although Armstrong attempted to promote the *Southern Workman* as a nonpolitical "instructive monthly," the paper, which expressed vividly his ideas of black reconstruction, sided with conservative political groups who wanted to disfranchise the freedmen and create a legal and customary racial hierarchy. Two years after the founding of the *Southern Workman*, a black newspaper concluded that Armstrong's monthly had "become so conservative that it leans the other way," meaning that it had become reactionary. (p. 37)

In his earliest writings for *SW* (March 1903), Jones reaffirmed the founding mission of Hampton and attempted to contemporize Armstrong. Utilizing Armstrong's language, he wrote about "the construction of mental and moral worth," "self help," "development of character and mind," "economic independence," and "the development of sane and sound leadership for Negro and Indian communities" (pp. 142–144). His discussion on leadership reiterated that a few worthy individuals should be groomed to lead their people.

Over the next few years, Jones became more familiar with Booker T. Washington's economic and political views. Washington's convening of the Tuskegee Conferences nudged Jones to further consider Black entrepreneurship (*SW*, April 1905). Believing that Blacks were forever disposed to agrarian pursuits, Jones may have been surprised at the entrepreneurial impulse. He noted that rural Blacks were saving money, selling wool from sheep, buying land, building homes, and financially supporting schools and churches. Jones cited census data that Negroes had "saved more than $300,000,000 worth of taxable property and owned 173,352 farms in the 12 southern states" (*SW*, April 1905, p. 207).

Throughout 1905, Jones committed himself to the serious study of Black issues. Subsequent articles in *SW* reported voluminous data on education attainment, health conditions, and population demographics.

His many articles in *SW* placed Jones in a prominent position in Black education. Drawing from his background in immigrant training and citizenship education, Jones significantly contributed to the "solution of the Negro question" by promoting continued subservience, accommodationism, gradualism, and the promise for a better tomorrow.

### Hampton Social Studies

Jones authored the *Hampton Social Studies* (*HSS*), which was published initially (by section) in *SW*, between 1905 and 1907. It became a primer for Negro education. Intended as a classroom curriculum, it was a statement of political philosophy. It taught Negroes their place in a society in transition from agricultural slavery to mechanical industrialization. It addressed the vexing questions of how Blacks should fit into the new social order without disruption. *HSS* was a treatise on politics, economics, and the sociology of race. It signaled Jones's ascendance as a major architect of Black education.

*SW* became the vehicle and organ through which Jones would introduce *HSS*. In the December 1905 issue, he set forth a rationale in an article entitled "Social Studies in the Hampton Curriculum: Why They Are Needed," which began as follows:

> Slavery and the tribal form of government gave the Negro and Indian but little opportunity to understand the essentials of a good home, the duties and responsibilities of citizenship, the cost and meaning of education, the place of labor, and the importance of thrift. (p. 686)

Denied knowledge and participation in social and political life, the minorities must be taught. Jones noted that morality and a less "emotional" religious orientation must become part of their new training. Traditional education should be scrapped in favor of this new "special education" (Bullock, 1967) required by the rapidly changing society. Such new education must serve the evolutionary requirements of the people.

The proposed *HSS* would serve the cause of "race development." It would teach civil government, economics, democracy, civic responsibility, and race relations. The first lesson of *HSS*, entitled "Social Studies in the Hampton Curriculum: Civics and Social Welfare," appeared in the January 1906 issue of *SW*. Discussing the development of government, government and public welfare, and the machinery of government, Jones urged Blacks to work so that they might soon be fit for democratic civilization.

The "Economics and Material Welfare" lesson (*SW*, February 1906) addressed consumer issues. It scoffs at the Negro's preference for non-nutritious food, expensive garments, and other poor consumer choices. Additionally, it discusses the virtue of saving money, vocational planning, and agricultural efficiency. Jones expresses relief that the "socialistic notions so prevalent among the working classes of the North" have not proliferated. He concludes by claiming great flexibility and promise for the industrial organization of society. If the colored races will study the dynamics of credit, transportation, monopolies, profit, interest, rent, wages, labor efficiency, and so on, they too can prosper in the new age.

Another lesson on the census urges Hampton students to chart and graph the conditions and progress of their people. While Jones viewed Black people as mostly agrarian labor, he understood that some would advance in the increasingly industrialized economy.

The most ideological of the lessons is the fifth, "Sociology and Society." Here Jones frames social and political outlooks on the organization of society and the appropriate behavior for individuals within that society. He reprises the "social mind" concept, that is, classifying people by mental and moral type. He asserts that rational and intellectual types should lead because the impulsive and emotional types could wreck society.

Retreating to the "scientific" racism of the mid-nineteenth century, Jones, like his mentor Giddings, raises the "climate" argument: "The colored people of Piedmont, Virginia . . . are less irritable, impulsive, and emotional than those of Tidewater, Virginia, with its warm, moist climate" (*SW*, December 1906, p. 691).

This lesson also considers effective social organization. Jones argues that social organization is "necessarily coercive" in circumstances of inequality and adversity, suggesting that only a homogeneous society could be truly efficient and fully functioning.

The final lesson, "The Progress of the Indians," is primarily a statistical census report, in which Jones presents data on population, disease, reservations, literacy, per capita income, and so on. It concludes that Native Americans, like America's other minorities, are on an "upward" path to progress.

## Reviewing the Hampton Years

Jones's years at Hampton were a matter of destiny. He was the right person in the right job at the right place at the right time. He was the quintessential ideological curricularist. He created a political curriculum intended for the classroom and for life. He presented himself as a progressive liberal, and his program of gradual, evolutionary change through religious and political education became sociopolitical doctrine.

Lybarger (1981,1983) writes that Jones's influence went far beyond *HSS* in that his conception of citizenship education became the consensus view of the Committee on Social Studies, and ultimately his ideas became an ideological cornerstone of the broader social studies movement.

In 1912, Jones agreed to chair the Committee on Social Studies, which was part of the U.S. Commission for the Reorganization of Secondary Education. This body was one of several early-twentieth-century federally commissioned groups established to study curriculum, higher education, college admissions, and teacher training. Jones's ideological leadership was crucial in shaping the final report, *The Social Studies in Secondary Education* (U.S. Department of the Interior, 1916). The report advocated a citizenship-training component in social studies programs, and stated that "secondary school teachers have a remarkable opportunity to improve the citizenship of the land" (p. 2).

Lybarger (1981) researched this seminal report extensively. He explores the social, political, and economic philosophy of its members; deconstructs the prevailing contemporary political philosophy of the ASSA; and examines the role of municipal reform groups influencing citizenship training. Among his conclusions is that Jones was interested in establishing "the ideal American or Anglo-Saxon character" (p. 176). He wrote:

> In the minds of members of the Committee on Social Studies, the "improvement of the citizenship of the land" involved the cultivation of the virtues of "obedience, courtesy, punctuality, honesty, self-control, industry and the like." (Lybarger, 1981, p. 82)

Lybarger suggests that this cluster of values, projected by Jones and others, provided a particular kind of outlook in the social studies. The good citizen was obedient rather than active, assertive, or demanding of societal and political participation. Accommodationism is promoted as desirable social behavior.

Lybarger concludes that Jones was firmly in line with the prevailing social evolutionist and "citizenship" ideology of his time. This new school subject called social studies was seen as an important vehicle in the ideological engineering of the new industrial nation.

## ON TO THE PHELPS STOKES FUND

As a result of Jones's role on the Committee on Social Studies, he became a known curriculum theoretician, allowing him to move on. His new life at the Phelps Stokes Fund allowed him to graduate from curriculum ideologist to policy maker at the national and international level.

### Preparing for Phelps Stokes: The Report on Negro Education

With a growing reputation as an expert in Negro education and Negro affairs, Jones left Hampton Institute in the summer of 1909. The federal government commissioned him to gather statistical data for the Bureau of the Census. Jones supervised the special "Negro Census," a job for which he was well rehearsed and well situated. During his next several years in Washington, DC, he also taught sociology courses at Howard University and joined its Board of Trustees.

The Phelps Stokes Fund, discussed extensively in Chapter 5, was established in 1911. As the Fund expanded and focused its work on Negro education, its directors commissioned Jones to head up a massive study on Negro education jointly underwritten by the Fund, the Bureau of Education, several universities, and various corporate philanthropies.

Taking 3 full years to complete, this was the largest and most comprehensive study ever undertaken of Black segregated schools in the United States. Examining 791 schools, the report looked at funding, facilities, administration, attendance, teacher training, curriculum, entrance requirements, and so on. The final report, entitled *Negro Education: A Study of the Higher and Private Schools for Colored People in the United States*, was published in two volumes in 1917. The report concluded that these schools were woefully underfunded and generally in poor shape. On the positive side, it concluded, great progress was being made in expanding education to Black America. The report provided documented rationale for continuing and expanding assistance from those philanthropic agencies that commissioned the study.

Ideologically, the report reflected Jones's ongoing support for industrial education, character training, and social evolutionism. Correia (1993) summarized Jones's views reflected in the document:

> Jones also argued that the relative poverty of African-Americans made industrial education even more necessary, and that "educational result is even more necessary for the Negro than for the white, since the Negro's highly emotional nature requires for balance as much as possible in the concrete and definite." Although Jones wanted the report to present unbiased statistics, he was unable to provide any empirical data to support the claim of the "Negro's highly emotional nature." (p. 272)

As the lead researcher and first author on this massive study, Jones attracted wide attention, again expanding his personal contacts.

## The Phelps Stokes Years: Refining Philanthropy in Black Education

Jones joined Phelps Stokes in 1912. He spent the next 32 years as its educational director and became an influential White architect of Negro education.

He guided Phelps Stokes to its position as a leading foundation concerned with Negro education. Under his stewardship, Phelps Stokes influenced foundations shaping Black education, including Rockefeller, Jeannes, Slater, and others. Additionally, Jones worked with national and international missionary associations that cooperated with the corporate philanthropists. His work expanded quickly to the African continent where the Hampton–Tuskegee accommodationist education model was exported to British Tropical Africa (King, 1971; Watkins, 1989). Beyond the funding and establishing of scores of schools, teacher-training programs, curricula, and so on, his embrace and cultivation of the ideology of corporate charity was of great consequence.

Unprecedented accumulations of wealth in the post–Civil War period allowed large industrial corporations to financially surpass church-sponsored missionary charity associations in gifts to Black education. Although different in outlook (Anderson, 1988), missionary and corporate philanthropic activities were joined in common effort as a result of Jones's influence.

Ideological consensus was not difficult to achieve among corporate foundations. Unregulated by government, the foundations allotted funds to agencies that promoted their version of human progress and Western culture. Education, science, the arts, and projects aimed at uplift would become the recipients of foundation gifts. The foundations' commitment to Western culture coincided with Jones's views developed from his study of the "social gospel," his settlement house work, and his Hampton activities.

Jones became a committed theoretician and practitioner of corporate-industrial philanthropy. He understood that funding Black schools was part of a larger philanthropic objective of social engineering whereby neither unbridled capitalism nor racial subservience would be fundamentally altered. Only gradual and planned social change was acceptable to the corporate elite. In fact, social change would be sponsored by those most invested in maintaining the status quo.

The impact of Phelps Stokes and Jones should not be underestimated. On both sides of the Atlantic, they demonstrated that colonial education could be advertised as progressive social change. Further, they showed that foundations successfully could inject their own views into the cultural and ideological life of oppressed peoples.

## EXPLORING A DECADE OF JONES'S WRITINGS

Examinations of Jones, such as Arnove (1980), Correia (1993), King (1971), Lybarger (1981), and Watkins (1989, 1990, 1991, 1993, 1994, 1995), find him a man of great activity as he took over and shaped Phelps Stokes's educational activities. His work within the national and international missionary societies, historically Black colleges, teacher associations, and the corporate philanthropic community more than occupied his time with administrative and policy-making activities. Scholars have examined his *Hampton Social Studies* (Jones, 1905–07), the Committee on Social Studies report (U.S. Department of the Interior, 1916), in which he played a central role, and his *Negro Education* (Jones, 1917), but little energy has been committed to his writings in the 1920s. This decade witnessed significant refinement in school policy, especially curriculum selection.

Jones wrote two major theoretical works in the 1920s. The *Four Essentials of Education* (1926) is a statement of his views on the social aims of education. The second, *Essentials of Civilization* (1929), represents the most exhaustive statement of his social and political views.

### The Four Essentials of Education

This work is a critique of contemporary social science education. He opposes the "accretion method" in which school knowledge was organized with little relationship to human activity and the realities of societal development. Jones calls for "liberal training," that is, preparation for the needs of life. Education must include "training for social civic responsibilities; health; recreational and aesthetic participation; and practical and occupational efficiency" (p. 9). He argues that the central objective of the curriculum should be "consciousness of community," which translates to education for civic responsibility, the common good, and the essentials of group life.

Jones's signature theme, the "four essentials of education," lists health and sanitation, appreciation and use of the environment, the household and the home, and the recreations of culture as the indispensable elements of societal cohesion. The essentials represent for him "foundations and universals of human society" (p. 20) and the centerpiece of the school curriculum.

For Jones, public education, especially Black education, must serve a civilizing mission. It must mold and develop character, especially the political character. He argues that the central government must assume the task of socializing the citizenry through schooling.

Jones acknowledges that he draws the four essentials largely from his Hampton experience, whereby he came to believe that education properly aimed at shaping people for obedience to the social order defines citizenship. He believes that education for citizenship, crucial in minority education, is relevant for "every boy and girl."

## The Essentials of Civilization

The notion of rudimentary or fundamental education and training would continue as a theme in Jones's scholarship. His magnum opus, *Essentials of Civilization: A Study in Social Values* (1929), represents his most ambitious effort in social theorizing.

Jones introduces this work by describing the problems of "cleavages, classes and misunderstandings of sectional, racial, national and international dimensions" (p. xxv). He finds the dynamics of sociocultural organization intriguing. Like Aristotle and Durkheim, Jones wants to explore how societies hold together. He argues that Western civilization is strong because it possesses essential values. Early in the work, Jones reprises the "four essentials," discussed above, as the building blocks of civilization. He then elevates his essentials to the level of universal truth.

He surveys the world's dominant economic ideologies, capitalism and socialism. Deeming socialism despotic and antidemocratic, Jones fears that unless citizens observe his four essentials, the internal conflicts within capitalist organization could sharpen.

He questions the professional educational community, asking whether they really understand the social mission of schools. Again, he identifies the four essentials as panacea.

Beyond education, Jones shares his views on religion and its role in shaping society. Religion, he believes, should play a prominent part in human affairs. Upon embracing the four essentials, the church should help ameliorate society. Political direct action should be avoided in favor of spiritual enlightenment:

> Standards of living, a living wage, hours of labor, prevention of poverty, child labor, rights of the consumer, the place of capital, collective bargaining, strikes and lockouts are all susceptible of study by the ministerial student. (p. 129)

For Jones, even the vexing race problem should be given over to the church through whose work true enlightenment would prevail. The divinity ultimately would govern humankind.

Jones reiterates that philanthropy is a cornerstone of his social philosophy. Christian charity sponsored by people of goodwill aids the downtrodden as they begin the process of catch-up, that is, proceed along the natural evolutionary path. Christian charity is God's way of improving society. He associates the Protestant Reformation with the democratic revolution. Thus, Christian charity must accompany the new democratic impulse. Leading the way, corporate industrialists will be joined by the artistic, literary, scientific, and cultural communities in the noble effort of building civilization.

Finally, Jones believes in the triumph of the West. He proclaimed that the future of America is the future of the world. Only the West is capable of civilizing and unifying its people.

## From Racial Cooperation to Eternal Truth

Jones believed that the blend of social evolutionism, gradualism, and Christian charity was more than good theory and good sociology. It was a formula for how to employ education and social institutions in the service of building civilized nations out of fragmented peoples. His agenda of "essentials" provides a social blueprint for the new order.

He understood that industrial democracy had replaced agrarian social organization. The new order could not operate optimally with uncontrolled ethnic divisiveness. His worldly experiences taught him that the old politics and bare-knuckled colonialism of the past did not serve the new order. If the Western world were to maintain economic supremacy, it needed to alter its methods.

Jones endorsed a "democratic" hegemony that would come to characterize twentieth-century politics. He never rejected racial supremacy or Western superiority. He wanted racial cooperation to be a component of the new world. Democracy could then be made compatible with the most unequal society.

This formula, for Jones, was historical destiny. The great civilization of the Western world could be realized. Racial subservience need not conflict with evolutionary social progress. Cooperation could prevail over class struggle and racial conflict. God's will could be done.

A major address delivered at the dedication of the Frissell Memorial at Hampton summarized the guiding precepts in Jones's life. Aligning himself with the accommodationist educator Frissell, Jones believed that their mission of minority education and civilization building was a most noble calling. Their beliefs were eternal truths. Their work was to be everlasting. They were shaping a world. He wrote: "Our work is not for Frissell; it is not for Hampton; it is not for white or negro; it is not for America. Our work is for the Kingdom of God, here and hereafter" (Jones, 1931, p. 7).

## DuBOIS'S OPPOSITION TO JONES

As mentioned, Dr. Carter G. Woodson and other Black leaders and educators opposed the actions of Jones. The most formidable challenges to Jones, however, came from Dr. W. E. B. DuBois. Both having taken up the "Negro problem" in general, and Black education in particular, were ideologically on a collision course.

Much was at stake in the discourse on Black education in the early twentieth century. Programs, curriculum, and practices to be established would influence a century of American education. Educational practices adopted at this time determined the social and political future of Black Americans.

By the early 1900s DuBois was a maturing scholar. His publications in popular and scholarly journals, public lectures, and activities on behalf of civil rights gave him growing recognition. In *The Souls of Black Folk* (1903) he turned his attention to the critique of colonial education, especially the views of Booker T. Washington.

The aforementioned two-volume report, *Negro Education* (Jones, 1917), provoked a public response from DuBois against Jones. DuBois believed the report to be quintessential accommodationism. Several themes in the report irked DuBois. Among them were the suggestions that southern Blacks were essentially rural and required agricultural education; that Black schools overemphasized book learning; that the transition from White to Black teachers was happening too rapidly; that the economic prosperity of the Black South rested with manual labor; that northern wealth and political power were needed to continue to shape the South; that Black private education was woefully inadequate and producing inferior students; that only three Black colleges—Fisk, Meharry Medical, and Howard—were truly institutions of higher learning; and that elementary education was to be the focus of Negro education. DuBois (1918) considered the report praiseworthy yet "dangerous and in many respects [an] unfortunate publication" (p. 173). He continued:

> He shows that there are (in proportion to population) ten times as many whites in the public high schools as there are colored pupils and only sixty-four public high schools for Negroes in the whole South! He shows that even at present there are few Negro colleges and that they have no easy chance for survival. What he is criticizing, then is not the fact that Negroes are tumbling into college in enormous numbers, but their wish to go to college and their endeavor to support and maintain even poor college departments.

... As Mr. Jones several times intimates, or is it rather a desire on the part of American Negroes to develop a class of thoroughly educated men according to modern standards? If such a class is to be developed, these Negro colleges must be planned as far as possible according to the standards of white colleges, otherwise colored students would be shut out of the best colleges of the country.

The curriculum offered at the colored Southern colleges, however, brings the author's caustic criticism. Why, for instance, should "Greek and Latin" be maintained to the exclusion of economics, sociology, and "a strong course in biology?"

The reason for the maintenance of these older courses of study in the colored colleges is not at all, as the author assumes, that Negroes have a childish love for "classics". . . . So, in a large number of cases the curriculum of the Southern Negro college has been determined by the personnel of the available men. . . .

This, Mr. Jones either forgets or does not know and is thus led into exceedingly unfortunate statements as when, for instance, he says that the underlying principle of the industrial school "is the adaptation of educational activities whether industrial or literary to the needs of the pupils and community," which is, of course, the object of any educational institution and it is grossly unfair to speak of it as being the object of only a part of the great Negro schools of the South. Any school that does not have this for its object is not a school but a fraud. (DuBois, 1918, pp. 173–174)

While Jones talked of racial cooperation between Blacks and Whites in the South, DuBois believed that such talk was a thinly veiled ploy for conservative politics. In the same essay, he wrote: "Mr. Jones inserts in his report one picture of a colored principal and his assistant waiting on the table while white trustees of his school eat" (p. 176).

DuBois (1918) challenged Jones and the philanthropies, observing:

... the great dominating philanthropic agency, the General Education Board, long ago surrendered to the white South by practically saying that the educational needs of the white South must be attended to before any attention should be paid to the education of Negroes ... it is this Board that is spending more money today in helping Negroes learn how to can vegetables than in helping them to go through college. It is this board that by a system of interlocking directorates bids fair to dominate philanthropy toward the Negro in the United States. (p. 177)

By 1921, DuBois believed that the influence of Jones on Black education in America deserved thorough exposure. DuBois wrote an article in *The Crisis* entitled "Thomas Jesse Jones." An annoyed DuBois questioned how this White man, whom he had referred to in another essay as the "evil genius of the Black Race" (DuBois, 1919, p. 9), of immigrant origins could emerge into the thick of the Black discourse. He attributed Jones's rapid rise to prominence to three factors.

He observed that "Mr. Jones' career would call for no special notice were it not that it illustrates in a peculiar way the present transition period of the Negro problem" (DuBois, 1921, p. 253). Second, given the politics of race, the voices of

Blacks would be either silenced or diluted and non-Blacks would continue to speak for Black people. DuBois noted that after the death of Booker T. Washington, "there has been no Negro spokesman whom the white South could trust to voice its demands for the Negro" (p. 253). Third, he observed that Jones was in the right place at the right time; Hampton had become a center of Negro educational and cultural life.

DuBois's opposition to Jones was at the heart of the great polemic of the early twentieth century: Which way for Black America? How would the grievances of the poor and powerless be addressed? How would social reform be exercised? How would the education of Blacks be undertaken?

## THOMAS JESSE JONES:
## "CHAMPION" OF NEGRO EDUCATION
## OR COLONIAL EDUCATOR?

Upon Jones's death in 1950, an obituary in the *New York Times* hailed him as "Champion of Negro Rights." Longtime friend and employer Anson Phelps Stokes eulogized Jones for his service to "minority and underprivileged people," his belief in "interracial cooperation," and his embrace of "religious faith and ideals" (Phelps Stokes et al., 1950, p. 17). The Phelps Stokes Fund published a *Memoriam* (1950), which contained tributes and resolutions from individuals, newspapers, journals, schools, missionary societies, and educators. Even the Indian Rights Association offered a resolution praising Jones for his "brilliant mind, deep interest in people and dynamic spirit" in his efforts to uplift Indian people (p. 31).

The passage of another half-century has afforded time to better understand this important figure in America's sociological and educational history. There is little doubt that Jones enjoyed support from the Black and Native American communities. Educators of color lauded his successful efforts to call attention to the educational needs of their people. Beyond studies and reports, he brought philanthropic funds to build schools, train teachers, and organize curricula. In that regard, his contributions stand. Of more contemporary significance is his role as colonial educator, social scientist, racial sociologist, political theoretician, and idea broker in the new America.

Jones must be viewed within the context of the building of America. The break with European monarchial tradition, the Civil War, and the emergence of industrial capitalism all signaled the end of the old ways. America, in the twentieth century, rejected despotic social relations. History demanded a new way for the new world. Now ideology, social science, and philosophic views must appear to rationalize the new America. Forging a functioning society out of this racially, ethnically, and economically diverse country would be no easy task. The social and political views that took hold and survived this formative period drew from selected traditions of the past, but were not of that past. Jones understood this theoretical dynamic better than most and helped craft an educational, racial, and sociopolitical philosophy for the future.

The product was an outlook that joined accommodationism to social progress. Jones ideologically reconciled the irreconcilable. He brought backwardness and progress together as social policy. He promoted both Anglo-Saxon superiority and racial cooperation. No "champion" of the minorities, he envisioned a new America where Blacks might progress despite assignment by history to inferior social status. Jones absolved the social structure and political order of responsibility. His blend of views captured support from both the oppressor and the oppressed.

Religion, nature, and social evolutionism provided the justification for Jones's eclecticism. Existing society, he argued, was not the product of hegemonic structural arrangements, but rather of God's rendering. The natural order was shaping events and the gradual improvement of the lower groups would occur within its processes.

Absent from Jones's views was a critique of the abusive role of corporate power, property relationships, and the hegemony of wealth in the political processes. Pointing only to the ameliorative capacities of corporate wealth, he ignored the partisanship of vested interests and did not recognize the effect of the maldistribution of wealth on the politics of race.

Embracing structural functionalism, Jones offered only charity reform. His great fear, perhaps paranoia, of mass action ultimately rendered him an antidemocratic democrat. His belief that the ruling order could reform itself has come to help define "acceptable" social change.

Finally, Jones's colonial, socioeducational, and curricular views and activities had major consequences in the twentieth century. Problems of racial and class privilege now plague our society. Disparities in education have done irreparable harm. The hope for democracy, equality, and tolerance has given way to a nightmare of hatred, discrimination, and violence.

# 7

## Rockefellers and Their Associates:
## For the "Promotion of Education
## Without Distinction of Race, Sex, or Creed"

No NAME IN THE HISTORY of the American republic is more synonymous with accumulated wealth and power than Rockefeller. Known primarily for its business enterprises in oil and banking, the family also has been deeply engaged in philanthropy.

For over a century and a half of "gift giving" following the Civil War, the Rockefeller family and its associates were major actors in shaping "scientific," early-twentieth-century corporate philanthropy and its accompanying political philosophy (Howe, 1980). Rising to prominence following the Civil War, the Rockfellers helped forge an economic and social culture for the new America. That culture of wealth, individual acquisition, and avarice would greatly influence twentieth-century America. As dominant figures in the new corporate-industrial state, the family supported and, more important, sponsored ideas and institutions conforming to its national and world views.

Bearing in mind the family's early business reputation as monopolists, manipulators, and price fixers, family philanthropic activities quickly focused on issues such as health care, education, and the arts. This inquiry is concerned with the Rockefellers' intense and broad interest in and involvement with education. The Rockefellers came to view education, and especially higher education, as an important building block for the new social and economic order. An important component of that concern was the education of Black Americans, newly freed from slavery. Ultimately, millions upon millions of dollars were committed to Negro education, as this family concentrated on becoming financiers, ideologists, and architects of Black education.

This account will not attempt to reconstruct the entire saga of Rockefeller activities since the Civil War. That work has already been carried out by Allan Nevins (1959, 1969), Silas Hubbard (1904), Jules Abels (1965), and Rockefeller employee and loyalist Raymond B. Fosdick (1952, 1956, 1962), along with many others.

This investigation looks at the Rockefeller family's promotion of curriculum and ideology in Black education between the late nineteenth century and

World War II. The Rockefellers' operation was a family effort that associated with and hired influential and effective individuals committed to colonial and accommodationist race relations and education for early-twentieth-century Black Americans.

Major actors in Rockefeller-sponsored education include, first and foremost, John D. Rockefeller, Sr., family patriarch and business pioneer. Next is John D. Rockefeller, Jr., or "Junior," as he was called, who greatly expanded the family's public activities. Reverend Frederick T. Gates, family theoretician, theologian, and trusted advisor, guided the family's political, religious, and philanthropic activities. Wallace Buttrick headed the family's General Education Board, discussed later. In that position, he was an overseer of Negro education. This chapter will discuss those individuals, then explore several conferences instrumental in forging Negro education. Finally, an assessment will be offered of the activities and ideology of the all-important General Education Board through which one family influenced Negro education as few others could.

## JOHN D. ROCKEFELLER, SR.

John D. Rockefeller, Sr., was born in lush and beautiful Tioga County in western New York State on July 8, 1839. His mother, Eliza Davison, was strictly religious. His father, William Avery, was an entrepreneurial trader who owned a farm. The family moved around New York State but eventually settled in the greater Cleveland, Ohio, area in 1855. Growing up, John D. was reared as a strict Baptist and imbued with an entrepreneurial spirit (Nevins, 1959). He enrolled in Folsom Commercial College in 1855 where he studied business computation, bookkeeping, mercantile practice, and banking. In 1859, John D. took up partnership with Maurice B. Clark, profitably selling salt, mess pork, breadstuffs, and other commodities.

The Civil War was a boon to Clark and Rockefeller, who began to sell clover seed, Timothy seed, farm implements, and minerals to the northern armies (Nevins, 1959). By 1863, Clark and Rockefeller was an established and prosperous firm. Rockefeller, however, was distracted by the speculative commercial oil business begun in Titusville, Pennsylvania. From this point, the "venture in oil" made history. Rockefeller struck out on his own, became a skilled and ruthless businessman, married Laura Celestia Spelman, continued to worship as a devout Baptist, and then became the richest and one of the most powerful men in the world.

Examinations of the socio-intellectual and political influences on John D. vary. Some suggest he was interested in involving himself and his business operations in social engineering in general and the education of Black Americans in particular. Other accounts point to a reluctance to participate in such matters. One persistent assessment of him holds that he was a person without developed societal, philosophical, and political views. This line suggests that his primary interest was money.

Compassion for the less fortunate, which included most Black Americans, was not immediately obvious in his writings. Accounts of relationships with his employees demonstrated the same kinds of attitudes that surfaced throughout his business dealings. He rejected unionism as a concept, maintained espionage systems among his employees, and quickly dismissed or neutralized troublemakers in his employ (Abels, 1965).

His religious practices have been a topic of much inquiry. While many in the charity movement were inspired by some altruistic theological doctrine, Rockefeller accepted the more puritanical and equally popular notion that godliness was in league with riches. Powerful writers and critics in his day, such as H. L. Mencken and Thorstein Veblen, commented on Rockefeller's church attendance. They suggested that for Rockfeller and other magnates, strong religious faith coexisted with their business practices. The non-charity-minded corporate industrialists did not appear to be driven by concern for the human condition.

Rockefeller's interest in Negro education very much conforms to his notion of the progress of civilization. Education for all would be an important building block in national and societal advancement. Black Americans too would have to be part of the nation's progress, although perhaps not equally.

This portrait of Rockefeller suggests that his central philosophical focus was on maintaining and expanding the avenues for individual and societal wealth. Neither an ideologue nor an egalitarian, Rockefeller never rejected the prevailing cultural, including racial, views of the day. As will be illustrated, he consistently would give full support to his segregationist advisors and associates on education in the South.

## ROCKEFELLER JUNIOR: EXPANDING FAMILY HORIZONS

It has been suggested that John D. Rockefeller, Sr., may have been less a lecturer on social ideas than a hard-boiled businessman. He dedicated his productive adult years to the building of his corporate operations. The job of expanding the family's influence into the social and political life of the country fell to Junior. The extent of the family's social consciousness, desire to participate in public life, and involvement in Black American education is debatable. That question is not the crucial one. The point is that history and political destiny demanded the family's involvement, as the corporate, banking, and industrialized economy was reshaping a nation forever and abandoning the backwardness of agrarian and chattel slave relationships. The new economy would fundamentally reshape the country's institutions as well as its economic, social, political, and cultural life.

John D. Rockefeller, Jr., was born January 29, 1874, when his parents and four older sisters were living comfortably in Cleveland, Ohio. Unlike his father,

Junior acquired a broad and structured academic foundation. A solid, but not brilliant, student at Brown University, Junior took all the required courses. Graduating in the class of 1897, Junior soon joined his father's corporate operations in New York City.

Accompanying his increasing skills in running the family businesses, Junior demonstrated great willingness to listen to and be persuaded by family advisor Rev. Frederick Gates. By the turn of the century, Gates had become increasingly interested in education, medicine, and health projects as a target for family philanthropy.

## Turning to Education

The roots of the family's interest in education and especially Negro education remain curious. Several factors must be considered. It has been argued that John D., Sr., preoccupied with business, was guided to (educational) philanthropy and a consciousness of social issues by advisors, particularly Rev. Gates. Nevins (1959) and Fosdick (1956) have linked his core religious beliefs more with Puritanism than with charity-mindedness and missionary sentiment. At the same time, evidence suggests that the Spelman family, his mother's family, was more inclined toward altruistic missionary views. Family friend and biographer Fosdick (1956) places more emphasis on the family's inherited tradition in education. Fosdick wrote of Junior:

> There is a sense in which Mr. Rockefeller's interest in education was inherited. His [Junior's] father founded the University of Chicago and had established a well-defined pattern of contributions to colleges and universities, and particularly to Negro schools in the South. (p. 369)

Fosdick suggests that both father and son shared a tradition of interest in Blacks and their education. He hints that Junior perhaps had more time and possibilities to engage such views:

> As we have seen, the younger Rockefeller shared with his father and mother, as well as with his Spelman grandparents, a deep and abiding interest in the education and welfare of the Negro race. The traditions of abolitionism and of the Underground Railroad, the memories of the Civil War and the great days of emancipation, were living influences in that home on Euclid Avenue in Cleveland; and although he was born nine years after Lincoln's death, the younger Rockefeller was reared in an atmosphere that still reverberated to the song of "John Brown's Body." (p. 373)

In that account, a picture begins to unfold of a man with a lifelong interest in Negro education. As a boy, Junior was taken on trips to Hampton and to Spelman College in Atlanta, named for his maternal grandmother. A lifetime of gift giving and attention to Negro education would follow.

Not unlike other families engaged in large-scale corporate philanthropy, Rockefeller public rhetoric was high-minded. While associates such as Robert Ogden, discussed in Chapter 8, Wallace Buttrick, discussed later in this chapter, and William Baldwin, discussed in Chapter 8, aggressively supported accommodationist industrial education for containment and continued racial subservience, Junior spoke publicly about "enrichment," "fairness," and "fundamental values."

It might be argued that while Junior and the family did not publicly advocate racial subservience, they accepted it by virtue of their continued support of colonial educators and their views. Publicly, Rockefeller Jr. spoke of the inequities of the past. He presented the "Negro problem" as the shame of the nation. No matter what others thought or did, he was personally outraged and would do everything in his power to right the wrongs of the past. Junior wanted to convince the world that he and his family consistently had combated the evils of the past.

Upon dedicating a chapel at Spelman College to the memory of several female ancestors, he said:

> The religion which dominated the lives of my mother and my aunt, was a religion of the finest kind, not something apart, put on with the Sunday garments and laid off at the close of the day, but which permeated every waking hour of their lives. . . . [Their] love was unselfish, all embracing and unfailing. . . . Girls of Spelman, the mantle of these sisters falls upon you, their younger sisters. (in Fosdick, 1956, p. 375)

Thus, the historically Black college became a cause célèbre for Junior. He would lend his name to the United Negro College Fund and present numerous speeches at Hampton, Fisk, Spelman, Tuskegee, and other schools. For him, the Black college would properly establish the Negro's place in the new social and industrial order. At one speech before the United Negro College Fund, he remarked: "We of the white race owe a debt of gratitude to our fellow citizens of the Negro race for having conceived and brought into being the idea of the educational chest, the value of which is so generally recognized" (in Fosdick, 1956, pp. 377–378).

As a sponsor of ideas, Junior knew full well of the Black American's key socioeconomic importance. For big business to operate effectively, an orderly South had to be maintained. A contained Black populace, providing cheap labor, was a key ingredient to an orderly South. Political advisors William Baldwin, a railroad man who employed thousands of southern Blacks, and banker Robert Ogden had written and spoken often about Black labor. Junior was well briefed on the desirability of cheap labor for the economy. In a retrospective talk in 1949 on Black education, he said of Black economic significance:

> The Negroes were a vital factor in the early development of this country and its wealth; and still are. . . . There are potentialities in the Negro race which, if given adequate opportunities for development, will make for the broad enrichment of the country,

but which if suppressed will inevitably lead to national embitterment. (in Fosdick, 1956, p. 374)

Further illustrating his understanding of the significance of Black labor to the economy, he said in a 1951 nationwide radio address:

> We must make our freedom of opportunity a freedom for all Americans without regard to race, color or creed. This we should do in testimony of our faith in our pattern of freedom. This we should do in common decency. After all, we are Americans. . . . I have in mind, specifically, the lack of educational opportunities for Negro youth. This lack has had its inevitable effect not only upon the health, morale and efficiency of our fifteen million Negro citizens, but upon every American as well, upon you and upon me. It has served to undermine national unity and stability. (in Fosdick, 1956, p. 378)

Thus, we see Junior carrying forth his father's tradition in both business and philanthropy. Like his father, he relied heavily on the advice of Gates, whose understanding of the role of Negro labor and Negro education in the new social order was becoming increasingly clear. Junior established the family's centrist position in national politics, which carries over even to the present day. Always considered either liberal Republicans or moderate Democrats, the Rockefeller family remains active participants in the social and political life of the nation.

## FREDERICK T. GATES

Of the scores of Rockefeller associates, employees, and family members, none had more impact on the family's political and philanthropic activities than did Rev. Frederick T. Gates. Gates emerged as senior advisor and confidant to both Rockefeller Sr. and Jr. Like his counterpart at the Phelps Stokes Fund, Rev. Thomas Jesse Jones, Rev. Gates was the family's resident theoretician, social engineer, and guru, helping to propel the family to become architects of Black education.

Frederick T. Gates was born on a farm in Broome County, New York, in 1853. His father, who studied medicine before becoming a Baptist minister, passed on those dual interests to his son. Most often pastoring small rural churches and working in the home mission service, the elder Gates never escaped poverty.

After his father was assigned to Forest City, Kansas, young Frederick entered Highland University in 1868. His education, more at a high school level than that of a university (Nevins, 1959), was short-lived. Repairing to the world of work, Frederick taught school before moving on to banking. Throughout his early work life, his commitment to religion intensified. As the time came to choose his life's work, he rejected acting and the law in favor of the ministry. In 1877, Gates enrolled in the Rochester (New York) Theological Seminary.

After ordination, he moved to Minneapolis and began pastoring a small Baptist congregation. It was during this period that Gates would be molded for his life's work. In the spirit of the previously described "social gospel movement" gathering momentum in the urban east, Gates turned his attention to the social issues of the day, taking up the study of economic, sociological, and political problems. Writing essays and speaking publicly, Gates attracted the attention of magnate George A. Pillsbury of flour milling fame. The socially conscious and philanthropic-minded Pillsbury and Rev. Gates struck up a relationship that culminated in Gates's planning and dispersal of Pillsbury's huge bequest to Baptist schools and religious projects upon his death. Becoming known in the religious-philanthropic-education community, Gates left his pastorate to investigate other career opportunities.

Having formed the American Baptist Education Society in the mid-1880s, Gates demonstrated keen insight not only in religion, philanthropy, and education, but also in the world of business. By 1889, Rockefeller Sr. was so impressed with Gates's essays and activities that he invited Gates to join their company. In September 1891, Gates, at age 38, took up permanent employment with the Rockefeller corporate conglomerate while phasing out his involvement with the Education Society.

## Rockefeller's New Lieutenant

Nevins (1969) calls Gates one of the "new lieutenants" of the family's activities. From the beginning, Rockefeller Sr. seemed enamored with Gates's views and integrity. Overwhelmed with the demands of business, he needed Gates to handle the "gift giving" to which both were committed. Gates not only helped, but also offered rationale, theory, and suggestions on the targeting and expanding of gifts. Gates assessed his own role as a new lieutenant:

> I did my best to soothe ruffled feelings, to listen fully to every plea, and to weigh fairly the merits of every cause, I found not a few of Mr. Rockefeller's habitual charities to be worthless and practically fraudulent. But on the other hand I gradually developed and introduced into all his charities the principle of scientific giving. (in Nevins, 1969, p. 268)

Beyond managing the philanthropic activities, a chemistry developed between Rockefeller Sr. and Gates. Rockefeller admired Gates's business acumen and quickly expanded his responsibilities to include managing certain investments. Biographers of Rockefeller, such as Nevins (1969) and Abels (1965), agree that by 1892–93, his massive corporate investments and the accompanying demands were taking their toll on his health and personal well-being. So pleased was Rockefeller with Gates's varied activities that by 1893, "all of Rockefeller's files were thrown open to Gates" (in Nevins, 1969, p. 289).

## Gates's Social Views

Unlike many of his contemporaries in the sociology community, Gates seemed to reject theoretical Social Darwinism and social evolutionism in favor of a pragmatic realism. He knew that the American aristocracy was not blessed by any special "selection." He understood that economic power could shift to other groups in different circumstances.

Gates offered "responsible" corporate-mindedness for his social outlook. Corporations and American business in general were to be hailed for their accomplishments. It was they who created wealth, order, and progress. More important, corporations "rationalized" and "reformed" the social order. Thus, Gates presented the corporate community as the legitimate wielders of power and logic. They would create and rationalize prosperity, democracy, and social life.

Gates's views on race were best expressed by continued support of White supremacists Baldwin, Buttrick, and Ogden, all discussed later. Gates accepted God, capitalism, corporate charity, and Black subservience as part of a package to advance American civilization in the twentieth century. Never opposing segregation, Gates made it abundantly clear that labor, both Black and White, drove industry and thus the greatness of the country.

There can be little doubt that Gates's influence and ideas contributed to the Rockefellers' acceptance of a corporate view of philanthropy, Negro education, political development, and social change. Within their larger historical interests, education would be but another building block. Higher education was the corporate way, that is, the "rational" way.

Individuals, including Negroes, were simply cogs in the corporate machine. The role of people was to obediently work for the corporate good and the nation's good. Hence, cheap labor was desirable, subservience was acceptable, and prevailing segregationist practices were tolerable.

## DR. WALLACE BUTTRICK

No discussion of the Rockefeller family's inner circle of advisors, ideologists, and friends would be complete without the inclusion of Dr. Wallace Buttrick. Abels (1965) calls Buttrick "another of the remarkable men who were involved in the Rockefeller philanthropies in their germination" (p. 290).

Wallace Buttrick was born October 23, 1853, in Potsdam, New York. Tracing his ancestry directly to the Mayflower, Wallace received his early education first at the Ogdensburg Academy and later at the Potsdam Normal School, both in New York. After attending the State University of New York in 1871–72, he took a job with the railroad. Having worked as a brakeman and postal clerk for the railway in northern New York for several years, he became attracted to the ministry in his late 20s. He enrolled in the Rochester Theological Seminary and he was graduated in 1883.

After pastoring churches in New Haven, Connecticut, St. Paul, Minnesota, and Albany, New York, Buttrick became active in the American Baptist Home Mission Society, which was connected to the missionary charity movement. Emerging as a leader in this group, he became closely acquainted with Frederick Gates, who later promoted his selection as secretary and executive officer of the General Education Board (GEB), to be discussed later, in 1902.

Lacking extensive knowledge of Negro education, Buttrick committed himself to the serious study of economic, social, and educational conditions of the southern states. During the course of his introduction to the field, he adopted accommodationist politics and education, thus becoming a forceful advocate for industrial education for the Negro. Buttrick became president of the GEB in 1917, succeeding his close associate Gates.

While on the GEB's Executive Board, Buttrick developed a keen interest in economic development in the South. Efficient farming, Buttrick believed, would allow the Negro economic viability. He is credited with infusing farm demonstration projects into the GEB's educational and sponsored projects. Family biographer Nevins (1959) writes: "The four men whose ideas dominated the early work of the General Education Board were Baldwin, Buttrick, Gates and John D. Rockefeller Jr." (p. 291).

Beyond his hard work and diligence, Buttrick represents a firm ideological position in the inner circles of the GEB and the larger Rockefeller consortium. Like colleagues Ogden and Baldwin, Buttrick was a committed White supremacist. Anderson (1988) explores the belief that the philanthropies funding Negro education represented the joining of southern White supremacists and northern moderates and liberals. Anderson (1988) believes Buttrick was perhaps the most representative of the northerners in this undertaking. He writes:

> Thus historians have revealed only a half-truth in arguing that it was the white South that insisted on a second-class education to prepare blacks for subordinate roles in the southern economy. The northern philanthropists insisted on the same. White supremacists themselves, northern reformers were not perturbed by the southern racism per se. They also viewed black Americans as an inferior and childlike people. Peabody maintained that black people were "children in mental capacity." Likewise, Southern Education Board and General Education Board trustee Wallace Buttrick said: "I recognize the fact that the Negro is an inferior race and that the Anglo Saxon is the superior race." Ogden also spoke of the black man's "childish characteristics" and argued that blacks were thriftless, careless, shiftless, and idle by disposition. (p. 92)

During his years as both executive officer and president of the GEB, Buttrick remained a vehement and uncompromising supporter of Hampton-style education. Having completed his early study of Black education in the South, Buttrick filed a report to the GEB in December 1903. In it he castigated several of the Black colleges for offering a classical liberal curriculum, arguing it was impractical and not geared to prepare Black youth for useful citizenship and productive efficiency (Anderson, 1988).

Buttrick consistently recommended that funding should be provided only for Black schools that offered "the true education of the Negroes" (Anderson, 1988, p.134), that is, manual, industrial, and agricultural training. Anderson (1988) captured Buttrick's philosophy well:

> Black private institutions in general, as Fort Valley in particular, had to be transformed because the principles were not modern in that they held to the classical liberal curriculum. The schools were not "Hamptonized" as they taught Latin, Greek, piano music, and other academic subjects aside from the "three R's." The industrial courses, when offered, were designed to produce skilled workers and not to train industrial teachers who would socialize black children to be common laborers and servants in the South's caste economy. How could the black private institutions be changed? "Do not give them a dollar," advised Buttrick, "unless they accept supervision, do genuine work, and hold to a course of study in which there is orderly progress from the elementary to the secondary." His report and recommendations were read by John D. Rockefeller, Jr., and Frederick T. Gates and, according to Gates, "We have no doubt of the justice of your observations." Gates concluded that the philanthropists should use all their influence toward the ends set forth by Buttrick. (p. 134)

Thus Buttrick was indeed, as Nevins argues, one of the four principal architects of the GEB and Negro education. He enjoyed the full support of Gates and Rockefeller Jr. Viewed as an expert on educating Blacks, Buttrick became a powerful force even beyond the influence he exerted over his colleagues. He was truly a molder and shaper of Rockefeller policy.

## THE GENERAL EDUCATION BOARD

Robert C. Odgen, a Philadelphia businessman, discussed at length in Chapter 8, represents the northern corporate community's emergent perspectives on the South. Favoring industrial and accommodationist education, Ogden brought 50 prominent northerners by chartered train to the South in 1901. This trip came to be known as "Pullman car philanthropy" (Harlan, 1968). From that trip came two subsequent dinner meetings leading to the founding of the GEB. John D. Rockefeller, Jr., a guest on the train, called the trip "one of the outstanding events of my life" (GEB, 1964, p. 3). As previously mentioned, Dr. Wallace Buttrick and Rev. Gates guided the GEB in its early years.

## Founding

The GEB was founded by John D. Rockefeller, Sr., in 1902 and incorporated by an act of Congress on January 12, 1903. Its purpose, specified in the charter, was "the promotion of education within the United States of America, without distinction of race, sex, or creed" (GEB, 1964, p. vii). The Articles of Association, or charter of the GEB lists the following officers: Chairman, William H. Baldwin, Jr., Treasurer, George Foster Peabody, Secretary, Wallace Buttrick, additional board members, J. L. M. Curry, Frederick T. Gates, Daniel C. Gilman, Morris K. Jessup, Robert C. Ogden, Walter H. Page, and Albert Shaw.

Upon the formal signing of the charter by President Theodore Roosevelt, Junior immediately wrote to Baldwin: "The immediate intention of the Board is to devote itself to studying and aiding to promote the educational needs of the people of the Southern States" (Baldwin, n.d., p. 4). To that end, $1,000,000 was pledged, with more to follow.

The initial gift of $1,000,000 was allocated expressly for educational needs of the southern states. Between 1905 and 1921, 12 additional gifts totaling $128,000,000 were made. The largest single gift was $50,000,000 made in 1919 (GEB, 1957). The story of the founding of the GEB tells of its rationale, political outlook, leading personalities, and activities.

The country's social, political, and economic dynamics at the turn of the twentieth century were taking shape. Industrial production, and its accompanying social organization, concentrated in the northern states, would supplant agriculture and rural politics. The South was thoroughly re-annexed, although vestiges of secessionism and ill will toward the North persisted.

Within race relations, Black subservience and the sharecropping system of debt farming and peonage continued in the South. In 1895, hard-core South Carolina segregationist Ben Tillman held a popular convention aimed at totally disfranchising Blacks. The Supreme Court's "separate but equal" ruling in *Plessy v. Ferguson* (1896) guaranteed legal enforcement of American apartheid. Inequality came to be seen as a "higher law" (Harlan, 1968). The rapidly consolidating northern corporate industrialists were, through their philanthropies, sponsoring a popular ideology consistent with their sociopolitical objectives.

Within education, sentiment for common schooling had gained tremendous momentum. Educators and social thinkers held out great hope for mass, tax-supported education. For Negro education the transition from self-help, charity, and church/missionary-sponsored schools to state-funded schools was on hold. In 1900, not a single state-sponsored K–12 school existed for Blacks (GEB, 1964). Harlan's (1968) exhaustive study concludes that the meager allotments for Blacks were but a fraction of those for Whites. Georgia, for example, expended only one-sixth as much on elementary education for Blacks as for Whites. Additionally, Thomas Jesse Jones's (1917) famous study found that per capita annual expenditures of the southern counties in the aggregate were $22.22 for Whites as opposed to $1.78 for Blacks during the turn-of-the-century period.

## Program of the General Education Board

Junior had been told in no uncertain terms by southerners that if he was going to assist the Negroes, he had better support the education of Whites lest there be big conflict. Henry St. George Tucker, president of Washington and Lee University, cautioned:

> If it is your idea to educate the Negro, you must have the whites of the South with you. If the poor white sees the son of a Negro neighbor enjoying through your munificence benefits denied to his boy, it raises in him a feeling that will render futile all your work. You must lift up the poor white and the Negro together if you would approach success. (GEB, 1964, p. 3)

Thus, the GEB always stated that it supported southern education, not Black education. Indeed this was not simply rhetoric. Expanding education to all southerners was the objective of these political and social engineers. However, it was their embrace of colonial or accommodationist education for Blacks that is of most interest here. With those broad interests, the GEB politically turned its attention to Black education. It wrote:

> The General Education Board's initial investigations and conferences led to the conclusion that for Negroes, as for whites, the first step was to interest the southern states in providing educational facilities for the Negro, and more specifically in developing publicly supported schools at the primary and secondary level. (GEB, 1957, p. 33)

## Industrial Training for Blacks

The GEB assembled a group of theoreticians and ideologists to work alongside its money managers and administrators. The Capon Springs (described in Chapter 8) crowd, along with others, agreed on the type of education most appropriate for Negroes. The Hampton model embodied the political, social, and philosophical outlook supported by Rockefeller advisors.

The work and writings of one of the Black GEB field agents and school inspectors, W. T. B. Williams, became important to the Rockefeller family's efforts. Williams published a comprehensive study entitled *Hampton Institute* in June 1906 that explained the institute's curriculum. The report was shared with the GEB and came to be viewed as a kind of position paper supporting industrial education. Early in the report, Williams quoted Hampton founder Armstrong in establishing the mission of the school:

The aim of Hampton Institute is the aim expressed by its founder thirty-six years ago: "To train selected youth who shall go out and teach and lead their people, first by example by getting land and homes: to give them not a dollar they can earn for themselves; to teach respect for labor; to replace stupid drudgery with skilled hands; and, to these ends to build up an industrial system, for the sake not only of self-support and intelligent labor, but also for the sake of character." (p. 2)

Reviewing the Hampton curriculum, Williams listed the four courses of study: academic, agriculture, trade, and graduate. The academic offerings consisted largely of Jones's civics, economics, and sociology courses, along with some rudimentary arithmetic, English, and other courses. The trade course offered the largest cluster and included blacksmithing, tailoring, carpentry, shoemaking, and plumbing. The graduate courses offered study of domestic science, public school teaching, and library methods. Of the quality of the teaching, Williams (1906) wrote:

It is fairly safe to say that no better teaching is done in any school in the South. Most of the instructors are white lady teachers from the North who have had experience in good Northern schools. Some of them are college graduates . . . ([for example,] Jones). (p. 6)

The heart of his discussion demonstrates that agriculture and the trades would be at the core of learning at Hampton. Williams wrote:

Thus to an extent unequaled by any other school I know are all the students at Hampton trained for agricultural life. Manual training is given the girls and the boys in the day school. Night school boys get more than the equivalent of this in their trades. Manual training here means more than merely the acquiring of some little skill in the use of ordinary tools. It is all that with strong trade tendencies besides, especially in the case of the boys. (p. 8)

Williams offered a lengthy discussion of Hampton's academic program. He emphasized that such work would be corrective and geared to rudimentary skills. Most important, Williams advised the GEB and the larger interested community that the academic curriculum was prescribed and tightly controlled. Negro education would not be left to chance. For example, he wrote that there was a "progressive line of reading" for juniors at Hampton (p. 11). Sample readings included B. T. Washington's *Up from Slavery*, Dickens's *A Christmas Carol*, *Robinson Crusoe*, and *Life of Lincoln*.

The political curriculum, that is, history and the social sciences, was of significant interest to Williams. He reported that the trusted Dr. Jones was responsible for this package of offerings. He explained that religious training would be the centerpiece:

History, economics, and sociology are taught by Mr. T. J. Jones, Ph.D. History runs through three years. It begins in the second year of the course and comprises the study of the Hebrew people "from the tribal state through the agricultural activities which they took up in Palestine, to the commercial form of society which they adopted before the Captivity. This includes a presentation of the evolution of their religious notions and ethical standards from polytheism and the narrow selfishness of the tribe to monotheism and the broader sympathies of national life, ending finally in the great truths of the New Testament—the Fatherhood of God and the brotherhood of man." The principal textbook of the course is the Bible, particularly the Old Testament, supplemented by books on Ancient History. This course is justly, I think, held in high esteem at Hampton. It serves to supplement and correct the ideas the students already have of the Bible. It is felt that "The contribution of this course to the pupil is the knowledge of the Bible, and acquaintance with ancient civilization, the numerous lessons which that civilization teaches undeveloped races, and more accurate conception of religion and its relation to morals." The results I think justify this estimate. (p. 13)

Williams, himself Black, emphasized that Eurocentrism and Christianity would be the focus of study of advanced students:

In the last year General History is studied. The emphasis is placed upon the great events of Western Europe in the mediaeval and modern periods. The development of the Christian Church and its influence upon the social and political life of the races of Western Europe are studied. The elements which contribute to the progress of European nations can be noted. (p. 14)

The ideologically important economics and sociology curriculum avoided social and critical inquiry in favor of lessons on thrift, savings institutions, insurance and benefit societies, and the "efficacy of different races on labor" (p. 15). The study of character and character improvement was important in the curriculum.

Williams saw spiritual development and worship as Hampton's enduring strength. Noting that it had been referred to by the poet Whittier as "the Christlike school" (p. 30), Williams argued that the religious environment created a certain kind of student and person. This student would be gentle, sweet, and neighborly. More important, graduates could live in harmony with the other races no matter their circumstances.

## Teacher Training at Hampton

A significant part of Hampton's attractiveness as a model program was its focus on training teachers. GEB deliberations, documents, and correspondence are replete with references to the broad possibilities for Hampton-trained teachers. The Board realized that to maximize influence in Negro education, perhaps thousands of disciples of industrial education and accommodationist politics could be trained who would spread the views of self-help and obedience. The following is from a GEB-produced document entitled *Negro Education*:

> A crying need in Negro education is the development of state supported schools for the training of Negro teachers. Several of the Southern States have made more or less promising beginnings in the way of providing state normal schools for the Negro. We believe that a small fund properly administered would stimulate the states to make larger contributions. (GEB, 1916, p. 3)

Buttrick (1905), GEB secretary, set forth a rationale for the training of teachers:

> One great need of the South, perhaps the greatest need, is of competent teachers for Negro schools. My work as General Agent of the John F. Slater Fund has opened my eyes to this great need. We need teachers who not only can teach the "three R's," but well poised men and women who can teach the Negro children *how* to work intelligently, how to till the soil, how to repair farm implements, how to build farm buildings, how to keep accounts, how to shoe a mule, how to judge the value of stock, how to fertilize the soil, rotate crops, etc., etc. The people of the South are ready to support such teachers of Negro schools. (pp. 2–3)

## The General Education Board in Retrospect

The GEB itself summed up its 62-year existence in a final report issued in 1964. It described its formation as a response to conditions existing in the South: "The low standards of education were particularly exaggerated in the Southern-states where the economic chaos and poverty following the Civil War and the Reconstruction period brought complication that could not be easily overcome" (GEB, 1964, p. 1).

The GEB saw itself as having performed a historically significant task. It stepped in when the southern states would not soil themselves with funding or initiating Negro education. Participants believed they performed a task of destiny. Education and the solving of the "Negro question" were crucial to the furthering of the new corporate industrial state.

The GEB members saw themselves as practical people getting things done. In their language, they sowed seeds that were harvested. They described theirs as a mission accomplished. In their summation, they wrote: "The first aim of the General Education Board was the improvement of elementary schools in the South" (1964, p. 4).

They claimed to have supported industrial education because it was politically expedient and practical. They insisted that they were in harmony with the prevailing attitudes of the South:

> This emphasis, for which the General Education Board was later to be criticized, should be understood in the light of its educational era. The manual training idea—

"education by doing" had been vigorously pushed in the last three decades of the nineteenth century, and at the start of the twentieth century had made its way from the urban schools to rural areas. What is more, these ideas bore a somewhat harmonious relationship to Southern prejudices: they provided a concept of Negro education the South found easiest to accept. (GEB, 1964, p. 18)

The importance of the GEB should not be underestimated. In large measure, it enabled big northern philanthropy to act in southern, and especially Negro, education. Through its early connection to the Southern Educational Board, an "interlocking directorate" (Anderson, 1988) was established. Anderson argues that the Peabody, Slater, and Jeannes Funds were greatly influenced by the GEB. He also argues that the Phelps Stokes Fund acted in coordination with the GEB. The GEB, in fact, by virtue of its funds and connections, became the overseer of Negro education. Most important, close connections with racial and political ideologists such as Ogden, Baldwin, Curry, and Buttrick allowed the GEB to simultaneously engage in educational uplift and embrace racial subservience.

## THE ROCKEFELLERS IN NEGRO EDUCATION AND NEW PHILANTHROPY

The Rockefeller family and its associates were major actors and architects of Negro education. Unlike others directly and explicitly proclaiming abolitionist, reform, missionary, or altruistic sentiment, Rockefeller Sr. was busy shaping a business empire that foreshadowed twentieth-century corporate-mindedness and competitiveness. That he was drawn to Negro education seemed more a function of shaping the new industrial social order than a personal passion.

Lacking extensive personal knowledge, Rockefeller Sr. was drawn to existing philanthropic activity in which Negro education had been targeted by the Slater Fund, Peabody Fund, and a variety of church and business-sponsored programs that brought their respective outlooks to this undertaking. The role of Frederick T. Gates in this process must not be diminished.

Ideologically, the religious influences of Frederick Gates never conflicted with, and most often endorsed, the hard-nosed business objectives of Robert Ogden or the White supremacy of William Baldwin. A major accomplishment of the Rockefeller consortium is that it brought these outlooks together in such a way as to fit Negro education into the political and social life of the country. What, then, was achieved by the activities of the Rockefellers, their advisors, their considerable funds, and their two educational boards?

First, they assembled and linked a disparate group of people and interests into a power bloc. Regional loyalties, distrust of big wealth, and partisan outlooks meant that the assembling of individuals was most important. The Rockefeller forces skillfully brought together the aforementioned northern industrialists, corporatists, bankers, railroad people, and merchandisers with philanthropists, southern segregationists, politicians, and southern educators, including university presidents and other advocates of expanded public schooling. Those gathered had political power, widely known reputations, and attitudes favoring continued racial subservience. This assemblage was easily positioned to effect consensus for action and the shaping of social policy.

Second, and more important, the Rockefeller people contributed to articulating ideological strategy and tactics for the new corporate industrial order. Numerous meetings, especially the Conferences for Education in the South, described in Chapter 8, along with assorted essays and lectures by Ogden, Baldwin, and Buttrick, and other activities, articulated a national political agenda and demonstrated how Negro education fit into it. The broad objectives called for a thoroughly reannexed and orderly South, the expansion of public schooling for all, the maintenance of cheap Black labor, and the continuation of Black subservience and segregation. Thus, a strategy for advancing the corporate agenda was successfully advanced.

Third, the philanthropists in general, and particularly the Rockefellers, committed themselves to the expansion of education for all. Not only would they support education, but they also would lead education for White and Black alike. Their support for colonial education for Blacks was subsumed by the broader call for mass education. Consequently, the Rockefellers and their associates do not appear as promoters of Black subservience, but rather as advocates of mass education, which they undoubtedly were.

Fourth, there is the matter of the curriculum of Hampton, or the Hampton model, endorsed and supported by the GEB and the Rockefeller associates. Industrial and vocational education taught manual skills at a time when machinery and mass production were clearly the wave of the future. Mechanization would forever render manual labor obsolete in industrialized twentieth-century America. Teaching manual labor was reactionary, to be sure and perhaps even "antediluvian" (Harlan, 1968). It would condemn Black Americans to a lifetime of subservience and backwardness and hardly would contribute to the leveling and equalizing of society. All the evidence points to unqualified Rockefeller support of Hampton-style education.

In advancing "scientific" philanthropy, the Rockefeller group demonstrated how gift giving could shape education and public policy. Throughout its existence, from 1902 to 1964, the GEB alone expended $324,600,000 in gifts (GEB, 1964). Tens of millions were spent between 1902 and 1912, whereupon southern state legislatures began providing funds for secondary schools for Black Americans. Rockefeller activities showed that "scientific" philanthropy was, in effect, ad hoc law making. Private interests were making and executing public policy.

Finally, Rockefeller projects provided a model for early-twentieth-century corporate support for Negro education. Subsequent philanthropies, such as Phelps

Stokes, discussed in Chapter 5, built upon the ideology and practice of the GEB and its satellite groups. The interlocking directorate, which included the GEB, the Southern Education Board, and core foundations, expanded after 1912 to include members from other philanthropic agencies. The interlocking directorate thus became a cabal of architects of Black education who accepted and carried forth the politics of separate and unequal.

# 8

## *Ogden and Baldwin:*
## *Northern Businessmen in Negro Education*

ROBERT C. OGDEN and William Henry Baldwin were major participants in the forging of America's colonial education for Blacks following the Civil War. Both were mainstream nineteenth-century Christian patriots and entrepreneurs. If northern business was to dominate the new union, "moderates" with a broad political and economic vision and embracing conciliatory politics must lead the way. The partisanship of hard-line regionalists would only add divisiveness, further inflaming an already fragile union.

Ogden and Baldwin became major actors. As northerners, both were detached from the heat and passion of southern politics and accompanying race relations. As entrepreneurs, both understood and promoted social policy that would contribute to stability and a political climate through which national unity and the corporate-industrial agenda could advance.

Neither was trained in the social science disciplines or education. However, as politically astute businessmen with broad views, both came to see the valuable role of Negro education in the new order. Owing to the great respect both had cultivated among high elected officials, clergymen, and fellow capitalists, they were able to galvanize an important section of the country's leadership around their vision of Negro education.

The two spent many years together working on the General Education Board, defining policy directions for Negro education, and rallying influential leaders to their cause. Both men believed in the superiority of the White race and, at the same time, both understood the political economy of Negro labor in the new South and the new industrial order. Finally, both became indefatigable supporters of the Hampton–Tuskegee model of industrial training.

### ROBERT CURTIS OGDEN: "THE UNOFFICIAL STATESMAN"

Robert C. Ogden in many ways epitomized the ideology and sociopolitical stance of other architects of Black education. A wealthy nineteenth-century Christian patriot and businessman, Ogden was a trustee and influential figure at Hampton Institute for 40 years. During his long life and career, he came to be known as a leader of Negro education. Because of his prudence and accomplishments, he was referred to by many as "unofficial statesman."

Central among his strengths was an ability to calmly, privately, and quietly bring together the northern business community with recently conquered "enlightened" southern leaders who understood that the old South was dead. It should be said that some of those leaders were not so enlightened but acted from more narrow motives. Thus, a significant wing of southern educators joined this effort. They were led by J. L. M. Curry of Alabama, who will be discussed in Chapter 9; Charles Dabney, a University of North Carolina professor; Charles McIver, a college president in North Carolina; Edwin A. Alderman, President of the University of North Carolina; Philander P. Claxton, future Federal Commissioner of Education; and others who grasped the new political realities. That is, White southerners could maintain racial and social privilege within the South, but would become economically and politically dominated by Wall Street and the North. Ogden was a major force in promoting that outlook.

Ogden became publicly known for his celebrated annual train rides, discussed later, to Hampton Institute and other points south. On those train excursions, Ogden invited northern millionaire business philanthropists to join southern moderates, educators, and important political figures to learn about educational initiatives in the South. During the trips, the Hampton concept was aggressively promoted. As mentioned, John D. Rockefeller, Jr., described his train ride in 1901 as one of the defining periods of his life.

## The Early Years

Robert C. Ogden was born June 20, 1836, in Philadelphia, Pennsylvania. His father, Jonathan, worked as a modestly successful woolen merchant, while his mother, Abigail (Murphey), reared Robert and five siblings. Jonathan was at one time president of the Long Island Insurance Company of Brooklyn and was a Republican member of the New York State Legislature in 1879 and again in 1880. He died in 1893.

In 1850, Market Street was the center of Philadelphia's commercial and shopping district. While a student in the Thomas D. James private school, Robert Ogden began his career in one of the area's hardware stores as an errand boy for $1.50 a week. He later became a clerk in a dry goods store.

Jonathan moved the family to Brooklyn, New York, where he became a partner in the clothing firm Devlin & Co. Robert soon joined that same firm, where he learned more about sales, marketing, and merchandising. Robert then moved on to the Philadelphia retail merchandising firm John Wanamaker, where he became a manager in 1879. Over the next 15 years, the Wanamaker firm prospered and expanded to other cities. In 1896 Robert returned to New York to become resident manager of a substantial Wanamaker division.

It was as a senior partner at Wanamaker that Ogden was able to act and interact at the highest levels of business, philanthropy, and public policy. The Wanamaker–Ogden relationship appears to have been mutually beneficial. From this corporate position, Ogden launched his educational and civic activities.

What motivated Ogden to participate in Black education? Unlike fellow architects, he was neither missionary, nor educator, nor politician. His involvement points to the keen interest the business community had in Negro education. As with many of the other architects, Ogden hailed from a sociofamilial background in which Christianity, patriotism, civic-mindedness, and nationalism were joined with the prevailing racial, economic, and social views of the emergent industrial and political order.

## On Religion, Philosophy, Politics, and the Negro

Ideologically, Ogden is an interesting study. His views were representative of the nationalistic, industrialist, Christian-patriotic, reformist, "progressive," White supremacist, and anticommunist outlook that dominated, and perhaps defined, early-twentieth-century America. Disdaining aristocracy, this outlook and its advocates generally sought to intellectually reconcile capital with labor, social welfare with avarice, Christianity with barbarous action, and White supremacy with racial subservience. It envisioned an America without caste or nobility, a "classless" society without the pesky problems and social turmoil of many European countries.

Not a scholar in the classical sense, Ogden was very much a thinker and nationalist visionary. His views, forged during the Civil War and accompanying tumult, were aimed toward regional reunification, moderation, and bringing together a country that could be economically viable and socially stable. Education would serve as a key vehicle toward this objective. He believed that he was helping to shape a nation and, ultimately, the world. He was cautious and prudent in his public and private pronouncements. Personal correspondence sometimes cautioned that he could not speak freely, as much was riding on his efforts to build a "United" States (Ogden, 1906a).

Alongside many associates in the corporate philanthropic community, he joined business with political objectives. Christian activism provided a rationale for action. Christian-patriotic activism was an ideological building block of the Ogden credo. It might be argued that because Ogden lacked the broad and stately education of his peers, Christian discourse served as his intellectual guidepost. The joining of Christianity, business, education, and politics is evident in his writings.

## Observations on Christian Duty, Activism, and Church Schooling

Although he exchanged scores of letters with clergy and Christian activists, one of his most developed essays, *Sunday School Teaching: Two Addresses*, was published by the evangelical publisher Revell in 1894. Written to the Presbyterian Sunday-School Superintendents Associations, it summarizes his then nearly 60 years of living.

In this essay, Ogden offers his assessment of looming political, racial, and moral problems that, if not addressed, could undermine the nation. Like many others in the business community, he feared political radicalism as a cause for alarm. Class conflict and the uncertainty of a solution to the race problem threatened all:

> We are in a physical world of most beautiful order. . . . The social organism is sick, the symptoms of disorder plain. Throughout all the world labor is arrayed with its sad complaints against capital. The socialist halls gather everywhere tens of thousands at the very hours when the churches are open for worship and instruction. In our own land politics are corrupt, millions of Afro Americans are without education, industrial, mental, or moral, the liquor saloon is potent in its debasing grasp of millions, corporate organizations are powerful in control of executives and legislatures, vice flourishes in a thousand forms, extravagance is rampant, luxury of living is spreading its debasing influences with rapidly widening circles. (Ogden, 1894b, pp. 14–15)

Ogden's search for direction and solutions to social problems led him to consider several of the popular theories of the day. He philosophically rejected man-made solutions, favoring divine panacea. For example, he dismissed as fanciful the notion that Anglo-Saxons would rescue the world. He believed that social and economic inequality were the most menacing of problems. He thought Christianity held the key:

> Some are beginning to feel that if America is to be saved for Christ, if Christianity is to solve human ills . . . the church needs to be awakened to readjustment of thought and method, to be reformed in dogma and in practice, backward to the simplicity of Christ's teachings. (Ogden, 1894b, p. 21)

His version of "Christian socialism" and Christian action would solve the class struggle:

> We want employers who will put the New Testament into the question of wages and labor, who will look less to the aggregate of money to be made than to the way in which it is made, carefully keeping in view, not the world's standard of ethics, but Christ's standard. . . . We need working-people who will take the Christ view of the obligations of labor. (Ogden, 1894b, p. 26)

His writings demonstrate that, for him, Christian doctrine requires social activism. This activism demands an ordered society in which commerce emerges as the central feature of social and political organization. His discussions of business further illustrate that point.

## The Business of Duty and the Duty of Business

Like his contemporaries in the corporate-philanthropic community concerned with Negro education, Ogden identified a special social and political role for big business and the big businessman. He understood that as possessors of great wealth and employers of millions, these men were in a position to influence both the public policy and the ideology of the country.

His life and writings indicate that Ogden favored a benevolent capitalism wherein captains of industry and finance would demonstrate social responsibility and public-mindedness. He wrote and spoke often about "business idealism" that acknowledges the possibilities for great wealth to influence society. One of his most heralded essays, "Business Idealism," published in *The Business World* in 1905, explained his views: "While the priest and the soldier were the heroes of past generations, the captain of industry will prove to be the hero of the future" (1905a, p. 277).

Ogden believed that a moral and responsible social policy was not only possible but also probable if influential parties avoided extremes and stuck to a middle course. He disdained authoritarian government and argued against plutocracy. He sought an influential role for the corporate community wherein it would not usurp the role of government (Ogden, 1905a).

Responding to the criticism of the left, Ogden did not believe that America's version of industrial capitalism necessarily created despair. Business and corporations are capable of the highest ethical and moral good. They can and should serve God, humanity, and the highest well-being of civilization.

For Ogden, the business idealists were those who gave life to their ideas in practice. They fostered and practiced morality and ethical conduct in their daily affairs. They were people of character and leadership. These ethical creatures understood that they had a debt to history. The notion of debt was prominent in Ogden's (1905a) philosophical credo as it signified a mandate to contribute to society:

> Are we ready to pay our honest debts? To find out our debt to the past, our debt to the present, our debt to the future? They are all to be paid together—a settlement of what we owe the future settles all. The chief business of each generation is to prepare the rising generation for future responsibility. (p. 281)

Finally, the business idealist must participate in social service. Such views supported a kind of philanthropic participation that might save a society from collapse.

## Civic Ideology

There is little evidence in Ogden's statements or writings that he had any great love for or felt any responsibility to the Black people. He participated in Negro education mostly because of his corporate mentality, politics, and patriotic desire to contribute to community and the public good. For him, business and the public good were inextricably connected. His Christian mandate suggested that one could not be disinterested in the plight of humanity. Mitchell (n.d.) romanticizes Ogden's civic ideology:

> According to the Roman view, a man's life *negotium* was the time given to public affairs, while his leisure *otium* was taken with private matters, such as earning a livelihood. The careers of few men in our country illustrate this distinction so well as does that of Mr. Ogden. (pp. 344–344A)

Thus, we find a man of many interlaced dimensions. A man not in conflict but perfectly at peace with a sociophilosophical creed that honored both capitalism and social progress. In fact, for him, the corporate-industrial society was the ideal vehicle for societal advancement and racial justice. His deep involvement in Negro education was consistent with those views.

## Why Negro Education? Toward a Motive

Acknowledging his embrace of civic responsibility, the question remains: What would drive this northern businessman with no apparent familial or emotional ties to the South to so deeply dedicate much of his life to the region's thorny problems?

Ogden mused about his own situation. He was primarily a northern merchant. Although his main commercial venues were in Philadelphia and New York, he possessed some investments in southern businesses, thus entrenching him in matters of the South.

The educators, industrialists, financiers, missionaries, and philanthropists connected to Ogden seem to share several common objectives even in light of their differences. All were committed to rebuilding and reuniting a fractured nation following the Civil War and Reconstruction. Most, even the southerners in this group, understood that northern industry and banking would dominate the nation's economy and wealth-creating processes. Most accepted some version of White superiority, often rooted in a social evolutionist justification. All foresaw America's successful economic emergence if it could discourage further divisive regionalism and maintain an orderly South (Anderson, 1988). Finally, all agreed that educating southern Whites and providing some minimal, for example, industrial, training for Blacks would contribute to their larger political goals. Where, then, did Ogden fit? He raised that very question himself: "Myself—not a Southerner, not a manufacturer, not an educator. All combine in presenting the question, Why am I here?" (Ogden, n.d.b, p. 1).

He wrote and spoke of reasons to be involved in such endeavors. One of his most pointed discussions was a written speech delivered to the Southern Industrial Association. His thesis held that an educated populace was good for business and that business was good for the country. He wrote: "Commerce and Education are twins. Industry creates commerce. Commerce inspires education. Intelligence promotes both" (Ogden, n.d.b, p. 2). His discussion then argues for industrial education for the entire South as an underdeveloped region:

> Its tendency is to create technical skill plus character; to give academic knowledge by industrial methods; to bring the student in contact with practical life; not to ignore books, but keep them in their proper relation to things. (Ogden, n.d.b, pp. 2–3)

In part, Ogden's interest in the "Negro problem" was a result of his lifelong relationship with General Armstrong. Ogden and Armstrong first met in 1859 when Armstrong was en route to Williams College in New England. Armstrong was 20 and Ogden was 23 years of age. Both shared missionary, religious, and puritanical background and sentiments.

While Ogden was interested in civic and commercial issues, Armstrong was focused specifically on questions of race and social development. It was he who dramatized the race question for Ogden. In 1913, Ogden wrote to Seth Low:

> The first and greatest blessing came to me through my intimacy with General S. C. Armstrong, whom I have for many years regarded as the first thinker and practical exponent of means by which two divergent races might live together in peace and harmony. (Ogden, 1913)

Ogden developed a deep reverence for Armstrong. In a Founder's Day address at Hampton, he said of Armstrong, "You were the greatest man I have ever been privileged to know" (Ogden, 1894a, p. 28).

Ogden's interest in Negro education was also connected, in part, to his desire for social stability. Education, he believed, helped to mold such stability. He wrote to H. W. McKinney: "The purpose of the Hampton School is to furnish district school teachers, well equipped with all the necessary knowledge of domestic science, for practical missionary work among the colored people" (Ogden, 1898). Ogden became even more involved in the Hampton School when he was named chairman of the Board of Trustees in 1874.

## Commitment to the Hampton Idea

By the mid-1870s, Ogden had developed firm beliefs about education in the South and especially Negro education. The underdeveloped and underindustrialized South needed an orderly citizenry and trained work force to catch up. He believed that both Whites and Blacks could benefit from industrial training, as it imparted skills needed for industrialization. Of great importance for Ogden, was the place of the Negro in this evolution. Ogden and the community of northern corporate philan-thropists were concerned about the political economy of southern development and Negro education within that process. They wanted trained Negroes, not economic equality of the races. They wanted Blacks who would remain in the South, main-tain its agricultural prosperity, and assume the unskilled and semiskilled jobs asso-ciated with industrial development. They wanted an obedient and stable Black popu-lation and work force. Hampton-style education fulfilled all such requirements:

> "Our great problem," said Ogden, "is to attach the Negro to the soil and prevent his exodus from the country to the city." In Ogden's view, "The prosperity of the South depend(ed) upon the productive power of the black man." He embraced the Hamp-ton model of black industrial education as a vehicle to hold blacks to southern rural society, stating specifically that Tuskegee's "first and large work" was in the area of "industrial leadership, especially in Agriculture." "The purpose of the Hampton school," said Ogden, "is to furnish district school teachers, well equipped with all the necessary knowledge of domestic science for practical missionary work among the colored people." He believed that the Hampton–Tuskegee program would help fit blacks into the southern agricultural economy as wage laborers, sharecroppers, and domestic workers. (in Anderson, 1988, pp. 88–89)

Another advantage of Hampton-style education was that it helped prepare Blacks for the service industries, particularly domestic service. This was consis-tent with Ogden's vision that Blacks should stay in the lowest-level occupations. Anderson (1988) observed:

> Ogden also spoke of the black man's "childish characteristics" and argued that blacks were thriftless, careless, shiftless, and idle by disposition. Hence he believed that the Hampton program was good for blacks all over the nation. "I have many times thought that a school of domestic training for colored people in New York City would be of immense advantage, and in certain ways I have had the opportunity to promote the idea in a practical fashion in this city," wrote Ogden in 1903. "The English, Irish, French and Swiss," he continued, "are holding places in domestic service in the city that would naturally belong to the colored people, but the latter are distanced in the competition because of ignorance and easy going ways." (p. 92)

Education, Ogden believed, allowed Blacks to be gradually uplifted. Hampton-style education contributed to both citizenship and character:

> The right education of the negro is at once a duty and a necessity. All the resources of the school should be exhausted in elevating his character, improving his condi-tion and increasing his capacity as a citizen. The policy of an enforced ignorance is

illogical, un-American and un-Christian. It is possible in a despotism, but perilous in a republic. If one fact is more clearly demonstrated by the logic of history than another, it is that education is an indispensable condition of wealth and prosperity. Ignorance is a cure for nothing. (Ogden, 1904b, p. 2)

## THE CONFERENCES FOR EDUCATION IN THE SOUTH

Several conferences on Negro education around the turn of the twentieth century brought together the major actors involved in Negro education of the period. Corporate philanthropists, missionary association people, businessmen, politicians, and school professionals came together to observe model projects, have discussions, and assess efforts in Negro education. Ogden emerged as the central organizer and a major contributor to these conferences.

### Establishing Ideological Guideposts

Edwin Abbott called the initial Conference for Education in the South in 1890. It was held at Lake Mohonk in the Catskill Mountains. As Anderson (1988) points out, the conferences were patterned after the annual American Indian conferences previously held at Mohonk. No Blacks attended. A passage of the opening address, delivered by former President Rutherford B. Hayes, helped set the tone for subsequent discussions:

> A century or two ago the ancestors of the great majority of the present [Negro] population of the United States were African barbarians and pagans of the lowest type. . . . They had no skill in any kind of labor, nor industrious habits, and knew nothing of any printed or written language. This heathen people, brought from the Dark Continent, after several generations in bondage, followed by few years of freedom, have all of them learned to understand and speak the English language. All of them have been taught the first, the essential lesson in civilization: they can all earn their own living by their own labor. (in Carruthers, 1994, p. 47)

A second Lake Mohonk Conference was held in 1891. Leading voices in this conference included Samuel Armstrong, Hollis Frissell, and Rutherford B. Hayes, then chairman of the Slater Fund. The Hampton idea received strong support from this group. Carruthers (1994) writes that by the end of the second conference the policies and direction were established. The primary goals of Black education would be "morality and the dignity of labor (i.e. working for white folks)" (Carruthers, 1994, p. 46).

The Lake Mohonk gatherings set the stage for the more substantive meetings that took place at the Capon Springs resort in the Blue Ridge Mountains where Virginia meets West Virginia. Dr. Abbott again called the first Capon Springs meeting on June 29, 1898. The influential J. L. M. Curry and Hollis Frissell attended. Called the Conference for Christian Education, it elected Bishop U. U. Dudley of Kentucky as chair. Northern philanthropists and like-minded White southern educational reformers attended this meeting (Anderson, 1988). Again, no Blacks were invited. As gunfire was being exchanged in the Spanish–American War, the 35 delegates at Capon Springs were well aware that America, race relations, and a new international status meant that the country would be forever transformed (Mitchell, n.d.).

The second Capon Springs conference was held in 1899. J. L. M. Curry was named president and Ogden, vice president. Curry's address to the conference demonstrated the political importance of the issues at hand. He argued that both races in the South must be educated in the interest of racial peace and national unity. Southern education was inextricably linked to national salvation.

Unable to attend the third Capon Springs meeting in 1900, Ogden sent a paper, which said: "The Conference can find a wide sphere of salutary influence by bringing the whole subject of popular education urgently before the business men of the South as business proposition" (in Mitchell, n.d., pp. 139–140).

## Capon Springs Conferences

Participants at Capon Springs were not equal rights advocates attempting to smash Jim Crow politics. Rather, they were social engineers trying to fashion a South that would fit into the new socio-industrial order. That order would demand a dominant North and an obedient South, with no more secessionist movements and no more separatist political actions. Racial subservience must be maintained, but the South must be a part of a northern hegemonist agenda. Statements coming from the leading figures supported an accommodationist educational and political agenda. Here is how Anderson (1988) evaluates a statement by Hollis Frissell of Hampton Institute:

> He [Frissell] maintained that slavery had been a "civilizing" influence on the "barbarous Negroes" and recommended Hampton's model of industrial education as a system that would complete the "education" begun under slavery. J. L. M. Curry, recognized as the Horace Mann of southern educational reform, laid the groundwork for a racially qualified form of dominance and subordination in the South: "The white people are to be the leaders, to take the initiative, to have the directive control in all matters pertaining to civilization, and the highest interests of our beloved land." Still, when Curry spoke of universal education he had in mind common schooling for both blacks and whites, demonstrating that there was no inherent conflict between white supremacy and the advocacy of universal education. At the second Capon Springs Conference, in 1899, William H. Baldwin, Jr. advised black southerners to accept racial subordination: "Avoid social questions; leave politics alone; continue to be patient; live moral lives; live simply; learn to work . . . know that it is a crime for

any teacher, white or black, to educate the Negro for positions which are not open to him." Baldwin also saw the Hampton–Tuskegee curriculum of industrial training as the only answer to the race problem. After three annual meetings the northern and southern participants in the Capon Springs conferences recognized that they shared beliefs in universal education, white supremacy, and black industrial training. They also held similar ideas regarding the promotion of public welfare, the training of laboring classes, industrialization, and the efficient organization of society. Having fortified their social and educational ideology from within, they were ready to take on the whole south. (p. 84)

Capon Springs set the ideological parameters for Negro education in the early twentieth century. Participating philanthropists, industrialists, educators, and political figures generally agreed that industrial-style education should be extended among southern Blacks. These leaders were also in general agreement on White supremacy, the need for subservient Black labor, and the new corporate social order of efficiency and labor peace (Anderson, 1988).

Capon Springs preceded the formation of the General Education Board, discussed in Chapter 7. The personalities, political ideology, and educational outlooks directly transferred from these conferences to the GEB. Anderson (1988), who examined the Capon Springs meetings, argues that they "launched the southern education movement" (p. 82). Anderson (1988) writes:

Capon Springs coalition . . . was an intersectional partnership of white northern industrial philanthropists and white southern businessmen and middle-class professional educators. At the center of the philanthropic northerners were Robert C. Ogden, George Foster Peabody, and William H. Baldwin, Jr. Prominent members included Wallace Buttrick and two southerners transplanted to the North, J. L. M. Curry and Walter Hines Page. (pp. 83–84)

Capon Springs articulated a position on Negro education that invited the support of a broader section of important and powerful individuals. Anderson (1988) reports support from segregationist Governor Charles B. Aycock, University of Tennessee president Charles W. Dabney, Georgia State Superintendent of Education G. R. Glenn, and a host of congressmen and other influential people.

Following the Capon Springs conferences, a subsequent Conference for Education in the South was held in Winston-Salem in 1901. Leaders of the conferences established the Southern Education Board to investigate and promote southern education and the GEB to fund it. The officers and governing boards of both consisted of many of the same individuals. As mentioned in Chapter 7, both boards were organized as a kind of interlocking directorate. The GEB, which later absorbed the work of the Southern Education Board, emerged as greater in importance.

While Capon Springs was historically significant, it attracted little public and media attention (Mitchell, n.d.). The subsequent Conferences for Education in the South did, however, receive much attention. Ogden's personal influence was felt everywhere. Every aspect of the conferences was planned meticulously to influence the businessmen, educators, members of the media, and politicians who participated.

## The Famous Train Rides

The train rides that Ogden organized to begin the conferences were works of artistry. Here is how Mitchell (n.d.) described the journey to the conference held in Winston-Salem in 1901:

> The train was the finest that the Pennsylvania Railway could furnish, and in the compartments fresh flowers were placed daily, not to speak of innumerable other courtesies that only the foresight of Mr. Ogden could have devised. Sometimes there were two diners, so that all the guests might be seated at once, while there were frequent visits from room to room and in the observation car a constant interchange of views. The effect of these intensive associations, as the group passed from community to community visiting schools and mingling with people, was to knit sympathies, to face the facts, to appreciate the difficulties encountered by the South in providing separate schools for two races, and to put to the fore the whole problem of education. (p. 144)

By 1901, Ogden had emerged a central figure in these deliberations. He chaired several conferences, succeeding Curry. For the next 13 years, the conferences would galvanize the corporate-philanthropic community around the Hampton–Tuskegee model of Negro education. The conference at Winston-Salem in 1901, the fourth consecutive annual meeting counting from Capon Springs in 1898, represented a major turning point (Mitchell, n.d.). With Ogden as new president, the participants got a clearer sense of their mission and the possibilities for accomplishment. That gathering was addressed and attended by many nationally prominent figures, including Governor Charles B. Aycock of North Carolina, Charles K. McIver, Charles W. Dabney, Carleton B. Gibson, John Graham Brooks, Francis G. Peabody, and P. P. Claxton, among others. The presence of these individuals signaled that decisions would go beyond talk and into action. They took up such issues as school betterment, qualifications for citizenship and suffrage, school enrollments, teacher salaries, and industrialization in the South. Ogden was seen as the "soul" of the conference (Mitchell, n.d.).

When John Graham Brooks was asked in 1902 if he planned to summer in Europe, he replied, "No, I am going on a much more interesting journey. Mr. Ogden's trip through the Southern States has a fascination that no European trip can equal" (Mitchell, n.d., p. 201). Between 1902 and 1912, Ogden oversaw 11 more conferences held in southern cities.

## Later Conferences

The fifth conference met in 1902 in Athens, Georgia. Ninety of Ogden's guests traveled first to Hampton, then on to Richmond and other points south. The conference itself was significant in consolidating the numerous new organizations that had begun fund raising and establishing an ideological direction for Negro education. The Southern Education Board, GEB, Peabody Fund, and Slater Fund led the way. Their interlocking directorates guaranteed united and coordinated activity. The conference heard reports on community organizing, mass meetings, teacher training, and fund raising (Mitchell, n.d.).

In 1903, the Conference for Education in the South met in Richmond, Virginia. This meeting paid tribute to Thomas Jefferson and the great university he established. With its ever-popular excursions and social events, the conference took place shortly after the death of J. L. M. Curry, one of its most spirited participants.

The seventh conference in 1904 convened in Birmingham, Alabama. The train was greeted with public receptions in Auburn, Troy, Tuskegee, Montgomery, and Calhoun, Alabama, among other cities. The conference discussed the Co-Operative Education Association, a Virginia initiative calling for 9 months of schooling for every child, rural high schools, improved teacher training, better libraries, and so on. Rallying around the theme of universal education, President Ogden declared that Virginia was leading the way. Also at this conference Blacks were urged to raise money for their own neighborhood schools.

The 1905 conference met in Columbia, South Carolina. En route, Mr. Ogden and his guests were invited to the Vanderbilt mansion where they spent a weekend. This was the year the famous Ogden train crashed with a switching freight train. Nevertheless, the conference proceeded and followed up on many of the issues raised the previous year. At this point, some referred to the conferences as the Ogden Movement.

The 1906 conference, held in Lexington, Kentucky, joined the issue of economic development to the discussions of education. The general consensus was that the education of both Blacks and Whites was essential to southern development. Additionally, there were discussions of farmers' co-ops, rural life, and more healthful living.

The tenth conference, in 1907, held in Pinehurst, North Carolina, found an aging Ogden rededicating himself and the conference to the cause of Negro education and addressing the issues of the South.

Memphis, Tennessee, hosted the eleventh conference in April 1908. Many well-known clergymen, authors, and Britain's Ambassador to the United States addressed the gathering. Much of the rhetoric at the conference was about nation building, democracy, and leadership. The subjects of higher education, the role of colleges and universities, and the education of women rounded off the agenda.

The 1909 conference was held in Atlanta, Georgia. For the first time, southern state superintendents of education participated in discussions of rural education, along with a review of model projects.

At the thirteenth conference, held in Little Rock, Arkansas, in 1910, Ogden supported the creation of a federal Department of Education, lectured on civic-mindedness, and praised the work of the Southern and General Education Boards. After thanking John D. Rockefeller for his generous gifts over the years, Ogden spelled out three general objectives for the coming period: the promotion of practical farming in the South, the further establishment of public high schools in the South, and the advocacy for increasing higher education throughout the entire country.

The fourteenth conference was held in Jacksonville, Florida, in April 1911. The exemplary work and contributions of the Jeannes Fund were acknowledged.

The last conference attended by Ogden was held in Nashville, Tennessee, in April 1912. Much discussion about health problems in the South, especially hookworm, took place. Additionally, problems of economic development, particularly the farm credit issue, were discussed. Owing to ill health, Ogden was unable to attend the Richmond conference in 1913.

Under Ogden's leadership, the Conferences on Education in the South accomplished several goals of educational and political importance. They raised consciousness about the "Negro problem," a problem that could usher in grave consequences if not addressed. The nation could be thrown into a state of instability, even chaos. Second, the conferences set a conciliatory tone between North and South. Prevailing voices made it clear that regionalism and extremism would only be counterproductive. All must recognize the national interest, the prospects for economic progress, and the new social realities. Third, the conferences further popularized industrial education for the Negro and other southern citizens. Advocates successfully argued that providing this type of training would not disrupt racial and social privilege but rather guarantee its continuation. They argued that training Blacks would help the South and, indeed, the entire nation. They made Negro education nonthreatening to those skeptical of its outcomes. Fourth, the conferences helped prepare Blacks and the country for the final transition from slavery to segregation. Last, the conferences brought northern philanthropists, politicians, and moderate southern educators into a community. That community provided communication, trust, and, most important, funds to carry forth this highly political endeavor.

## OGDEN AND BLACK EDUCATION

As mentioned earlier, Ogden was more businessman than scholar. However, in matters of Negro education, he cast himself as a person of broad knowledge and intellect. Because of his public visibility and power in Black education, he drew the glare of the Black intelligentsia, especially those concerned with education. Of great interest is how Ogden negotiated both his public and private relationships with Dr. DuBois, whose ideas, he believed, undermined the Black agenda prepared by the northern industrialists. Ogden was concerned with DuBois's opposition to industrial education and Booker T. Washington.

## On Dealings with DuBois and the Black Intelligentsia

While "the Doctor," as DuBois was called by adoring students and friends, opposed accommodationist politics and industrial training, increasing corporate support in the early years of the twentieth century compelled him to speak out. In *The Souls of Black Folk*, published in 1903, he publicly attacked Booker T. Washington:

> His programme of industrial education, conciliation of the South, and submission and silence as to civil and political rights, was not wholly original. . . . It startled the nation to hear a Negro advocating such a programme after many decades of bitter complaint; it startled and won the applause of the South, it interested and won the admiration of the North; and after a confused murmur of protest, it silenced if it did not convert the Negroes themselves. (p. 80)

This broadside coincided with the early Conferences on Negro Education in the South and Ogden's increasing influence in Black education. As mentioned, Ogden was extremely prudent and cautious in his public pronouncements. Black intellectual and writer T. T. Fortune wrote in the *New York World* (1905) that Ogden was trying hard to avoid public discussion of Negro education, which he viewed as divisive. Correspondence suggests that Ogden fundamentally disagreed with Dr. DuBois. He wrote to philanthropist George Foster Peabody:

> I write you on the installment plan, this time concerning DuBois. It would be difficult for an enemy to place him in a more unfortunate position than he makes for himself by this letter to you. Detailed discussion would be useless concerning opinions so fundamentally wrong, conceited and prejudiced as those of Mr. DuBois. . . . Perhaps, the foregoing is prejudiced, but Mr. DuBois has established clearly to my mind his own lack of honesty. (Ogden, 1904a)

Another letter to a colleague read:

> The more I see of the Negro race the more impressed I am with childish characteristics and this is often deeply emphasized in the cases of Negroes having a higher education without the capacity to assimilate and the character to use it. From what I hear of DuBois he is, in his personal relations petty and childish to an extreme. (Ogden, 1904d)

Regarding some publishing matters, he wrote to C. L. Stebbins:

> Tomorrow I will send you copy of the introduction I have written for the book on Negro education. I have not seen the contribution of Prof. DuBois, which I may say in strict confidence is the only one concerning which I should have serious doubt. (Ogden, 1905b)

Ogden had contact with noted Black professor Kelly Miller of Howard University. He felt comfortable privately expressing his concerns about DuBois to Miller:

> A large part of the discussion upon the race question—North and South, Saxon and Negro—is irrelevant and much of it insane. . . . The spirit of your discussion is good and your forms of statement admirable—a marked contrast to large current discussions and criticism. . . . While I cannot express my views fully, I am yet convinced that Dr. DuBois is very unfair toward Mr. Washington, and I have feared from his article in "The Booklover's Magazine", and his "Soul of Black Folks", that he is compromising his intellectual integrity. He is not constructive. He in common with much cultivated colored men, is subjected to conditions that are provoking and bitter. (Ogden, 1903)

Ogden believed that he needed to be informed about the discussions and activities of Black intellectuals. Before DuBois's public polemics on industrial education, Ogden quietly helped fund DuBois's widely respected sociological study, *The Philadelphia Negro* (1899). That endeavor, in which DuBois interviewed thousands of Black residents, was the first statistical-sociological survey of Black Americans by a Black researcher. Ogden regarded the survey as important for its revealing data on the lives and status of Black Americans. In a letter to Dr. William Jay Schieffelin, Ogden wrote:

> I was one of three persons who called DuBois to Philadelphia for the study of the Negro. I contributed the first money for that purpose, but . . . never appeared publicly in the matter. The whole of that work which is a piece of statistical study was very important, was placed to the credit of the University of Pennsylvania. (Odgen, 1906b)

Ogden was committed to the construction of Black education with little Black input. He confided to a friend that he respected only six colored men. He was committed to Negro education because it was the salvation of America. He wrote to J. R. Miller: "The work in which we are engaged is colossal. . . . It affects both races and has something to do with the happiness of millions of our people. . . . The white people are now suffering more from the curse of slavery than the black" (Ogden, 1904c).

## On the Negro Question: An Overview

The central issues facing Ogden, the educational philanthropists, and the entire country about Black Americans were: How should they be viewed? What should be done with them? What would be their role as the country moved toward northern industrial hegemony and world influence?

Ogden's evolved view of the Negro question was consistent with the prevailing view in American social and political policy and practice. He rejected the reactionary, violent, regional racism of the conservative South, while supporting a moderate and viable position that would not disrupt traditional race relations. This practical approach or conciliation would allow the country to proceed with the business of business.

For Ogden, the patriot, building the nation was of preeminent importance. An orderly South was crucial to the process. All southerners had to have education, since mass illiteracy could not serve social and political stability or the ends of twentieth-century democratic industrialization. The advocacy for Negro education was motivated by political objectives. Ogden's moderate, even "progressive," stance on Black education thus had a posture that allowed it to be cloaked in and associated with a kind of social humanitarianism. Ogden represented a clear political vision that the powerful corporate-philanthropic community could support. In an article entitled "The Problem of the Negro" (n.d.a), Ogden's pragmatism about social and racial views belies his disdain:

> The education and the development of the unprivileged masses of our white people is, we must believe, the supreme question of the South. And yet we cannot forget that the Negro presents a question which silence has never dissipated and which indifference cannot answer. He imposes an issue which no man in the South can evade. He is here among us. We are face to face with him. I may wish that he were not here, but my wishing so would not provide him either with adequate transportation or with another destiny. We must take him where we find him and talk about him as he is. The problem he presents is one which bitterness may always intensify but which bitterness has never solved. Nor do I pretend to solve it. The more I know about it, the more clearly I perceive that nobody knows enough about it to play the role of either the dogmatist or the busybody. (pp. 9–10)

## Ogden as Nation Builder and Political Architect

Ogden's role as a national political figure is undeniable. He was widely respected by the corporate-philanthropic community, northern politicians and southern moderates alike. He was the ultimate diplomat and negotiator. He showed how to reconcile the seemingly irreconcilable. He defined a path of moderation whereby northern business could organize and stabilize national commerce, and the South could maintain White privilege and racial subservience.

Politically, Ogden repeatedly proclaimed his undying support for the Republican Party, as it was the source of conciliatory politics. Given America's system of federalism, Ogden supported the constitutional equality of Blacks, understanding that the culture of states' rights would assert itself. He wrote to President Theodore Roosevelt on December 3, 1904:

> I think I am better informed concerning the unjust operation of the franchise laws in the South than the great majority of Northern men. I am a sincere Republican and have voted for every Republican nominee for the Presidency since Abraham Lincoln. I believe in the Fourteenth and Fifteenth Amendments to the Constitution, but admit the great injuries done the South in the Reconstruction period. (Ogden,1904e)

Always searching for the conciliatory middle ground, Ogden felt it imperative that the strident voices of reactionary racism be muzzled. For Ogden, the racial order could continue on, but in quiet tones. Blacks had to be allowed limited participation in the labor market and the social life of the country in the interest of stability. In that same lengthy letter to Roosevelt, Ogden wrote of his belief that only controlled social change would be successful:

> It was your discretion alone that proves superior to the error of others and eliminated the race issue from the campaign. Thus the demagogue of the South was crippled in the use of his only remaining weapon, the Negro as a political issue; the country was saved from an attack of increased sectional bitterness; the Negro was protected from fresh aggravation of the present over-acute race hatred and the quiet power of the constructive educational work now proceeding was not hindered. The danger of an opposite course to that pursued by you is but little understood. The race issue in the late campaign would have turned back the wheels of progress many years. (Ogden, 1904e)

Further, he wrote:

> Our friends that advocate Congressional action concerning the franchise in the South are either mistaken or reckless. If they desire to help the Negro they are dealing ignorantly with the situation. If they are using the question for political notoriety they are little better than the demagogue of the South who trades upon the prejudice and fear of Negro domination that is born of ignorance. It is bad philanthropy and worse politics. . . . The intelligent influence of the North and the Negro are important in the adjustment of our race question. But the vital solvent must come from the best South. Only Southern voices will be heard and heeded in the South for criticism, for justice to the Negro, for enlightened progress. . . . Perhaps, it may truly be said that Slavery has harmed the poor white more than the Negro. They should have sympathy, pity and patience, not resentment and bitterness, even though they are very provoking and trying. They are a dead weight upon the whole body politic. They must be educated. The joint intelligence of black and white, created by painful steps and slow, is the only basis of hope. (Ogden, 1904e)

## WILLIAM HENRY BALDWIN: RACIAL AND RACIST EDUCATOR

In many ways the life and activities of William Baldwin paralleled those of Robert Ogden. Along with Ogden, Baldwin was one of the influential northerners involved in southern Negro education. Known initially as a railroad businessman, Baldwin was connected to the South and its issues by the expansion of his railroad interests to that region. Like the other architects, he too understood that the Negro question required a workable solution. His attention also was drawn to education. He spent many years as a trustee of Tuskegee and also as a trustee of the Southern Education Board, and he was the first president of the Rockefeller-inspired GEB.

Like Ogden, he represented big business, patriotism, and nationalism. Also, he supported the marriage of northern hegemony and southern racial privilege. Finally, like Ogden, Baldwin saw himself occupying moral high ground. He was guided by religion and ethical conduct. Although Baldwin has rarely been cast as a colonial educator, his philosophical contributions and activities positioned him as a prime ideologist and architect of Black education.

### Formulating Lifelong Views

William Henry Baldwin, Jr., was born in Boston on February 5, 1863. He was the sixth child of William Henry and Mary F. A. (Chafee) Baldwin. Educated at the Roxbury Latin School, he later attended Harvard. Student records indicate that while at Harvard he participated in sports, glee club, drama, writing, and various fraternal associations (*Harvard Graduates Magazine*, 1905).

When he completed his education, his career choices narrowed to business, the law, or the ministry. Choosing business, he went to Omaha in 1886 to take up railroad accounting with the Union Pacific Railroad. Baldwin rose through the ranks quickly and became a manager for Union Pacific.

In the rough-and-tumble world of railroading, corruption and trickery were commonplace. Bribery, price fixing, and deception abounded. Outraged at the lack of ethics in the business, Baldwin publicly declared that he would operate honestly and openly, and he engaged in a discussion on "railroad philosophy" (Brooks, 1910/1981), through which he posited that the railroads were indispensable to the national interest and should benefit owner and user alike. Beyond simply being a business, the railroads were great contributors to the nation and, indeed, civilization. He spoke of how the railroads benefited the welfare of the nation and how through them "flows the life of the people" (p. 110). He equated the strength of the nation to that of the railroads. The railroad was able to join together remote regions and shape commerce in ways previously unseen. The railroads were part of vital national interests, he argued. Mismanagement and corruption should not be tolerated.

The evolution and articulation of Baldwin's "railroad philosophy" foreshadowed and became part of a larger body of economic, social, political, and racial
theorizing. As he matured and grew in importance, Baldwin spoke out more on
the pertinent issues of the day. Prior to his deep involvement in Negro education,
he spent considerable time addressing the conduct of business. Of special interest
to him were the roles of business ownership, unions, and the public interest.

His business views offered the scaffolding for his views on Blacks and their
education. The notion of educating Blacks was tied to the common good. The
common good could best be achieved by the progress of business. Educating southern Negroes was not a matter of humanitarianism or altruism, but rather a matter
of social order and commerce. It was indeed a necessity.

## On Business, Race, and the Public Good

Baldwin believed that commerce would drive the nation. The principal mechanism of commerce was the corporation, which must be made to function well. He
believed that the corporation must truly serve the public's interest and the common good. Corporations, he argued, should serve the commonwealth, not simply
benefit a few individuals (Brooks, 1910/1981). A social point of view should be
applied to corporations. Dividends and profits should be widely distributed so as
to expand social benefits. Generous returns should be paid for stock investment.

He spoke out aggressively against deceptive practices whereby big companies
often paid dividends on watered down stock. He called for honest capitalization and
proper rewards. Surplus should be extended to the shareholders and public.

Baldwin's views on labor issues were interesting. His involvement with the
Southern Railway during the 1890s occurred at a time of great labor unrest. Strikes
were acrimonious and the opposing sides were reluctant to compromise. Unlike
many of his hard-line colleagues, Baldwin always saw a limited place for the
existence of organized labor. He believed that labor and capital did not have to be
antagonistic because both were part of the community and, ultimately, the national
interest. Beneath his public rhetoric, which favored unions, however, was a call
for their diminished power. Blacks could and should be used to break the backs
of (White) unions that became too demanding:

> The union of white labor, well organized, will raise the wages beyond a reasonable
> point, and then the battle will be fought, and the Negro will be put in at a less wage,
> and the labor union will either have to come down in wages, or Negro labor will be
> employed. The last analysis is the employment of Negro labor in the various arts
> and trades of the South, but this will not be a clearly defined issue until your compe-
> tition in the markets of the world will force you to compete with cheap labor in other
> countries. . . . I believe, as a last analysis, the strength of the South in its competi-
> tion with other producing nations will be in the labor of the now despised Negro,
> and that he is destined to continue to wait for that time. (in Anderson, 1988, p. 91)

He viewed the emerging corporate arrangements as permanent. Much like today's captains of industry, he declared that capital and labor were compelled to work together. To continually fight each other, he believed, was folly.

## On Race Matters

By the early 1890s, Baldwin was fully engaged in the "Negro problem." He understood well that the nation's future was inextricably tied to the issues of Blacks and the South. As his railway had designs on the South, Baldwin became fascinated with the issue. His biographer describes in the following lengthy passage how absorbed Baldwin became:

> A friend much with him in the South said of Baldwin, that while he had enthusiasm for about everything that came his way, he "agonized" over the negro problem. The work is a strong one, but it fairly expresses the intensity of feeling which this grave issue came to inspire in him. After he took service on the Southern Railway in 1894, his private letters are filled with references to this subject. Now he excuses himself for delay in writing to some member of the family because Booker Washington is with him; their plans "absorbing every spare hour of the day." Again, he sends regrets to his wife that he cannot get home for Sunday because of extra conferences on plans to help on southern matters. He went into the South with opinions about the negro, common among New Englanders of his rearing and traditions. It was doubtless better that he had not read much upon the subject. He was too young to carry with him any embittered legacy from the War of Secession. He goes as a businessman whose responsibilities compel him to take practical account of the question. He lives and works upon the moving train. From the blackest to the whitest belts, he meets the negro. He has a special fondness for talking with him. At many points, colored labor enters into the constructive service of the railroad system. In future undertakings, he needed the cooperation of thousands of these negroes. (Brooks, 1910/1981, pp. 172–173)

Baldwin's view of the Black American was an aggregation of stereotypes, mythology, and common racism prevalent then and now. He believed that slavery, despite its horrors, was a step up from the perceived barbarism of Africa. America, he believed, no matter how adverse, provided a civilizing experience for Blacks. Still, beyond all these notions, it was the labor issue that intrigued Baldwin. The unpaid wages from slavery had allowed great accumulations of wealth for the slavocracy. Baldwin believed that the same formula, that is, the expropriation of labor, could serve the new order. He explained:

> The potential economic value of the Negro population properly educated is infinite and incalculable. In the Negro is the opportunity of the South. Time has proven that he is best fitted to perform the heavy labor in the Southern States. "The Negro and the mule is the only combination, so far, to grow cotton." The South needs him; but

the South needs him educated to be a suitable citizen. Properly directed he is the best possible laborer to meet the climatic conditions of the South. He will willingly fill the more menial positions, and do the heavy work, at less wages, than the American white man or any foreign race which has yet come to our shores. This will permit the southern white laborer to perform the more expert labor, and to leave the fields, the mines, and the simpler trades for the Negro. (in Anderson, 1988, p. 82)

The Reconstruction period greatly interested Baldwin. He believed that it was a historical disaster in that Blacks had been totally unprepared to assume their freedom. Preparation for full liberty had to be cultivated, but the right time in history had not yet occurred. He came to see education as part of that cultivating process for Blacks. Certainly no egalitarian, Baldwin nonetheless realized that Black Americans were a permanent part of America's ethnic landscape and represented a significant population in the South. As such, he believed they must be fitted as both workers and consumers for the ever-expanding economy, including his railroads, through a certain kind of education.

## On the Education of Black Americans

By the mid-1890s, Baldwin had developed a close relationship with Booker T. Washington. After having ignored invitations to visit Tuskegee for some time, Baldwin finally made the visit. He had rejected classical, or liberal, education for Blacks. He viewed such education with skepticism, claiming it would not serve these illiterate southerners. Tuskegee left a dramatic imprint on Baldwin.

He referred to the Tuskegee model schools as the "good country schools" that suffered no frivolous enterprises. He wanted students to be trained rather than educated. Brooks (1910/1981) suggests that he was touched by the "success stories" of young Black males and females learning a vocation while "constructing" their mental and moral framework:

Thirty years ago General Armstrong's inspiration planted the seed at Hampton. The result of his work the whole world knows; but it remained for a Negro to transplant his work to the black belt of the South. Booker T. Washington was his interpreter, the Moses; Tuskegee his creation, his life, and the hope of the race. Come with me a moment and let us feel the atmosphere at Tuskegee. A thousand boys and girls from fifteen to twenty years of age; a corps of teachers, all negroes. Here is a building for the trades; the blacksmiths are at the forges; the tinsmiths at their benches; carpenters and wheelwrights in the shops; the shoemakers with their lasts; the sawyers in the mills; below we see the brickmakers at the kilns; the farmers in the fields sowing the crops, reaping the harvests, caring for the herds, or working in the dairies. Here is the agricultural building, where scientific farming is taught, not only for the benefit of the negro student, but for the benefit of the white farmer as well. (pp. 204–205)

Further:

> The girls, too, are at their work, making dresses, hats, or clothes for the students, laundering or learning to cook or serve. Forty buildings stand about, planned and built by the boys. And out of it all comes a modest air of hope, of ambition, and of zeal to work with the hands. They are taught to have simple tastes and few wants; wants that can be satisfied. The Tuskegee student is taught how to work with the hands, and he has to work hard. He is taught the dignity of manual labor; and with this industrial teaching the students are taught from the books in all studies suitable for their needs. (p. 205)

His optimism and praise for Hampton and Tuskegee were boundless. Their model of education and curriculum was, for him, the solution to the "Negro problem." Hampton–Tuskegee would cultivate citizenry. Their model would provide culture to a people lacking in it. Those trained could go out and spread the good news to those not trained. Importantly, Whites and American society gained as much as did Blacks. Brooks (1910/1981) observed:

> But the eight millions of southern negroes are touched by these influences only on the outer fringe. "The problem," as he saw it, was to make the Tuskegee discipline racewide and race-deep. In the coming century, he says, "let no child escape." What Tuskegee has done for the happy few, let it through a thousand other centres, do for all. This is the safety of the negro, but it is every whit as much the safety of the white. (p. 210)

While supporting the type of industrial training and character building provided by Hampton–Tuskegee, Baldwin adamantly opposed higher education for Blacks. Anderson (1988) assesses Baldwin's outlook:

> "Except in the rarest of instances," Baldwin proclaimed, "I am bitterly opposed to the so-called higher education of Negroes." To be sure, he recognized that racial segregation of necessity required the existence of limited black higher education and professional opportunities to train needed professionals such as doctors, nurses, and social workers. Explicit in Baldwin's statements was the philosophy that higher education ought to direct black boys and girls to places in life that were congruent with the South's racial caste system as opposed to providing them with the knowledge and experiences that created a wide, if not unlimited, range of social and economic possibilities. Further, the needs of the South's racially segregated society were to determine the scope and purpose of black higher education, not the interests and aspirations of individual students or the collective interests of black communities. As the first chairman of the General Educational Board and an influential voice among northern industrial philanthropists, Baldwin helped channel the funds of these philanthropic foundations into black industrial schools and white colleges. (pp. 247–248)

## Baldwin's Socioracial Views

In addition to his promotion of Hampton–Tuskegee-style education, Baldwin thought about and spoke out on other aspects of turn-of-the-century Negro life. His persistent thesis suggests that the stability of the country depended on the stability of the South, and the stability of the South rested on the viability of the southern Black. The South would be only as strong as its bottom rung. "The South cannot rise unless the negro rises. . . . So long as the negro is down, the white man will stay down. . . . Eight million ignorant negroes must be an eternal drag on their white neighbors" (Brooks, 1910/1981, pp. 210–211).

Similar to his views on labor and capital, Baldwin blurs the distinctions between Blacks and Whites as though they came together as equal social forces. Thus, collaboration and cooperation among the races were his operating themes. Baldwin understood that America could not move forward in an environment of social turmoil and disruptive racial antipathy. Racial conflict had to be "managed," for it certainly would not disappear.

Baldwin, who accepted the racial attitudes of the day, pursued a kind of theoretical accord among the races. His discourse focused on the notion of "duties" rather than "rights" (Brooks, 1910/1981). He attached himself to Booker T. Washington's notion that Blacks should forget the past, forget slavery, and move forward to a new period of accommodation and cooperation. He felt that dredging up questions of blame and responsibility for the past was counterproductive. The savageries of the past should be left there. The new social and industrial order held out hope for all.

## Baldwin's Impact

Although Baldwin can be coupled historically with Ogden in views and activities, he hardly had the quiet statesmanlike approach of Ogden. Baldwin was the hard-hitting vicar of northern capital. Education, for him, served the economic and social order. Blacks represented subservient labor and were to be used as such.

Within the context of his socioracial and political views, Baldwin's educational legacy rests on his formidable and tenacious support of Hampton's industrial training and accommodationist ideas. He found the Hampton idea the ideal solution to the Negro question (Anderson, 1988).

## CONCLUDING OBSERVATIONS

Robert Ogden and William Baldwin are two of the most important figures in Negro education. While they fully accepted the southern (and northern) racial and caste systems, they had a broader agenda. For them, the business of America was business. The social and political agendas of the country must not detract from commerce. Being northerners served them well. They could both sympathize with yet rise above the racial passions of the defeated South. Both, especially Ogden, were vilified in the mass media. For instance, hardened southerners such as Thomas Dixon, author of *The Clansman* (1905) (which provided the concept for the acclaimed movie *Birth of a Nation*), attacked Ogden for worshipping Negroes (Anderson, 1988). Others feared a threat to the prevailing racial privilege so entrenched in the region.

Ogden and Baldwin skillfully circumvented these pitfalls. Their appeal was not to the forces of reaction and the plantation, but rather to the new hegemony of which they were an integral part. They appealed to the millionaire northern magnates, bankers, and industrialists. Additionally, they addressed those clergy, politicians, and approachable southern educators who could work "within" the new political realities.

Supporting Booker T. Washington and the Hampton–Tuskegee philanthropic community, Ogden and Baldwin helped fashion something much greater than Negro education. They helped promote a blueprint for race relations and racial "progress" that shaped the entire twentieth century and beyond. That blueprint called for continued segregation, the limiting of Blacks to unskilled and semiskilled subservient labor, little or no Black participation in the political and electoral arena, and continued Black residency in the South. These two men helped shape and define the politics of "gradualism."

They were able to help maintain not only racial peace but also, indeed, class peace. They provided an admirable compromise: limited education, even higher education, in exchange for the maintenance of existing racial and economic social arrangements. We do not know whether these were men of genius or mere political expediency, but their work allowed a whole new era to unfold. The country was able to reunite, industry expanded in both the North and South, and, despite some violent eruptions, the races coexisted, for the most part peacefully, in a kind of uneasy détente. Ogden and Baldwin were major contributors to allowing the business of America, that is, business, to proceed.

# 9

## *J. L. M. Curry*

No other White architect of Black education is as flamboyant or interesting as Jabez Lamar Monroe Curry. Curry's nearly 80 years on this earth took him from the rural South to Harvard, through the Alabama state legislature, to the United States Congress, onward to the Confederate Congress, and finally into education administration. Along the way, he became an attorney, ordained minister, military officer, Ambassador to Spain, and college professor. An arch segregationist and staunch secessionist, Curry made his mark on the old South as an accomplished orator, defender of slavery, and indefatigable advocate for states' rights.

At a time when the country was being forever transformed, Curry quickly acquiesced to northern hegemony and the new social order. Believing that slavery once contributed mightily to the country's prosperity, Curry adapted easily to the inevitability of northern rule and corporate industrialization. Although a southerner in every sense, Curry, a Harvard graduate, interacted with and was accepted by "Boston brahmins" in the interest of patriotism and national unity. While other postbellum southerners wallowed in self-pity, regional hatred, and a romanticization of the old South, Curry changed and moved on. He readily grasped the new tasks at hand. The republic had to be preserved. His lifelong interest in mass education, combined with an obsession on the "Negro question," allowed for his ascendance to the highest levels of educational and political policy making.

He eventually became the General Agent for the Peabody Fund and sat on the Board of Directors of the Slater Fund, both influential in funding and shaping Negro education. From these important bases, he soon sat on the Board of Directors of both the General Education Board (GEB) and Southern Education Board. During the critical period of the establishment of the system of Black education, Curry was a major voice. A forceful advocate of industrial education for Blacks, he was a significant actor at Capon Springs and an intimate associate of Baldwin, Ogden, and the other major participants in the drama of Black education.

## ORIGINS AND BACKGROUND

J. L. M. Curry was born June 5, 1825, in Lincoln County in the northeastern part of Georgia. The "dark corner," as it was called, of northeastern Georgia was said to be a lawless and rowdy area where fistfights often arbitrated disputes. His father, William, and mother, Susan Winn, were of English, Scottish, Welch, and French descent. While he was an infant, tragedy struck when his mother and a younger brother both died in 1827. In 1829, William married a widow, Mary Remsen, who subsequently gave birth to one son.

During Jabez's youth, his father prospered in farming and business. Lincoln County tax records of 1834 indicate that he owned 7,000 acres of land, 42 slaves, and several thousand dollars worth of merchandise stock (Rice, 1949).

William, a man of some schooling, wanted the best education for his children. At age 10, Jabez was sent to the Willington Academy where he was taught by scholars with university degrees. Jabez interacted with great orators and southern men of culture. He later returned to the Double Branches school in Lincoln County. There, during his adolescence, he was tutored by University of Dublin graduate Daniel W. Finn in Latin, Greek, algebra, and geometry.

By his own accounts as well as those of others, Jabez was intelligent and well adjusted. He acknowledged occasionally playing with slave children. Consistent with the culture of the region, Jabez was deeply influenced by religion. He was known to attend many sermons throughout the area.

In 1837, the entire household, including the family, the slaves, and even tutor Daniel Finn, moved to eastern Alabama's rich land from which American Indians had been removed. On the new land, William operated a farm (with slaves), a store, and the area's post office.

Although the family had been away from Georgia for some time, members had fond memories of their former home. Thus, Lincoln County seemed attractive for the children's higher education. William sent sons Jackson and Jabez and stepson David to Franklin College, later the University of Georgia, for further training.

Franklin's focus on classical education suited the Curry boys just fine. Jabez did very well. Drawn to the literary and debating clubs, he became an accomplished orator. Since Athens, Georgia, was then a hotbed of political and intellectual activity, Jabez heard and experienced firsthand the provocative speakers and issues of the time. His political passions stoked, Jabez took his bachelor of arts degree with honors at 18 years of age.

The next step was Harvard Law School, which proved magical for Jabez. His twin interests, politics and literature, were further stimulated. He regularly heard lectures by Longfellow, Poe, Hawthorne, Elizabeth Barrett Browning, and other important literary figures. From the world of politics, he heard the likes of John Quincy Adams, Daniel Webster, and many others, as Whigs, Democrats, Liberals, and Republicans debated the burning concerns of the day.

Of great interest here is that Jabez, purely out of intellectual curiosity, went to several abolitionist meetings. He heard Frederick Douglass, Wendell Phillips, and William Garrison in person. He soon denounced the abolitionists as a "noisy and fanatical faction" (in Rice, 1949, p. 14). He viewed them as a small and isolated phenomenon.

Accounts suggest that Jabez had a broad intellectual curiosity that led him to seek out transcendentalist philosophers and writers, theologians, thespians, and educators. Horace Mann profoundly influenced him, as Curry grew interested in mass education: "Mann's glowing periods, earnest enthusiasm, democratic ideas, fired my mind and heart and ever afterward, I was an enthusiastic consistent advocate of universal education" (in Rice, 1949, p. 15).

The Harvard experience honed and fine-tuned Curry. After receiving a law degree in 1845, he returned to the South committed to involvement in the social, political, and educational life of the region and the nation. Strongly favoring slavery, states' rights, and southern regional interests, he, unlike most southerners, had experienced living in the North and would later adjust and become receptive to a broader national outlook.

The mid-1840s found Curry marrying, dabbling in the family business, and halfheartedly practicing law. Although lucrative, the family plantation did not hold his attention, as it was said that he "preferred books to overseeing Negroes" (in Rice, 1949, p. 25). In 1846, Curry joined one of the many popular volunteer units headed for the War in Mexico. He was promoted to second sergeant, but War Department bureaucracy and misadventures brought him quickly back to Alabama without seeing serious combat activity.

In 1847, Curry was elected to the Alabama state legislature. His term in the Alabama house of representatives found him refining a body of political beliefs. An active legislator, he served on many committees and councils, often assuming leadership positions. He was a staunch Democrat and a member of the "Calhoun group," that is, those who ideologically followed John C. Calhoun and the hard states' rights position.

In 1850, Curry's life changed quite a bit. His father gave him land with slaves in Salt Creek, Alabama. Without giving any reasons, Curry did not seek re-election, gave up the practice of law entirely, and repaired to plantation owner life. In 1852, he sold Salt Creek and purchased his brother's plantation in Talladega County. Talladega tax records indicate that by 1857, Curry owned 25 slaves. By 1863, that figure jumped to 40 slaves, 550 acres of land, $325 worth of vehicles, and $300 worth of household furnishings.

From 1850 to 1853, his expanding business holdings and prosperity afforded him more time to write and speak out on the intensifying states' rights issue. His considerable oratorical and intellectual skills quickly attracted attention.

His passion for politics and especially the burning regional issues led him quickly back to politics. He was re-elected to the state legislature in 1853. Over the next 4 years his interest in the states' rights issue, and politics in general, sharpened. In 1857, 2 years after the deaths of his infant son and his father, Curry was elected to the U.S. Congress from Alabama's seventh district.

Major political turmoil was brewing. Questions surrounding slavery, the terms of admission of new states to the union, and the rights of states were the major issues of the day. Regionalism and partisanship were dividing the country as never before. Curry aligned himself with the pro-slavery states' rights faction.

His unambiguous views and riveting oratory quickly made him a presence in Congress. After Curry's delivery of his maiden speech, a reporter for the *New York Tribune* wrote:

> Mr. Curry is evidently a man of talent, a scholar and a thinker. His speech commanded for an hour the full attention of the House, and was really worthy of it in style and manner, if not in matter. Most of the crack Southern orators of the floor have a palpably Africanized style of speaking, and harangue the House very much in the style of an Ashantee or Congo chief addressing a palaver of his sable brethren. Mr. Curry spoke like a white man, with the bearing of a gentleman. This may be accounted for, perhaps, by the fact that he was a graduate of the law school of Harvard College. He is certainly a powerful addition to the Pro-Slavery side of the House. (in Rice, 1949, p. 31)

## FRAMING AN IDEOLOGICAL PLATFORM

At Harvard Law School, Curry studied with respected legal minds of the time, including Joseph Story, Simon Greenleaf, and other luminaries. A recurring theme in his studies was the notion of individual rights. Curry's writings showed evidence that he associated individual rights with liberty, which, for him, did not mean anarchy or freedom without laws. Liberty meant restrained participation in civilization. Hence, his notion of liberty was connected to order and especially law. His ideal civilization was one that combined law with individual rights. He wrote a speech later in life entitled *Liberty and Law* (1900), which capsulized these views:

> Men babble of liberty while their limbs are fettered. The drunkard boasts of strength while paralyzed by weakness; of intellect while muttering inanities. Man's true liberty is not to be free from law but under restraint and guidance of the best law. (pp. 1–2)

Conjoined with his views on individual rights was a commitment to property rights. In Curry's time, ownership of property was a measure of substance. The propertied were considered endowed with the responsibility to deliberate issues, vote, and govern in the name of all. The owners of property were, in a sense, seen to be the builders of civilization, and civilization building was the cornerstone of Curry's world view.

The defense of slavery was of critical significance to Curry. He correctly attributed the region's, and ultimately the nation's, prosperity to a production system that utilized slave labor. Slavery meant prosperity, and prosperity contributed to the advancement of civilization. Slavery and White supremacy were building blocks of the Curry viewpoint. By far the most important element of Curry's political and ideological outlook was states' rights and the secession movement. These issues helped define his early life, as he devoted considerable time to writing and speaking about them. A more expansive look at his views on these political questions may be useful, as they composed his basic ideological viewpoints and foreshadowed his educational outlook.

## On Slavery and States' Rights

Curry's advocacy of states' rights was inextricably connected to his defense of slavery. His extensive writings exalted slavery as the birthright of the South. Slavery was God's labor agreement. It was natural. It was inevitable. It was fully anticipated and protected by the founding fathers, the Constitution, the Supreme Court, mother nature, and all that was holy.

Beyond his organic defense, Curry spoke extensively about the social and economic impact of the "peculiar institution" (Stampp, 1956). Slavery allowed for civilization to evolve in the South. Slavery also was the backbone of the South's prosperity. The rights of a state to maintain this institution were inalienable and must be protected at all costs. Southerners owed allegiance first to their states, not to the federal government.

Draft essays from a book he was preparing on Reverend Richard Fuller, a clergyman he greatly admired, were filled with summative discussions on slavery. He wrote of slavery's justification:

> For the Negroes it secured advantages and privileges never elsewhere enjoyed by the race. They came from the Dark Continent, from ignorance, superstition, barbarism, heathenism, slavery, the heritage of the centuries, and acquired a noble language, habits of industry and obedience, and a Divine religion. No one can compare the Negro in Africa and the Negro in the South except to the infinite advantage of the latter. (Curry, n.d., pp. 29–30)

Like many slavocrats, he argued that slavery had a salutary effect on Blacks. He articulated the following commonly held views:

> *First* of all, it must be recognized that the Negro, before importation, had, behind him and around him the effects, upon physical, intellectual and moral nature, of thousands of years of ignorance, poverty, equatorial climate, bondage, superstition, pagan-

ism and despotism. In this country, while greatly improved from his native condition, he has been a slave, of a superior class, it is true, and has learned therein the fundamental lessons of modern civilization—"the art of steady work and the language and the religion of the foremost Christian country",—but still he has been a slave, with the repression which that implies and involves, and without the opportunities for development which free institutions and citizenship and equality before the law give to those who enjoy these privileges. The progress of the race since 1865 has been marvelous, and such men as Washington, Price, Lynch, Jones, Corbin, Penn and Bruce demonstrate, beyond question, that the Negro can be educated and receive a high degree of culture and be fitted for stations of honor and usefulness. (Curry, n.d., pp. 39–40; emphasis in original)

Nowhere has the states' rights argument been better articulated than in a 12-volume set of writings entitled *Confederate Military History* (1899) edited by Clement A. Evans. All of the essays were written by "distinguished men of the South," explaining Confederate views. Curry's contribution, entitled "Legal Justification of the South in Secession," along with other essays, provided rationale for the next 100 years of states' rights advocacy. Curry's arguments were embraced by the likes of Senator Theodore Bilbo, Governor George Wallace, "Axhandle" Lester Maddox, and Senator Jesse Helms.

## THE CONFEDERACY AND CIVIL WAR ACTIVITIES

On January 19, 1861, Curry was elected to be a deputy from the state of Alabama to the new Confederate organization. A convention met February 4, 1861, to proclaim the Confederate States of America.

His initial activities included reviewing troops in the field when the Congress was not in session. Beyond offering speeches at churches and other gatherings throughout the South, Curry regularly assessed military strength, troop movements, morale, and leadership. He routinely corresponded with Jefferson Davis and leading generals on military matters.

When Congress was in session, Curry often presided and frequently was instrumental in policy decisions, such as prisoner exchange, relations with foreign nations, and the preparation of important public statements.

Soon Curry would be assigned Confederate Army duty as commissioner of habeas corpus. His task was to investigate charges of disloyalty or treasonous activity within the civilian population. This was no insignificant task, as "disloyalty" was widespread, especially in the northern part of Alabama where Curry had jurisdiction.

Other military assignments for Curry included special aide and staff positions for leading generals, including Joe Wheeler. Achieving the rank of Lieutenant Colonel, Curry eventually commanded units that saw combat. Toward the end of hostilities, Curry took a bullet in his coat, which perforated his folded copy of the *New York Tribune* (Rice, 1949).

## War's Aftermath: Toward a New Life

Losing the war, the South had to pay a stiff price. Soldiers and officials were war criminals, property was confiscated without compensation, and martial law was imposed. "Southern civilization" and the "cotton kingdom" would never be the same.

Unrelated to the war, Curry's wife, Ann, died in April 1865, as he was about to see the end of hostilities. Having lost his wife and his beloved South, Curry was placed under arrest May 30, 1865, despite an amnesty agreement issued by President Andrew Johnson. He was charged with engaging in armed rebellion, supplying materials for such rebellion, using and exchanging the illegal currency and bonds of the Confederacy, and other related crimes.

Curry called upon all of his resources. After appealing to acquaintances in high places; talking personally to President Johnson, who had been a Senator from Tennessee; and making a "payment" of $250, he was pardoned late in 1865. For understandable reasons, Curry began calling on the Lord more and more during this period. Much of his political polemics gave way to uttering Holy Scripture. The ministerial side of Curry asserted itself as he began delivering a whirlwind string of sermons. Shortly after his pardon, he was selected to be President of the Howard Baptist College in Marion, Alabama. He devoted the next year to successfully acquiring ordination. A more challenging task was the rebuilding of Howard's treasury, student body, and reputation. Amidst all these activities, he took a second wife.

Regarding the changes taking place in the new South, Curry wrote in his diary in 1866 that the "radicals" were taking over everything. In his view, the "radicals" were opening the doors for Negro activity. He also noted that Negroes were marching and engaging in public action. The South that Curry cherished was forever dead. While contemporaries ceaselessly lamented its passing, Curry quickly accepted reality. He readied himself for a new social order.

Over the next few years he continued working at Howard College and delivering sermons. Reviving Howard financially proved a most difficult task in an economically depressed environment. After declining several pastoral opportunities, Curry moved his family to Richmond, Virginia, where he accepted a professorship in history and English literature at Richmond College. The end of hostilities, accompanied by a new academic appointment, found Curry reflecting, speaking, and writing anew. The world, and especially his world, was being transformed. Questions surrounding the country's unity, Negro citizenship, mass education, and a host of legal questions were to be given urgent national consideration.

## IDEOLOGY IN THE NEW SOCIAL ORDER

In the second phase of his life, Curry was a man of some means, although he did not possess great wealth. Mending the union was most important to him. His South was lost, but heaven forbid that the entire country be lost to atavism and anger. Two interrelated issues captured his attention: national unity and public education.

Strategies differed on how to achieve national unity. For Curry and the White South, Reconstruction was particularly distasteful. Curry believed it to be an ill-conceived nightmare that must end. For him, there had to be reunification without Reconstruction. His attention turned to mass education and especially Negro education as a strategy to achieve a stable South in the new industrial order. There were many new issues and tasks facing Curry. These issues were, in fact, challenges in which the very life of the resuscitated union was at stake.

Reconstruction found Curry angry at the endeavor, while simultaneously developing new political and educational views. The rabid racist, segregationist, and states' rightist swallowed hard and provided a voice of moderation during a most fragile period.

### Reconstruction Versus Reunification

The enfranchisement of Blacks and their election to public office, disenfranchisement of unrepentant Whites, manumission, martial law, and passage of the Thirteenth, Fourteenth, and Fifteenth amendments effectively reordered the South, a reordering that Curry argued vehemently against. Regarding the broad Constitutional and legal revisions, Curry asserted that the national government usurped authority in the South. The North, he wrote, had to acquire a base of support if it was going to govern.

The Negro, still despised by many White southerners, would provide that base. Hence, the Freedman's Bureau, Constitutional amendments, special laws, proclamations, and executive orders were all designed to assemble Black support. However, Black political participation was unacceptable to Curry.

For Curry, these changes represented what he considered the violation of the "public trusts" and the "horrors of Reconstruction," as he believed the doors were opened to kleptocracy. Citing views he agreed with, he wrote, "Duplicity, ignorance, superstition, pauperism, fraud, robbery, venality, were in the ascendant" (Curry, 1895, p. 231).

Curry further argued that the great Caucasian people had been irrevocably divided. They had been, after all, on the way to building a powerful emergent civilization, which was in possible ruin. Poised to become a world power and demonstrate to the world its superiority in government, culture, and character, America had lost its way. The great dream might be forever lost.

Curry created for himself a rationale for reunification rather than Reconstruction. Reconstruction was conceived in irrationality, avarice, and misplaced passion. It was creating unnecessary social and political divisions. The sudden election of Black people to high office in the South was no doubt an irritant to Curry. Although he never articulated one, he demanded a more sane approach that acknowledged the mutual historical dependence of North and South.

Curry entered the Reconstruction years bitter and desperate, and emerged from them with a new nationalist spirit. It is difficult to assert that Curry changed during this period. Perhaps it was a pragmatism that he always possessed, (re)asserting itself. The South he knew was forever dead, but the nation must be saved. This outlook foreshadowed his emergent educational activities that contributed so mightily to national unity.

## FROM POLITICS TO EDUCATION: ON TO PEABODY

With his politics focused, he turned to the greater task facing the country, the education of its people. Progress, prosperity, and political stability depended on the nation's ability to train its people both socially and vocationally. Mass education would serve the country as it edged toward a new international status. Curry never lost sight of his New England experience and the influences of Horace Mann. He was persuaded that mass education was important to social order.

His background served him well for his new tasks. As a former politician, he understood people, power, and leverage. He could get things done. He knew the rural South as well as the effete Ivy League halls of academia. He knew the energies and the pulse of the sometimes rowdy, sometimes genteel, sometimes compassionate, sometimes barbaric White population. He also understood the yearnings and sentiments of Blacks for a better life. Curry had accumulated a wealth of experiences. International travel had made him worldly. The events of the previous decade sobered and seasoned him. He was a patriot committed to the nation's business. He came together with a new breed of businessmen, political people, and educators who all shared his general philosophical and political world outlooks.

### George Peabody and the Birth of the First Educational Foundation

George Peabody has been the subject of extensive research. Hundreds of monographs, articles, government documents, and pamphlets have examined his life, business endeavors, and philanthropic activities. Additionally, the Peabody Fund and its organs, the *Peabody Reflector* and the *Peabody Bulletin*, have published extensively on this man, sometimes called "the father of modern philanthropy." He had a pivotal role in Black education, as well as enjoyed a relationship with Curry.

The Peabody clan immigrated to America in the mid-1600s, settling in the area around Rowley, Massachusetts. George was born into a large family on February 18, 1795, and his childhood was taken up with school and work. By the time he was 11, the family could no longer pay for his education. He took a full-time job at Proctor's General Emporium, learning the skills of bookkeeping and store management. The teenage years found George learning merchandising, finance, and storekeeping. Most important, he learned the dynamics of credit and how to profit from it.

George enlisted in an artillery unit and served in the War of 1812. Seeing little actual combat, he was, however, stationed at Fort Warburton, Baltimore, with Francis Scott Key, composer of "The Star Spangled Banner" (Parker, 1956).

Family debt, combined with ill and irresponsible siblings, forced George to take on unwelcome financial burdens. His first significant business venture found him partnered with Elisha Riggs. Together, they successfully bought and sold consignments of goods from northern merchants connected to England. The passing years found Peabody expanding from local merchant to world trader. England became crucial to his enterprise, as he profitably marketed cotton, woolens, linen, and dry goods there. Although headquartered in Baltimore and shipping out of New York, Peabody was spending increasing time in London. He finally relocated to London in 1837.

The recession of the mid-1830s threatened the banking system and credit availability. The firm of William and James Brown, Brown Brothers, was a major source of credit in England. Affected by the monetary crisis, Brown Brothers nearly went out of business. The firm, rescued by Peabody, would later join him to dominate the financing of trans-Atlantic commerce. Brown Brothers has been a major force in international financing ever since.

Peabody was in the right place at the right time. The demand for tradable commodities was nearly insatiable on both sides of the Atlantic. Trans-Atlantic trade was booming in the 1840s and 1850s. Beyond the trade and sale of dry goods, Peabody was the first person to sell U.S. bonds in Europe. Those bond sales helped finance the building of the Baltimore & Ohio Railroad and the Chesapeake and Ohio Canals. Those sales also helped finance the federal government's military and commercial expansion into the western frontier. Additionally, Peabody-brokered bonds helped finance the Mexican War and the laying of the first trans-Atlantic cable (Parker, 1956). As Peabody's businesses flourished, he quickly joined the ranks of the world's wealthiest men.

In 1851, he organized a major trade and commodities exhibition at the Crystal Palace in London. Visited by 6 million people, the "Great Exhibition" is now observed as the first World's Fair.

Firmly ensconced in London, Peabody became almost a tourist attraction (Parker, 1956). Friends, businessmen, journalists, scholars, and robber barons visited him. It was during this time that he befriended the likes of Cornelius

Vanderbilt, journalist Horace Greeley, Colonel John C. Fremont, and the famous John Pierpont, or J. P., Morgan. In addition, dukes, duchesses, and a variety of royalty called on this man, who was regarded as a financial potentate.

Thoroughly committed to "gift giving," Peabody decided to set up a string of "Institutes" that would receive and administer his philanthropic gifts for education. He wanted to fund the "Lyceum" in many areas so that people could acquire knowledge. A half dozen or so of these institutions were established in major population centers in England.

By the mid-1850s, Peabody had entered into a relationship that elevated him into the stratosphere of money and power. He joined forces with fellow Massachusetts financiers and merchandisers Junius and his son J. P. Morgan. Committed to keeping their European businesses American, they became the first modern international finance capitalists or imperialists. This union captured a significant chunk of the world's wealth.

Withstanding cyclical crises in the uncertain and ever-changing world economy of the late 1850s and early 1860s, Peabody, the Morgans, and their associates always seemed to summon the resources to avoid financial catastrophe. As the Civil War approached, a seasoned Peabody increasingly turned his attention to philanthropy and education.

He was forever grateful to the people of London, his adopted home, where he grew so prosperous. Franklin Parker, a biographer, believes it was Peabody's desire to assist those communities, that nurtured him. This, in part, accounts for his philanthropic rationale. But scholar Merle Curti (1956) discusses a complex set of reasons for Peabody's gift giving:

> Several factors render Peabody's philanthropies remarkable. Unlike many donors, he does not seem to have been motivated by religious considerations. Nor is there any evidence that a sense of guilt figured in his decisions to give a considerable part of his fortune to philanthropy while he was living. His critics insisted that the vain desire for self-glorification was at the root of his benefactions. Such a motive was indeed present, but it was not the only one. Peabody never married and thus had no immediate heirs to whom to bequeath his wealth. . . . Two considerations seem to have been most influential in his philanthropies. One was a deep devotion to the communities in which he was reared or in which he made his money. The other was secular version of the Puritan doctrine of the stewardship of riches—his desire, in the simplest terms, to be useful to mankind. Having himself been deprived of opportunities for a formal education, he was eager to help others in a similar situation not merely to achieve vocational training but to open the doors to cultural self-improvement. (pp. ix–x)

Interested in assisting the "Ragged Schools," schools for the very poor, Peabody soon learned of their many problems. Trained teachers refused to work there and even parents did not want their children to attend, instead encouraging them to work to bring in wages. Thus, housing for the poor became a target for Peabody. Although more interested in education (Parker, 1956), by 1859 the Peabody Donation Fund was making substantial gifts to establish clean, livable housing in London.

The emergence and expansion of Peabody's organized philanthropy coincided with the outbreak of the Civil War in the United States. Looking to repatriate to the United States, he was distressed at the outbreak of hostilities. As a businessman, Peabody opposed the war. Dismissing ideological or political considerations, he felt that the war was bad for business. He believed that all disputes could be peacefully negotiated so that commerce could proceed uninterrupted.

During the Civil War, Peabody's philanthropic activities in England intensified. In 1862, his colossal gift of 500,000 pounds for housing in London was for "relieving the poor and needy of this great city, and to promote their comfort and happiness" (in Parker, 1956, p. 126). That gift was responsible for housing 14,600 people over the next 20 years (Parker, 1956).

In the middle of the war, Peabody journeyed to the United States with plans to retire from business activities but expand his philanthropic giving. Harvard, Yale, and other universities with a science orientation, attractive to Peabody, benefited. Harvard professor and "scientific" racist Louis Agassiz, described in Chapter 2, received $140,000 in 1867 from Peabody to expand his research.

It was during the 1866 trip to the United States that Peabody's rationale for his Fund would be established. Southern leaders, especially former South Carolina governor William Aiken, graphically explained the South's devastation to Peabody. They convinced him that the unity and progress of the country required a viable South. They argued that an illiterate, angry, financially devastated South would not serve commerce or progress. Black and White children required education. Peabody was soon convinced that industrial education was desirable, especially for Blacks.

The George Peabody Educational Fund's founding letter was drafted February 7, 1867. Targeted explicitly for the South and especially for Negroes, Peabody's first gift was $1,000,000 in 1867, followed by a second $1,000,000. Shortly after the second gift, Peabody died, on November 4, 1869 at age 74, never really seeing the impact of his Fund. While his money helped change forever the financing of Black education, Peabody himself was not really an architect of Black education. Those who administered and guided the Fund, however, certainly were.

In 1869, Robert C. Winthrop, Charles P. McIlvaine, Hamilton Fish, and Barnas Sears constituted the brain trust that had advised Peabody. With no blueprint, this group became important as they worked through the rationale and possible recipients for disbursements. Politically minded businessmen and educators, they charted the course, established the objectives, and framed the language for the new philanthropic thrust into Black education. They soon attracted Curry to their endeavor. The Fund's outreach activities greatly influenced Curry, but it was he who emerged as its leader, providing social and political ideology as well as charisma.

## Early Peabody Fund Activities

Barnas Sears, president of Brown University, emerged as a leading voice of the initial Peabody brain trust. Within a few years, Sears assumed the position of General Agent, a kind of CEO, for the Fund. Fund leaders deliberated and outlined policies and programs on mass education, industrial education for Blacks, funding, teacher training, curriculum, and other issues. They established several important objectives and policies. As noted, their earliest activities occurred during Reconstruction. Most southern states had primitive or no elementary schools. Favoring mass education, the Peabody management supported separate schools for the races.

Eventually, the flagship operation for the Peabody Fund came to be the normal school in Nashville, Tennessee. Having received significant funding in the late 1870s, the school came to be known as the George Peabody College for Teachers.

Under Sears's leadership, the Fund supported southern education in the broadest terms. Almost all the southern states benefited from this largesse. Part of the Peabody management approach was to lobby individual states to appropriate more funds for education.

Early Peabody activities assisted Negro education. The Peabody trustees supported the "wards of the nation" idea put forward after the Civil War by a variety of politicians and nation builders. It posited that the newly freed slaves should have a special temporary legal status. "Ward" status suggested semicitizenship. The "ward" argument could be utilized both to ask for financial support and to deny participation.

Sears and the trustees energetically supported industrial education for Blacks. Regular gifts were made to Hampton, while other moneys were given to programs at Fisk, Atlanta University, and a scattering of normal schools.

The death of Barnas Sears in 1880 caused great concern at the Fund. As the first organization of its type, its course was uncharted. The Fund's trustees realized that their task was to be a lengthy one, since Peabody had believed the Fund should exist for a minimum of 30 years. The choosing of the next General Agent was crucial.

## Curry and Peabody

Negro education as a political strategy to establish an orderly South was widely supported within the venues of economic and political power. The educational philanthropies became action arms of that power (Arnove, 1980). The Peabody endeavor attracted great attention. The list of candidates for the Fund's General Agent position read like a who's who of nationally recognized educators, university presidents, business people, and political figures. Nominees included Henry Barnard and Presidents Johnston of Louisiana State University, Seelye of Auburn, Angell of Michigan, and Lincoln of Brown, and a host of respected national leaders.

Curry's southern roots and his previous close relationship with Sears helped him win the appointment. The Peabody Fund, aimed at the South, felt that it could use a southerner to carry it through. The third phase of Curry's life, that of educational architect and theoretician, began to unfold. His early commitments were to both mass education and Hampton-style Negro education. In short order, Curry became a vocal advocate for state support of education, a supporter of normal schools, and a financial backer of Negro education.

He quickly emerged as a philosophical and ideological force. He declared that education was part of the natural right of man. Education would help mold men in God's image. Education was an important component of civilization building. Here is how biographer Rice (1949) characterized Curry's views during the early Peabody period: "He marshaled facts to prove education essential to prosperity, and argued that only the educated laborer could produce products that could sustain competition on the world markets. He argued that poverty was the inevitable result of ignorance" (p. 107).

Curry pointed out that democracy had triumphed in the United States. The patriotic and pragmatic Curry urged acceptance of this fact and of the fact that Negroes were citizens. He made clear his belief that the states could ill afford not to educate the Negroes. He challenged them to support Negro education. He derided those who spent time bemoaning the past instead of starting from where they were, accepting things they could not change, and building for the future. He warned of the dangers of illiterate voters and quoted for his listeners the illiteracy figures of their states. He scorned those who feared that the education of the laboring classes would lift them above the station they were meant to occupy.

## J. L. M. CURRY: SOUTHERN EDUCATOR, RACIAL EDUCATOR

Curry's writings and activities over the next few years catapulted him to new prominence. He wrote and spoke out on education and curriculum within the sociopolitical and economic context. He offered theories of schooling that would serve Whites, Blacks, the South, and the entire nation. Under the banner of mass education, Curry helped solidify a system of segregated schools that guaranteed decades of differentiated education for Black Americans. This lifelong segregationist was a major theoretician in the plan of separate but unequal.

## Rationale for Negro Education

While Curry supported mass education from the standpoint of liberty, nation building, morality, and industrialization, his views on educating Blacks were different.
Political expediency was at the heart of this endeavor. The proper positioning of
Blacks in the South and in the labor market was important to national progress. Blacks
would have a great impact on the wage system, civil order or disorder, and, ultimately, the nation's prosperity. For Curry, just as the slave system was prosperous,
so too would a new system without slavery have to be made prosperous.

First, Curry understood that Black Americans were inextricably woven into
the country's social, economic, and political life. Blacks would occupy America's
basement. Curry also understood that society's lowest levels could pull everyone
down. He spoke and wrote often of this paradox: "We are tethered to the lowest
stratum of society, and if we do not lift it up, it will drag us down to the nether-
most hell of poverty and degradation" (Curry, 1900, pp. 8–9).

Second, Curry was enamored, perhaps even obsessed, with the rule of law.
If the country was to survive, it had to be bound by covenant. The Thirteenth and
Fourteenth amendments granted citizenship and suffrage to Blacks, and those laws
had to be honored regardless of perspective. Curry himself despised both amendments. In his speech *Citizenship and Education* (1884), he called the Fourteenth
Amendment the "blunder of the centuries," believing that the "Negro question"
could have been solved without dramatic constitutional and legislative change.

Finally, Curry repeatedly advanced the notion of education for citizenship.
He presented a series of lectures in the early to mid-1880s that offered a primer
on political socialization. In those discussions he talked of avoiding perils that
might occur in the American version of democracy. Education, he believed, promoted citizenship.

## Education and the Negro Question

The civic-minded Curry never lost sight of the notion that educating Blacks after
the Civil War was, in some respects, high-risk politics. A program of minimalism
backed the rhetoric of liberty, equality, and self-actualization for the Negro. The
Negro must be semieducated for semicitizenship. Black Americans would be junior
partners in industrial America.

During the Peabody years, Curry became ever more convinced of the role of
education in southern Black life. He never tired of trying to persuade recalcitrant
Whites that this was the path. In a speech to the crusty Alabama legislature, he said:

> I have said the Negro problem was dark; but you may dip your brush in the colors of
> Erebus and make it blacker if you can. You may convert dangers into perils and
> speculations into facts, and pile Pelion upon Ossa, and I might not differ from you.

> When you have represented the present and the future in the most forbidding colors,
> I then assert with confidence that ignorance is no remedy for the situation, promises
> no relief, and only aggravates the evil. (in Rice, 1949, p. 149)

Curry agonized over the "Negro problem." His notes and diaries indicate that after returning from his mission to Spain, he began a manuscript on the issue but scrapped it, finding the project difficult and depressing (Rice, 1949). Among his concerns was the demographic presence of Blacks. Concentrated in the South, they could form a solid power bloc that could overshadow potentially fractured Whites.

Knowing the White South intimately, Curry was concerned for its unity. One can only speculate whether his Civil War experiences of divided loyalties played a role in his fears. He even went so far as to project widespread miscegenation as a possibility. He wrote that miscegenation in the South would create "an inert, degraded population" and that the southern United States would look like Central America (Rice, 1949, p. 157).

The ultimate apocalypse for Curry was Negro dominance. Whites should never allow Blacks to evolve to that political posture. A solid Negro vote, he argued, could "emasculate" the White South. Divine law, in his view, dictated White rule.

## Expanding Views on Negro Education: Joining Slater

During the decade of the 1880s, Curry came to be viewed as knowledgeable on the politics of the Negro question and Negro education. He advanced ideological positions that joined White racial superiority to the advancement of Negro education. It was to be the compromise around which northern industrialists and southern moderates could unite. Southern White racial extremists could only romanticize about an earlier time. Curry was making policy that forged race relations for the next century.

In 1891, Curry was chosen to succeed Atticus G. Haygood, Methodist minister and president of Emory College, as a trustee of the John F. Slater Fund. He was immediately made Chair of the Educational Committee, which gave him the same duties as General Agent (Curry, 1901). The Slater Fund became the second, after Peabody, of the large educational philanthropic foundations. Established in 1882 by John Fox Slater of Norwich, Connecticut, its governing board was chaired by Rutherford B. Hayes. Unlike Peabody, Slater money was to be used for Blacks exclusively. The stipulation accompanying the initial $1 million gift read that grants were for:

> [t]he uplifting of the lately emancipated population of the Southern States, and their
> posterity, by conferring on them the blessings of Christian education . . . for their
> own sake . . . and . . . for the safety of our common country, in which they have been
> invested with equal political rights. (Curry, 1901, p. 1)

The ten Slater trustees, led by Morris K. Jessup, Daniel Coit Gilman, and William Slater, had been deeply involved in defining Negro education. Curry fit right in and quickly joined their deliberations. Several concepts advanced by Curry and the Slater board became important fixtures for a generation of White architects of Black education to embrace and embellish.

First, Slater Fund leaders agreed that Negro education was to be "Christian education." They wanted Blacks to be "good men and good citizens" (Curry, 1901, p. 1). They wanted Blacks to develop duty toward God in the context of Holy Scripture. They wanted obedient and reverent people who could not be drawn to crime or insolence. Second, they wanted Slater schools to train good teachers. They had been appalled at the quality of teaching in Negro schools. The entire effort, they believed, could succeed only if teachers cultivated new leaders for the race. The third and most important component of the project was to advance industrial training as a curriculum and an ideology. Curry played no small role in helping to refine, package, and fund industrial education for Blacks.

## Commitment to Industrial Training

John Slater was a forceful advocate of industrial training for Blacks. The commitment of his Fund to this type of education offered a model for others to follow. The denial of intellectual or liberal education for Blacks was now a fait accompli. Here is how Curry, author of the Slater Report, assessed the Fund's position in the influential and oft-cited report of 1901:

> That industrial training simultaneously with mental and moral instruction should be taught in aided institutions, as making a more self-reliant and self-supporting population and furnishing some of the conditions of the best intellectual and moral discipline of the colored people, especially of those who were to be teachers and guides of the people. (p. 2)

Curry continued to build upon the industrial training tradition during his leadership at both Peabody and Slater. Throughout the 1880s and 1890s, Curry provided both ideological and financial justification. He argued that this was the best course of action for the Negro. It must be so because all the White administrators say so: "The concurrent opinion of all connected with industrial work is most favorable as to its benefits" (Curry, 1901, pp. 4–5).

Curry and his Fund colleagues knew full well that their prescriptions for Black education differed from what was conventionally accepted as liberal education for the world of business, manufacturing, and finance. Curry (1901) wrote:

> The accepted methods of education in their general scope are of doubtful application to Negroes. Some need the best intellectual training that they may become leaders of the industrial, social, intellectual, and religious life of the race, but, as things now

are, the great mass need to be fitted for domestic and mechanical and agricultural occupations which will produce the means of living and ensure self-respect and comfortable self-support. (p. 5)

The Curry-led group paid special homage to Hampton and Tuskegee as embodiments of their paradigm. They explicitly allocated dollars for Black colleges and programs that adhered to this model. Again, here is Curry's (1901) policy:

The policy has been persistently adhered to, of supplementing, or rather coordinating, academic with manual and industrial training, and the reports from the schools are uniform and emphatic in ascribing the origin and success of industrial departments to the timely and efficient aid rendered by this fund. (p. 4)

## J. L. M. Curry: Ruminations

Not only was J. L. M. Curry a man for his time, but some also might consider him a man for these times. He provided a nineteenth-century exemplar for some of today's figures. Black Americans look with great curiosity at the hard-bitten segregationists of yesteryear who now proclaim their undying love for the Black race. The George Wallace of 1998 was a far cry from the George Wallace of 1958. America's rapidly changing political environment creates fleeting political allegiances.

The contemporary corporate-industrial society responds best to profit. No cultural, racial, or gender mountains are too high. Yesterday's enemies are today's friends. There are no permanent associations, only permanent interests. Economic and political expediency are inextricably connected. Such is the legacy of J. L. M. Curry.

# Conclusion: Thoughts and Afterthoughts

HAVING SPENT SEVERAL YEARS thinking, gathering data, and writing and rewriting this project, I am left to reflect on several issues. I have no new arguments to make, as I have made them in the text. I would, however, like to recap major points and perhaps expand a few themes.

First, let us look at what the work set out to accomplish. I conceptualized this study as one in history, education, and political economy. It would be a study of colonial education and colonialism. It would be a study of how the political, economic, and cultural power structures came together to influence knowledge selection, shape educational policy, and consolidate a society stratified by race, class, and obviously gender. Above all, it was to be a study in ideology and how dominant economic and sociopolitical interests shaped schooling for Blacks, the curriculum, and ultimately the social life of the country.

I have always accepted that Black, and all, public education was a product of historically, politically, and socially constructed ideas. I have observed Black education as a "political" act. I have viewed this act as influenced by hegemonic social relationships, labor market economics, class stratification, and racial division. Although the project did not address democratic and oppositionist views extensively, they were an important part of the history. I reject rigid deterministic arguments that point exclusively to the role of powerful interests in history. History is made by people in struggle. Some win, some lose. Winners become losers, and losers become winners. The laws of dialectics are fiercely at work in the making of history. I acknowledge that schools, curriculum, culture, and social ideas are all contested terrain. America's division of wealth, property relationships, and race and gendered relationships have rendered social and economic interests mutually exclusive. Those who own and do not work can never be reconciled to those who work and do not own. As such, democracy does confront power. Common people do have ideas, engage in action, and, indeed, mightily influence social processes.

In the case of Black education, we know of the heroic self-help efforts during and immediately following slavery. We know that African Americans embraced education in significant ways. We also know that the stakes were so high that the ruling elite could not help but be involved.

In undertaking this work, I wanted to highlight the separate tradition and history in Black education. I wanted to examine the power dynamics influencing this formation. I wanted to place Black education in a context. I wanted to demonstrate how slavery, segregation, and America's politics dictated Black education. As a political sociologist, I have examined relationships between education and the state. More specifically, I have been concerned with how powerful forces influence education and the curriculum. In the case of this study, both the state apparatus and powerful economic forces joined in tandem to shape Black education.

With the establishment of the Freedman's Bureau, the federal government demonstrated that it was asserting not only involvement in, but also control of, such matters. Beyond the significant role of the federal government, I have identified other social institutions that had a hand in the enterprise of Black education. The activities of missionary societies represented the influence of the charity community. Finally, major commitments from corporate philanthropies and attention from civic reform associations indicated the profound policy significance of the endeavor. A broad array of public, private, and intellectual forces thus were joined in this initiative.

Black education experienced a separate tradition in funding, administration, teacher training, and curriculum. Black education became a central policy instrument in consolidating the unpredictable newly freed slaves, re-annexing the South, and guaranteeing a pool of cheap semiskilled and unskilled labor. This was as political an undertaking as we have known.

I have tried to tell a political story through the lives and activities of major players in the drama. The people chosen represent much more than action; they represent ideas, theories, and power. They were both shaped by and shapers of history.

Interestingly, when I embarked on this project, I expected that my chosen "architects" would all be simply evil men possessing the colonial mentality. The story I would tell would be easy—powerful evil men perpetrated evil deeds. As we have seen, it was not that cut and dried. These people indeed possessed the colonial mentality, but they were more complex and interesting. Their ideological stance can be attributed, in part, to the political history of the country.

America never experienced classical feudalism with its detached aristocracy, titles of nobility, and lack of social altruism. America's colonial masters practiced domination, but it was postfeudal in nature. These architects would embrace post-Renaissance, "enlightened" social and political relationships. They would acknowledge individual rights in the democratic social order.

Thus, their world was complex. Although they embraced privilege and racism, their task, as they saw it, was to create a viable political structure in which the privilege of wealth and race did not totally pre-empt democratic participation.

These people were, above all, nation builders, idea brokers, and agents of consensus. They knew what kinds of compromises it would take to shape twentieth-century America. They were above the petty, the mundane, and the superficial. They had a nation to shape. They didn't think in terms of permanent friends and permanent enemies, only permanent interests. J. L. M. Curry could, with great ease, transform himself from hard-core plantation segregationist to proponent of education for all. Never straying from racial supremacy, they were attempting to structure a social order that could function. These architects were men of expediency.

Christian patriotism and Christian nationalism seem to be common threads influencing and binding them. For them, God ordained America and its glory. They would carry on their Black education work in the name of God.

Above all, these architects were people of vision. They were engaged in the great compromise. If America was to work, they had to ideologically reconcile great wealth with social altruism. They had to wed democracy to plutocracy. Fortunately, America's unprecedented expanding industrial wealth allowed them to successfully complete that task. The gigantic automobile, steel, and rubber factories, alongside the mines, mills, and refineries, provided the newly freed slaves, the newly arrived immigrants, and the indigenous White proletariat with employment far beyond the agrarian dead end. The American experience would bring a new dimension to national development.

Of all the conclusions and assertions of this study, the overwhelming finding relates to the importance of Black education in America's political and racial history. We can assert without equivocation that Black education has been one of the singular most important issues of the past 150 years. It has transcended schooling to become a major policy issue. In broad terms, Black education has been at the heart of shaping modern America.

Politically, as I have argued throughout this work, the post–Civil War period was the defining juncture or watershed in America's history. Everything was up for grabs as a prostrate country lay bleeding and divided. The new society would be configured in the mid- to late nineteenth century. Of maximum importance, the "Negro question" had to be addressed and settled. Several conclusions were clear: Blacks would remain in America and become a subservient labor force. A recalcitrant southern planter class would yield monopolistic economic hegemony to northern corporations but maintain wealth. Moreover, they would maintain social and cultural dominance. An orderly South would be successfully, if reluctantly, re-annexed.

Situating Blacks would be key. Black education would become the critical issue for all. Education was always at, or near, the top of the freedom list for Blacks. Offering even humble educational opportunities would provide a history-making initiative. Black education thus became the central political weapon by which Blacks would be introduced and inducted into America's social organization.

Black education invited Blacks to participate in, without disrupting, the social order. Education could offer promise, vision, and dreams in the absence of immediate material prosperity.

As noted, accommodationist education was politically constructed. It taught the cultural values of the ruling order. It aimed to shape an ideological outlook for an entire people. It taught conformity, obedience, sobriety, piety, and the values of enterprise. Heavy emphasis on teacher training guaranteed that the word would be spread. As emphasized throughout, the architects understood the great ideological possibilities in Black education. The curriculum was thus geared to social engineering as much as anything else.

The shaping of race relations was inextricably connected to Black education. The objective of the ruling order was to wed Constitutional freedom with social subservience. Freedom became the form, subservience the content.

The issue of race would, as DuBois predicted, dominate America in the twentieth century. America needed class peace and race peace to get beyond its national adolescence and allow corporate industrialization to expand. America's apartheid had to be made workable. It needed to appear natural and ordained. Beyond that, Blacks needed to be convinced that their lot was improving.

As argued in the text, the creation of a Black middle class has been indispensable to the country's racial politics. No marginalized group in the American context is viable without a middle class. A compradore Black middle class, consisting of clergy, entrepreneurs, and clerks, would serve to anchor the race. Booker T. Washington's platform of uplift was rooted in the middle-class notion.

As we look back on the twentieth century, we observe that the consolidation of the Black middle class has long been completed. The path of the Black middle class has been a winding one. The viability of "mom and pop" businesses has been thoroughly undermined by giant corporate usurpation. The once-flourishing Black business districts from Oklahoma to Chicago's Bronzeville to the Black mecca of Harlem have long been defunct. The Black business middle class is rooted more in management than in ownership. Programs of giveaway and takeaway persist in cyclical fashion. Last year's "affirmative action" becomes this year's program cut.

While Black entrepreneurship remains tenuous, there can be no doubt that professionals, academics, civil servants, athletes, and entertainers anchor the middle class. In recent times, the Black middle class has shown decidedly new tendencies toward political and social conservatism, as its members become more distanced from the "struggle."

The contemporary Black middle class is firmly entrenched. While its lowest group fights to maintain its status, another group has found relative stability. A section of the Black middle class has become exceedingly loyal to America's economic and political system. That section, in most cases, has turned away from protest.

My final thought is about the larger political, social, and policy implications of Black education. In many ways the forging of this endeavor helped to teach America's corporate industrial ruling class how to rule.

We recall that prior to the Civil War, America's elites were landed gentry in both North and South. Industrialization, urbanization, and northern hegemony called upon new powers. As I have repeatedly insisted, America was up for grabs. Things could have gone quite differently.

New ways of deliberating and implementing policy had to be found. New explanations had to be rendered. New populations such as Blacks and immigrants had to be considered, although certainly not equally. New ways of compromise had to be explored. The North had to re-annex a recalcitrant South. The corporate ordering of society had to be undertaken. These were no small chores.

Black education became a model, perhaps even a template. The ruling class had a great exercise in how to rule. They learned how to compromise, how and when to be inclusive or exclusive.

# References

Abels, J. (1965). *The Rockefeller billions: The story of the world's most stupendous fortune.* New York: Macmillan.

Agassiz, L. (1850). The diversity of origin of the human races. *Christian Examiner, 49*: 110–145.

Anderson, J. D. (1980). Philanthropic control over private black higher education. In R. F. Arnove (Ed.), *Philanthropy and cultural imperialism: The foundations at home and abroad* (pp. 147–177). Boston: G. K. Hall.

Anderson, J. D. (1988). *The education of blacks in the south: 1860–1935.* Chapel Hill: University of North Carolina Press.

Apple, M. (1979). *Ideology and curriculum.* London: Routledge & Kegan Paul.

Aristotle, (trans. 1970). *Politics.* Munich: W. Fink.

Armstrong, S. C. *See Southern Workman.*

Arnove, R. F. (Ed.). (1980). *Philanthropy and cultural imperialism: The foundations at home and abroad.* Boston: G. K. Hall.

Baldwin, W. (n.d.). Historical statement. Box 337, Folder 3542, GEB Collection. Rockefeller Archive Center, Sleepy Hollow, NY.

Berman, E. H. (1969). *Education in Africa and America: A history of the Phelps Stokes Fund.* Unpublished doctoral dissertation, Columbia University, New York.

Berman, E. H. (1980). Educational colonialism in Africa: The role of American foundations, 1910–1945. In R. F. Arnove (Ed.), *Philanthropy and cultural imperialism: The foundations at home and abroad* (pp. 179–201). Boston: G. K. Hall.

Berman, E. H. (1983). *The influence of the Carnegie, Ford, and Rockefeller foundations on American foreign policy: The ideology of philanthropy.* Albany: State University of New York Press.

Biddiss, M. D. (1970). *Father of racist ideology: The social and political thought of Count Gobineau.* London: Weidenfeld & Nicolson.

Blauner, R. (1972). *Racial oppression in America.* New York: Harper & Row.

Bond, H. M. (1934). *The education of the negro in the American social order.* New York: Prentice-Hall.

Bontemps, A. (1972). *Young Booker: Booker T. Washington's early days.* New York: Dodd, Mead.

Bowles, S., & Gintis, H. (1976). *Schooling in capitalist America: Educational reform and the contradictions of economic life.* New York: Basic Books.

Brigham, C. C. (1923). *A study in American intelligence*. Princeton, NJ: Princeton University Press.

Brinton, D. G. (1890). *Races and peoples*. New York: N. D. C. Hodges.

Brooks, J. G. (1981). *An American citizen: The life of William Henry Baldwin, Jr.* New York: Arno Press. (Original work published 1910)

Brown v. Board of Education of Topeka, Kansas, 347 U.S. 483 (1954).

Bullock, H. (1967). *A history of negro education in the south: From 1619 to present*. Cambridge, MA: Harvard University Press.

Buttrick, W. (1905, February 14). Letter to Andrew Carnegie. Box 173, Folder 1620, GEB Collection. Rockefeller Archive Center, Sleepy Hollow, NY.

Carey, H. C. (1858–59). *The principles of social science*. Philadelphia: Lippincott.

Carruthers, J. H. (1994). Black intellectuals and the crisis in black education. In M. J. Shujaa (Ed.), *Too much schooling, too little education: A paradox of black life in white societies* (pp. 37–55). Trenton, NJ: Africa World Press.

Cartwright, S. A. (1851, May). *Report on the diseases and physical peculiarities of the negro race*. New Orleans Medical and Surgical Journal, pp. 691–715.

Clark, J. B., & Giddings, F. H. (1973). *Big business: Economic power in a free society*. New York: Arno Press. (Original work published 1888)

Commanger, H. S. (1957). *The American mind*. New Haven, CT: Yale University Press.

Correia, S. T. (1993). *For their own good*. Unpublished doctoral dissertation, Pennsylvania State University, State College.

Curry, J. L. M. (n.d.). Draft for book on Rev. Fuller. Curry Papers. Alabama State Archives, Montgomery.

Curry, J. L. M. (1884). *Citizenship and education*. Address to National Education Association. Curry Papers. Alabama State Archives, Montgomery.

Curry, J. L. M. (1895). *The southern states of the American union: Considered in their relations to the Constitution of the United States and to the resulting union*. Richmond, VA: R. F. Johnson.

Curry, J. L. M. (1899). Legal justification of the south in secession. In C. A. Evans (Ed.), *Confederate military history* (Vol. 1, pp. 3–58). Atlanta: Confederate Publishing. Family Archives, #677, Curry Papers. Alabama State Archives, Montgomery.

Curry, J. L. M. (1900, June 18). *Liberty and law, suggestions for educated youth* [Speech]. Curry Papers. Alabama State Archives, Montgomery.

Curry, J. L. M. (1901). *Slater report*. Curry Papers. Alabama State Archives, Montgomery.

Curti, M. (1956). Foreword. In F. Parker, *George Peabody: A biography*. Nashville: Vanderbilt University Press.

Darwin, C. (1859). *On the origin of species by means of natural selection or the preservation of the favored races in the struggle for life*. London: J. Murray.

deMarrais, K. B., & LeCompte, M. D. (1995). *The way schools work: A sociological analysis of education*. New York: Longman.

Dewey, J. (1916). *Democracy and education*. New York: Macmillan.

Dewey, J. (1938). *Experience and education*. New York: Macmillan.

Dixon, T. (1905). *The clansman, an historical romance of the Ku Klux Klan*. New York: Grosset & Dunlap.

DuBois, W. E. B. (1899). *The Philadelphia negro*. New York: Schocken.

DuBois, W. E. B. (1903). *The souls of black folk*. New York: Signet.

DuBois, W. E. B. (1918, February). Negro education. *The Crisis, 15*(4), 173–178.

DuBois, W. E. B. (1919, May). Negro education. *The Crisis*, pp. 9ff.

DuBois, W. E. B. (1921, October). Thomas Jesse Jones. *The Crisis, 22*(6), 252–257.

Durkheim, E. (1899). *Education and sociology.* New York: Free Press.

Ehrlich, P. R., & Feldman, S. S. (1977). *The race bomb: Skin color, prejudice, and intelligence.* New York: Quadrangle.

Evans, C. A. (Ed.). (1899). *Confederate military history* (Vol. 1). Atlanta: Confederate Publishing. Family Archives, #677, Curry Papers. Alabama State Archives, Montgomery.

Farrall, L. A. (1985). *The origins and growth of the English eugenics movement 1865–1925.* New York: Garland.

Fortune, T. T. (1905). Article in *New York World.* Ogden Letters, Box 15. Library of Congress, Washington DC.

Fosdick, R. B. (1952). *The story of the Rockefeller foundation.* New York: Harper.

Fosdick, R. B. (1956). *John D. Rockefeller Jr.: A portrait.* New York: Harper & Brothers.

Fosdick, R. B. (1962). *Adventure in giving: The story of the General Education Board, a foundation established by John D. Rockefeller.* New York: Harper & Row.

Galton, F. (1865). Hereditary talent and character. *Macmillans's Magazine, 12,* 165–166.

Galton, F. (1869). *Hereditary genius.* London: Macmillan.

Galton, F. (1889). *Natural inheritance.* London & New York: Macmillan.

Garrity, J. A., & Gay, P. (Eds.). (1972). *The Columbia history of the world.* New York: Harper & Row.

General Education Board (GEB). (1916). Negro education. Box 329. Rockefeller Archive Center, Sleepy Hollow, NY.

General Education Board. (1957). *Historical review 1902–1951.* Box 329, Folder 3467, GEB Collection. Rockefeller Archive Center, Sleepy Hollow, NY.

General Education Board. (1964). *General Education Board: Review and final report 1902–1964.* New York: Author.

Giddings, F. H. (Ed.). (1901). *Democracy and empire: With studies of their psychological, economic, and moral foundations.* New York: Macmillan.

Giddings, F. H. (Ed.). (1906). *Readings in descriptive and historical sociology.* New York: Macmillan.

Giddings, F. H. (1911). *The principles of sociology: An analysis of the phenomena of association and of social organization.* New York: Macmillan.

Giddings, F. H. (1922). *Studies in the theory of human society.* New York: Macmillan.

Giddings, F. H. (1932). *Civilization and society: An account of the development and behavior of human society.* New York: Henry Holt.

Gobineau, A. de (1967). *Essai sur l'inegalite des races humaines* [Essay on the inequality of human races]. New York: Fertig. (Original work published 1854)

Gould, S. J. (1981). *The mismeasure of man.* New York: Norton.

Grant, M. (1916). *The passing of the great race.* New York: Scribner's.

*Guntons Magazine.* (1890, June).

Haeckel, E. (1874). *Anthropogenie.* Leipzig: W. Engelmann.

Haller, M. H. (1984). *Eugenics: Hereditarian attitudes in American thought.* New Brunswick, NJ: Rutgers University Press.

Hankins, F. H. (1968). Franklin H. Giddings. In D. L. Sills (Ed.), *International encyclopedia of the social sciences* (Vol. 6, pp. 175–177). New York: Macmillan & Free Press.

Harlan, L. R. (1968). *Separate and unequal: Public school campaigns and racism in the southern seaboard states 1901–1915*. New York: Atheneum.

Harlan, L. R., et al. (Eds.). (1972). *The Booker T. Washington papers* (Vol. 2). Urbana: University of Illinois Press.

*Harvard Graduates Magazine*. (1905, March).

Hasian, M. A., Jr. (1996). *The rhetoric of eugenics in Anglo-American thought*. Athens. University of Georgia Press.

Herrnstein, R., & Murray, C. (1994). *The bell curve: Intelligence and class structure in American life*. New York: Free Press.

Hoffman, F. L. (1896). *Race traits and tendencies of the American negro*. New York: American Economic Association.

Hofstadter, R. (1944). *Social Darwinism in American thought*. Boston: Beacon Press.

Howe, B. (1980). The emergence of scientific philanthropy, 1900–1920: Origins, issues and outcomes. In R. F. Arnove (Ed.), *Philanthropy and cultural imperialism: The foundations at home and abroad* (pp. 25–54). Boston: G. K. Hall.

Howerth, I. W. (1897). A programme for social study. *American Journal of Sociology, 2*, 852–872.

Hubbard, S. (1904). *John D. Rockefeller and his career*. New York: Author.

Ireland, A. (1905). *The far eastern tropics: Studies in the administration of tropical dependencies: Hong Kong, British North Borneo, Sarawak, Burma, the Federated Malay States, the Straits Settlements, French Indo-China, Java, the Philippine Islands*. Boston: Houghton Mifflin.

Jarvis, E. (1844). Insanity among the coloured population of the free states. *American Journal of the Medical Sciences, 7*, 80–83.

Jefferson, T. (1955). *Notes on the State of Virginia*. Chapel Hill: University of North Carolina Press. (Original work published 1781)

Jensen, A. R. (1995, January). Psychological research on race differences. *American Psychologist, 50*(1), 41–42.

Jones, T. J. (1899). *Social education in the elementary school*. Unpublished master's thesis, Columbia University, New York.

Jones, T. J. (1902a). *Courage of our convictions* [Sermon].

Jones, T. J. (1902b). *Report of work in the university settlement house*. Occasional paper.

Jones, T. J. (1903). *Fatherhood of God* [Sermon].

Jones, T. J. (1904). *The sociology of a New York City block*. Doctoral dissertation, Columbia University, New York.

Jones, T. J. (1905–07). *Hampton social studies*. Serialized in *Southern Workman*.

Jones, T. J. (1917). *Negro education: A study of the higher and private schools for colored people in the United States* (2 vols.). Washington, DC: U.S. Bureau of Education.

Jones, T. J. (1926). *Four essentials of education*. New York: Scribner's.

Jones, T. J. (1929). *Essentials of civilization: A study in social values*. New York: Henry Holt.

Jones, T. J. (1931, January). Frissell of Hampton. *SW*, pp. 2–8.

King, K. (1971). *Pan Africanism and education: A study of race philanthropy and education in the southern states of America and east Africa*. Oxford: Clarendon Press.

Lindeman, E. C. (1936). *Wealth and culture*. New York: Harcourt Brace.

Linnaeus, C. (1964). *Systema naturae*. Nieuwkoop, Netherlands: B. de Graaf. (Original work published 1735)

Liston, D. P. (1988). *Capitalist schools: Explanation and ethics in radical studies of schooling*. New York: Routledge.

Lybarger, M. (1981). *Origins of the modern social studies curriculum 1900–1916*. Unpublished doctoral dissertation, University of Wisconsin–Madison.

Lybarger, M. (1983). Origins of the modern social studies 1900–1916. *History of Education Quarterly, 23*, 455–468.

Marable, M. (1986). *W. E. B. DuBois: Black radical democrat*. Boston: Twayne.

Meyers, M., Cawelti, J. G., & Kern, A. (1969). *Sources of the American republic: A documentary history of politics, society, and thought*. Glenview, IL: Scott, Foresman.

Mills, C. W. (1952). *The sociological imagination*. New York: Oxford University Press. (Original work published 1940)

Mitchell, S. C. (n.d.). *Robert Curtis Ogden: A leader in the educational renaissance of the south*. Ogden Papers, Box 27. Library of Congress, Washington, DC.

Morton, S. G. (1839). *Crania Americana or, a comparative view of the skulls of various aboriginal nations of north and south America*. Philadelphia: John Pennington.

Morton, S. G. (1844). Crania Aegyptiaca: Observations on Egyptian ethnography, derived from anatomy, history, and the monuments. *Transactions of the American Philosophical Society, 9*, 93–159.

Myers, G. (1936). *History of the great American fortunes*. New York: Modern Library.

Nevins, A. (1959). *John D. Rockefeller*. New York: Scribner's.

Nevins, A. (1969). *John D. Rockefeller: The heroic age of American enterprise* (Vols. 1 & 2). New York: Scribner's.

*New York Times*. (1950, January 6). Obituary (Thomas Jesse Jones).

Ogden, R. C. (n.d.a). *The problem of the negro*. In Ogden Papers, Box 22, Miscellaneous Notes on the Negro. Library of Congress, Washington, DC.

Ogden, R. C. (n.d.b). *Some observations upon southern educational conditions: Popular education, the power of industrial progress*. Ogden Papers, Box 22. Library of Congress, Washington, DC.

Ogden, R. C. (1894a, January 28). *Samuel Chapman Armstrong: A sketch*. Presented on Founders Day, Hampton Institute. Ogden Papers. Library of Congress, Washington, DC.

Ogden, R. C. (1894b). *Sunday school teaching: Two addresses*. New York: Revell. Ogden Papers, Box 21. Library of Congress, Washington, DC.

Ogden, R. C. (1898, April 30). Letter to H. W. McKinney. Ogden Papers. Library of Congress, Washington, DC.

Ogden, R. C. (1903, September 28). Letter to Kelly Miller. #125, Ogden Letters, Box 13. Library of Congress, Washington, DC.

Ogden, R. C. (1904a, January 5). Letter to George Foster Peabody. #308, Odgen Letters, Box 13. Library of Congress, Washington, DC.

Ogden, R.C. (1904b, April 27). Education for the negro. *New York Sun*. Ogden Papers. Library of Congress, Washington, DC.

Ogden, R. C. (1904c, May 2). Letter to Rev. J. R. Miller, D.D. #27, Ogden Papers, Box 14. Library of Congress, Washington, DC.

Ogden, R. C. (1904d, June 25). Letter to Col. Thomas Higgenson. #490, Ogden Papers, Box 14. Library of Congress, Washington, DC.

Ogden, R. C. (1904e, December 3). Letter to President Theodore Roosevelt. Ogden Special Collections, Box 7. Library of Congress, Washington, DC.

Ogden, R. C. (1905a, June). Business idealism. *The Business World: An Office Magazine*, *25*(6), 277–281. Ogden Papers, Box 21. Library of Congress, Washington, DC.

Ogden, R. C. (1905b, September 11). Letter to C. L. Stebbins, Esq. #810, Ogden Letters, Box 15. Library of Congress, Washington, DC.

Ogden, R. C. (1906a, March 20). Letter to Dr. Julius D. Dreker. #460, Ogden Letters, Box 15. Library of Congress, Washington, DC.

Ogden, R. C. (1906b, May 10). Letter to Dr. William Jay Schieffelin. #801, Ogden Letters, Box 15. Library of Congress, Washington, DC.

Ogden, R. C. (1913). Letter to Low. Ogden Letters, Box 15. Library of Congress, Washington, DC.

Parker, F. (1956). *George Peabody, founder of modern philanthropy*. Ed.D. dissertation, George Peabody College for Teachers, Nashville.

Peabody, F. G. (1927). *Reminiscences of present-day saints*. Boston: Houghton Mifflin.

Peery, N. (1975). *The negro national colonial question*. Chicago: Workers Press.

Phelps Stokes, A. (1918). *Educational plans for the American army abroad*. Anson Phelps Stokes Folder. Schomberg Center for Research in Black Culture, New York Public Library.

Phelps Stokes, A. (1924). *Confidential memorandum for the trustees of the Phelps Stokes Fund: Regarding Dr. Carter G. Woodson's criticisms of Dr. Thomas Jesse Jones*. New York: Phelps Stokes Fund

Phelps Stokes, A., Jr. (1948). *Negro status and race relations in the United States 1911– 1946: The thirty-five year report of the Phelps Stokes Fund*. New York: Phelps Stokes Fund.

Phelps Stokes, A., et al. (1950). Memoriam. In *Memoriam: Thomas Jesse Jones 1873– 1950*. New York: Phelps Stokes Fund.

Phelps Stokes, C. (1895). *Last will and testament of Caroline Phelps Stokes deceased and subsequent writings*. Folder 1, Phelps Stokes Collection. Schomberg Center for Research in Black Culture, New York Public Library.

Phelps Stokes, J. G. (1904a). *Public schools as social centres*. Box 76. Rare Book and Manuscript Library, Columbia University, NY.

Phelps Stokes, J. G. (1904b, September 29). *Ye have the poor always with you*. Box 76. Rare Book and Manuscript Library, Columbia University, NY.

Phelps Stokes, J. G. (1918). Address of J. G. Phelps Stokes at meeting of Inter-Party League for Restoration of Russian Freedom at Carnegie Hall, New York. Box 78. Rare Book and Manuscript Library, Columbia University, NY.

Phelps Stokes, O. E. (n.d.). Biographical sketch of Caroline Phelps Stokes. In *Educational adaptations: Report of ten years' work of the Phelps Stokes Fund, 1910–1920*. Folder 1, Phelps Stokes Collection. Schomberg Center for Research in Black Culture, New York Public Library.

Plessy v. Ferguson, 163 U.S. 537 (1896).

Rice, J. P. (1949). *J. L. M. Curry: Southerner, statesman and educator*. New York: King's Crown Press.

Ross, E. A. (1914). *The old world in the new: The significance of past and present immigration to the American people*. New York: Century.

Rush, B. (1799). Observations intended to favor a supposition that the black color of the negroes is derived from the leprosy. *Transactions of the American Philosophical Society, 4*, pp. 289–297.

Rush, B. (1812). *Diseases of the mind*. Philadelphia: Kimber & Richardson.

Selden, S. (1999). *Inheriting shame: The story of eugenics and racism in America*. New York: Teachers College Press.

Serres, E. (1860). Principes d'embryogenie, de zoogenie et de terratogenie. *Memoire de l'Academie des Sciences, 25*, 1–943.

Shockley, W. (1972, January). Genetics, dysgenics, geneticity, raceology: A challenge to the intellectual responsibility of educators. *Phi Delta Kappan*, pp. 297–307.

Slaughter, S. A., & Silva, E. T. (1980). Looking backwards: How foundations formulated ideology in the progressive period. In R. F. Arnove (1980), *Philanthropy and cultural imperialism: The foundations at home and abroad* (pp. 55–86). Boston: G. K. Hall.

*The Southern Workman (SW)*. (1876–1881, 1903–1905). Various issues.

Stampp, K. M. (1956). *Peculiar institutions: Slavery in the ante-bellum south*. New York: Vintage.

Stoddard, L. (1920). *The rising tide of color against white-world supremacy*. New York: Scribner's.

Takaki, R. (1990). *Iron cages: Race and culture in 19th-century America*. New York: Oxford University Press.

Takaki, R. (Ed.). (1994). *From different shores: Perspectives on race and ethnicity in America*. New York: Oxford University Press.

Talbot, E. A. (1904). *Samuel Chapman Armstrong: A biographical study*. New York: Doubleday, Page.

Tucker, W. H. (1994). *The science and politics of racial research*. Urbana: The University of Illinois Press.

Tyack, D. (1974). *The one best system: A history of American urban education*. Cambridge, MA: Harvard University Press.

*University Settlement Bulletin*. (1902).

U.S. Department of the Interior, Bureau of Education, Commission for the Reorganization of Secondary Education, Committee on Social Studies. (1916). *The social studies in secondary education* (A. W. Dunn, Compiler). (Bulletin #28). Washington, DC: Government Printing Office.

van Evrie, J. H. (1853). *Negroes and negro "slavery": The first an inferior race; the latter, its normal condition*. New York: V. L. Dill.

Wade, S., Thompson, A., & Watkins, W. H. (1994). Beliefs, ideology, and history texts. In R. Garner & P. A. Alexander (Eds.), *Beliefs about texts and instruction with texts* (pp. 265–293). Hillsdale, NJ: Erlbaum.

Washington, B. T. (1901). *Up from slavery: An autobiography*. New York: Bantam Books.

Watkins, W. (1986). *The political sociology of postcolonial social studies curriculum development: The case of Nigeria 1960–1980*. Unpublished doctoral dissertation, University of Illinois, Chicago.

Watkins, W. H. (1989). On accommodationist education: Booker T. Washington goes to Africa. *International Third World Studies Journal and Review, 1*, 137–143.

Watkins, W. H. (1990). W. E. B. DuBois vs Thomas Jesse Jones: The forgotten skirmishes. *Journal of the Midwest History of Education Society, 18*, 305–328.

Watkins, W. H. (1991, October). *A curriculum for colored people: The social and educational ideas of Franklin H. Giddings*. Paper presented at the Bergamo Curriculum Conference, Dayton, OH.

Watkins, W. H. (1993, Fall). Black curriculum orientations: A preliminary inquiry. *Harvard Educational Review, 63*(3), 321–338.

Watkins, W. H. (1994). Curriculum for immigrant and minority children. In T. Husen & T. N. Postlethwaite (Eds.), *International encyclopedia of education*. London: Pergamon Press.

Watkins, W. H. (1995). Pan-Africanism and the politics of education: Towards a new understanding. In S. Lemelle & R. D. G. Kelly (Eds.), *Imagining home: Class, culture and consciousness in the African diaspora* (pp. 222–242). London: Verso Press.

Weber, C. W. (1986, March 16). *The influence of the Hampton–Tuskegee model on the educational policy of the Permanent Mandates Commission and British colonial policy*. Paper presented at meeting of the Comparative and International Educational Society, Toronto.

White, C. (1799). *An account of the regular gradation in man and in different animals and vegetables and from the former to the latter*. London: C. Dilly.

Williams, W. T. B. (1906, June). *Hampton Institute: Essay directed to Frissell*. Box 173, Folder 1621, GEB Collection. Rockefeller Archive Center, Sleepy Hollow, NY.

# Supplementary Readings

Abbot, L. (1921). *Silhouettes of my contemporaries*. Garden City, NY: Doubleday, Page.

Alderman, E. A., & Gordon, A. C. (1911). *J. L. M. Curry: A biography*. New York: Macmillan.

Allen, F. L. (1949). *The great Pierpont Morgan*. New York: Harper & Brothers.

Apple, M. (1983). *Education and power*. Boston: Ark Paperbacks.

Armstrong, S. C. (1878, March 8). Letter to Ogden. Ogden Special Collections, Box 6. Library of Congress, Washington, DC.

Armstrong, S. C. (1892, December 7). Letter to Ogden. Ogden Special Collections, Box 6. Library of Congress, Washington, DC.

Barrows, I, C. (1969). *Armstrong: The first Mohonk conference on the Negro Question*. New York: Negro Universities Press. (Original work published 1890)

Binet, A., & Simon, T. (1911). *A method of measuring the development of the intelligence of young children*. Lincoln, IL: Courier.

Birney, C. H. (1885). *Sarah and Angelina Grimke*. Boston: Lee & Shepard.

Bond, H. M. (1966). *The education of the negro in the American social order*. New York: Octagon Books.

Brace, C. L. (1972). Commencement day with the colored students. In L. R. Harlan et al. (Eds.), *The Booker T. Washington papers* (Vol. 2, pp. 55–60). Urbana: University of Illinois Press. (Original work published 1875)

Burt, C. (1962). Francis Galton and his contributions to psychology. *British Journal of Statistical Psychology, 15,* 1–49.

Burt, C. (1972). The inheritance of general intelligence. *American Psychology, 27,* 175–190.

Butchard, R. E. (1994). Outthinking and outflanking the owners of the world: An historiography of the African-American struggle for education. In M. J. Shujaa (Ed.), *Too much schooling, too little education: A paradox of black life in white societies* (pp. 85–122). Trenton, NJ: Africa World Press.

Buttrick, W. (n.d.). [Untitled]. Box 304, Folder 3176. Rockefeller Archive Center, Sleepy Hollow, NY.

Buttrick, W. (1926). [untitled speech]. Box 304, Folder 3176. Rockefeller Archive Center, Sleepy Hollow, NY.

Buttrick, Wallace. (1932). In *National cyclopaedia of American biography* (Vol. 22). New York: James T. White.

Carnegie, A. (1899). *Gospel of wealth*. New York: North Amer. Rev. Publ. Co.

Carnoy, M. (1974). *Education as cultural imperialism.* New York: David McKay.

Carosso, V. P. (1987). *The Morgans, private international bankers, 1854–1913.* Cambridge, MA: Harvard University Press.

Carson, S. (1952). *Samuel Chapman Armstrong: Missionary to the south.* Unpublished doctoral dissertation, Johns Hopkins University, Baltimore.

Catalogue of officers and students. (1844–45). Harvard University. Curry Papers. Alabama State Archives, Montgomery.

Chapman, S. (1984). *The rise of merchant banking.* London: George Allen & Unwin.

Columbia University, Faculty of Political Science. (1931). *Bibliography of the faculty of political science, 1880–1930.* New York: Columbia University Press.

Cooper, A. (1989). *Between struggle and hope: Four black educators in the south 1893–1915.* Ames: Iowa State University Press.

Corey, L. (1930). *The house of Morgan: A social biography of the masters of money.* New York: G. Howard Watt.

Correia, S. T., & Watkins, W. H. (1991, April). *Thomas Jesse Jones: A portrait.* Paper presented at the annual meeting of the Society for the Study of Curriculum History, Chicago.

Curry, J. L. M. (n.d.). The outlook in the south. Box 2. Alabama State Archives, Montgomery.

Curry, J. L. M. (1860, December 21). Letter from Curry to John Haralson, Esq. *The Beacon*, Greensboro, AL.

Curry, J. L. M. (1898). *A brief sketch of George Peabody and a history of the Peabody education fund through thirty years.* New York: Negro Universities Press.

Curry, J. L. M. (1900, November 22). *Alabama legislature.* Curry Papers. Alabama State Archives, Montgomery.

Curry, J. L. M. (1901, April 19). [Untitled]. Curry Papers. Alabama State Archives, Montgomery.

Dabney, C. (1936). *Universal education in the south* (Vols. 1 & 2). Chapel Hill: University of North Carolina Press.

Darwin, C. (1871). *The descent of man.* London: J. Murray.

Davenport, C. B. (1911). *Heredity in relation to eugenics.* New York: Henry Holt.

Dickerman, G. J. (1907). *Twenty-five years ministry of the Slater fund.* Box 260, Folder 2685, GEB Collection. Rockefeller Archive Center, Sleepy Hollow, NY.

*Dictionary of American biography.* (1930). New York: Scribner's.

Dillingham, G. A. (1989). *The foundation of the Peabody tradition.* Lanham, MD: University Press of America.

Dooly, I. (1901). Northern philanthropy and the negro question. *Atlanta Constitution*, May 1.

DuBois, W. E. B. (1921, October). Thomas Jesse Jones. *The Crisis, 22*(6), 252–257.

Ford Foundation. (1968). *Annual report.* New York: Author.

Franklin, V., & Anderson, J. D. (Eds.). (1978). *New perspectives on black educational history.* Boston: G. K. Hall.

Fries, H. E. (1916). *In memory of Robert Curtis Ogden: True friend patriotic citizen unofficial statesman Christian gentleman.* Privately published. Ogden Papers, Box 1, Memorial Publications folder. Library of Congress, Washington, DC.

Gates, F. T. (n.d.). *Capital and labor.* Box 1, Folder 9. Rockefeller Archive Center, Sleepy Hollow, NY.

Gates, F. T. (n.d.). *Corporation privileges.* Box 1, Folder 17. Rockefeller Archive Center, Sleepy Hollow, NY.

Gates, F. T. (n.d.). *Corporations*. Box 1, Folder 17. Rockefeller Archive Center, Sleepy Hollow, NY.

Gates, F. T. (1905). Letter to the General Education Board. In Box 16, Folder 157, GEB Collection. Rockefeller Archive Center, Sleepy Hollow, NY.

Gates, F. T. (1926). *Thoughts on the Rockefeller public and private benefactions*. Box 3, Folder 57, Gates's Private Papers. Rockefeller Archive Center, Sleepy Hollow, NY.

Gates, Frederick Taylor. (1933). In *National cyclopaedia of American biography* (Vol. 23). New York: James T. White.

General Education Board. (n.d.). *Historical statement*. Box 337, Folder 3542, GEB Collection. Rockefeller Archive Center, Sleepy Hollow, NY.

General Education Board. (n.d.). *Training*. Box 173, Folder 1620, GEB Collection. Rockefeller Archive Center, Sleepy Hollow, NY.

General Education Board. (1906, March 26). *Hampton Institute, Hampton, VA*. Box 173, Folder 1621, GEB Collection. Rockefeller Archive Center, Sleepy Hollow, NY.

Giddings, F. H. (1896). *The principles of sociology: An analysis of the phenomena of association and social organization*. New York: Macmillan.

Giddings, F. H. (1901). *Inductive sociology: A syllabus of analysis and classifications and provisionally formulated laws*. New York: Macmillan.

Giddings, F. H. (1906). *Studies in the theory of human society*. New York: Macmillan.

Giddings, F. H. (1916). *The elements of sociology: A textbook for colleges and schools*. New York: Macmillan.

Giddings, F. H. (1918). *The responsible state*. Boston: Houghton Mifflin.

Giddings, F. H. (1924). *Perspectives in social inquiry: The scientific study of human society*. Chapel Hill: University of North Carolina Press.

Giddings, F. H. (1929). *The mighty medicine: Superstition and its antidote: A new liberal education*. New York: Macmillan.

Goddard, H. H. (1912). *The Kallikak family: A study in the heredity of feeble-mindedness*. New York: Macmillan.

Hampton Institute. (1904). *The Armstrong league of Hampton workers: Its story in brief*. Hampton, VA: Hampton Institute Press.

Harlan, L. R. (1983). *The wizard of Tuskegee 1901–1915*. New York: Oxford University Press.

Hearn, N. (1980). *George Peabody (1795–1869): "One of the poor's greatest benefactors."* London: Peabody Donation Fund.

Hidy, M. E. (1978). *George Peabody, merchant and financier, 1829–1854*. New York: Arno Press.

Hovey, E. V. (1938). *The life story of J. Pierpont Morgan*. New York: Sturgis & Calton.

Hoyt, E. P. (1968). *The Peabody influence: How a great New England family helped to build America*. New York: Dodd, Mead.

Jarvis, E. (1840). Reflections on the census of 1840. *Southern Literary Messenger, 9*, 346–347.

Jensen, A. R. (1969). How much can we boost IQ and scholastic achievement? *Harvard Educational Review, 39*(1), 1–123.

Jensen, A. R. (1981). *Straight talk about mental tests*. New York: Macmillan.

Johnson, A. (Ed.). (1929). Wallace Buttrick. *Dictionary of American biography* (Vol. 3). New York: Scribner's.

Johnson, A., & Malone, D. (Eds.). (1931). Frederick Taylor Gates. *Dictionary of American biography* (Vol. 7). New York: Scribner's.

Jones, F. N. (1965). *George Peabody and the Peabody institute*. Baltimore: Peabody Institute Library.

Josephson, M. (1934). *The robber barons*. New York: Harcourt, Brace.

Kincheloe, J. L., Steinberg, S. R., & Gresson, A. D. III (Eds.). (1996). *Measured lies*. New York: St. Martin's Press.

Leavell, U. W. (1930). *Philanthropy in negro education*. Nashville: George Peabody College for Teachers.

*A life well lived: In memory of Robert Curtis Ogden*. (1914). Ogden Papers, Box 1, Memorial Publications folder. Library of Congress, Washington, DC.

Marks, R. (1980). Legitimating industrial capitalism: Philanthropy and individual differences. In R. F. Arnove (Ed.), *Philanthropy and cultural imperialism: The foundations at home and abroad* (pp. 87–122). Boston: G. K. Hall.

Marx, K. (1935). *The poverty of philosophy*. In E. Burns (Ed.), *A handbook of Marxism* (pp. 348–370). New York: Random House. (Original work published 1847)

McDougall, W. (1924). *Ethics and some modern world problems*. New York: Putnam.

McDougall, W. (1925). *The indestructible union*. Boston: Little, Brown & Co.

Meier, A. (1963). *Negro thought in America 1880–1915: Racial ideologies in the age of Booker T. Washington*. Ann Arbor: University of Michigan Press.

Men of millions to redeem the south. (1901). *New York World*, April 28.

Miller, K. (1908, December). Forty years of Negro education. Box 260, Folder 2689, GEB collection, Rockefeller Archive Center, Sleepy Hollow, NY.

Montague, G. H. (1902). *The rise and progress of the Standard Oil Company*. New York: Harper & Brothers.

Morgan, T. J. (1899, September 22). American Baptist Home Mission Society to John D. Rockefeller, Jr. Box 89, Spelman College Folder. Rockefeller Archive Center, Sleepy Hollow, NY.

Morton, S. G. (1849). Observations on the size of the brain in various races and families of man. *Proceedings of the Academy of Natural Sciences, 4*, 221–224.

*Negro education*. (1916, January 24). Box 329, Series: Reports, GEB Collection. Rockefeller Archive Center, Sleepy Hollow, NY.

Northcott, C. H. (1948). The sociological theories of Franklin Henry Giddings: Consciousness of kind, pluralistic behavior, and statistical method. In H. E. Barnes (Ed.), *An introduction to the history of sociology* (pp. 744–765). Chicago: University of Chicago Press.

*Notes on Rockefeller family contributions to better racial understanding*. (n.d.). Box 20, Folder 111.1, Series: Welfare Interests. Rockefeller Archive Center, Sleepy Hollow, NY.

Obituary (Robert Curtis Ogden). (1913). *The Hampton Student*, August 15.

Odum, H. W. (1951). *American sociology*. New York: Longmans.

Ogden, R. C. (n.d.). *Concerning the negro*. Ogden Papers, Box 22. Library of Congress, Washington, DC.

Ogden, R. C. (n.d.) *Earnestness and intelligence the basis of all upward movement*. Notes of Robert C. Ogden. Ogden Papers, Box 22. Library of Congress, Washington, DC.

Ogden, R. C. (n.d.). *The great difficulty of a double system of education*. Ogden Papers, Box 22. Library of Congress, Washington, DC.

Ogden, R. C. (n.d.). *Sociology*. Ogden Papers, Box 23. Library of Congress, Washington, DC.

Ogden, R. C. (n.d.). Speech on 1895 anniversary. Ogden Papers, Box 21. Library of Congress, Washington, DC.

Ogden, R. C. (1896, November 18). [Untitled]. Address delivered at the opening of the Trade School. Ogden Papers, Box 21. Library of Congress, Washington, DC.

Ogden, R. C. (1902, February 18). Letter to Mrs. M. E. Berry. Ogden Papers, Box 13. Library of Congress, Washington, DC.

Ogden, R. C. (1902). [Untitled written speech]. Ogden Papers, Box 21. Library of Congress, Washington, DC.

Ogden, R. C. (1903, April). Letter to Mrs. Arthur Gilman. Ogden Special Collections, Box 6. Library of Congress, Washington, DC.

Ogden, R. C. (1903, April 15). Letter to Captain E. L. Zalinski. #500, Ogden Letters, Box 13. Library of Congress, Washington, DC.

Ogden, R. C. (1903, April 18). Letter to A. C. Kaufman. #568, Ogden Letters, Box 13. Library of Congress, Washington, DC.

Ogden, R. C. (1903, May 6). Letter to Archibald Hopkins. #625, Ogden Letters, Box 13. Library of Congress, Washington, DC.

Ogden, R. C. (1903, September 23). Letter to James A. Worden, D.D. #121, Ogden Papers, Box 13. Library of Congress, Washington, DC.

Ogden, R. C. (1903, November 10). Letter to Charles W. Dabney. #201, Ogden Letters, Box 13. Library of Congress, Washington, DC.

Ogden, R. C. (1903, November 12). Letter to Walker-Wilkerson Publishing Co. #204, Ogden Letters, Box 13. Library of Congress, Washington, DC.

Ogden, R. C. (1903, December 1). Letter to George Whitelock, Esq. #252, Ogden Papers, Box 13. Library of Congress, Washington, DC.

Ogden, R. C. (1903, December 21). Letter to Professor S. G. Atkins. #276, Ogden Letters, Box 13. Library of Congress, Washington, DC.

Ogden, R. C. (1904, February 26). Letter to W. H. Baldwin, Esq. #469, Ogden Letters, Box 13. Library of Congress, Washington, DC.

Ogden, R. C. (1904, February 27). Letter to W. B. Watkins, Esq. #478, Ogden Letters, Box 13. Library of Congress, Washington, DC.

Ogden, R. C. (1904, March 19). Letter to W. B. Weaver, Esq. #670, Ogden Letters, Box 13. Library of Congress, Washington, DC.

Ogden, R. C. (1904, May 6). Letter to Dr. George P. Phenix. Ogden Special Collections, Box 7. Library of Congress, Washington, DC.

Ogden, R. C. (1904). *Ogden party*. Occasional notes; roster of guests scheduled for the 1904 "trainride" south. Ogden Papers, Box 15. Library of Congress, Washington, DC.

Ogden, R. C. (1905, February 4). Letter to W. S. Coopeland, Esq. #500, Ogden Papers, Box 14. Library of Congress, Washington, DC.

Ogden, R. C. (1905, March 25). Letter to William MacDonald. #642, Ogden Papers, Box 14. Library of Congress, Washington, DC.

Ogden, R. C. (1905, May 23). Letter to Rev. William H. Yeocum. #361, Ogden Letters, Box 15. Library of Congress, Washington, DC.

Ogden, R. C. (1905, December 16). Letter to Rev. Duncan C. Milner. #325, Ogden Papers, Box 14. Library of Congress, Washington, DC.

Ogden, R. C. (1906, February 16). Letter to Rev. Rollin A. Sawyer, D.D. #316, Ogden Letters, Box 15. Library of Congress, Washington, DC.

Ogden, R. C. (1906, March 20). Letter to Rev. Rollin A. Sawyer, D.D. #454, Ogden Letters, Box 15. Library of Congress, Washington, DC.

Ogden, R. C. (1906, May 26). Letter to Dean David C. Barrow (University of Georgia). #872, Ogden Letters, Box 15. Library of Congress, Washington, DC.

Ogden, R. C. (1907, October 11). Letter to Frank Gilmer, Esq. #266, Ogden Letters, Box 16. Library of Congress, Washington, DC.

Ogden, R. C. (1909, April 4). Unveiling of the memorial tablet in memory of the late William H. Baldwin, Jr., Tuskegee Institute, AL. Ogden Papers, Box 20. Library of Congress, Washington, DC.

Ogden, R. C., et al. (1901, May 23). Social and industrial betterment in the south. In *The Get-Together Club*, No. 1. Ogden Papers. Library of Congress, Washington, DC.

Ohles, J. F. (Ed.). (1978). Buttrick, Wallace B. In *Biographical dictionary of American educators*. Westport, CT: Greenwood Press.

Parkhurst, C. H. (1912, October 7). Letter to the Friends of the Colored Race. Box 114, Folder 1030, GEB Collection. Rockefeller Archive Center, Sleepy Hollow, NY.

Payne, C. (1995). *I've got the light of freedom: The organizing tradition and the Mississippi freedom struggle*. Berkeley: University of California Press.

Peabody, F. G. (1898). *Founder's day at Hampton: An address in memory of Samuel Chapman Armstrong*. Boston: Houghton Mifflin.

Rockefeller, J. D., Jr. (1903). Letter found in historical statement. Document 810, Box 337, Folder 3542. Rockefeller Archive Center, Sleepy Hollow, NY.

*Rockefeller gives million to south*. (1902). *New York World*, April 22.

Ross, A. D. (1968). Philanthropy. In D. L. Sills (Ed.), *International encyclopedia of the social sciences* (Vol. 12, p. 78). New York: Macmillan.

Ross, E. A. (1905). *Foundations of sociology*. New York: Macmillan.

Satterlee, H. (1937). *The life of J. Pierpont Morgan*. New York: Author.

Semali, L. (1996). In the name of science and of genetics and of the bell curve: White supremacy in American schools. In J. L. Kincheloe, S. R. Steinberg, & A. D. Gresson III (Eds.), *Measured lies* (pp. 162–175). New York: St. Martin's Press.

Slater, J. F. (1932). *A letter of fifty years ago*. Washington, DC: John F. Slater Fund.

Small, A. (1915). Fifty years of sociology in the United States. In *American Journal of Sociology*, 20, 210.

Spencer, H. (1864). *Social statics*. New York: Appleton.

Spencer, H. (1874). *The study of sociology*. New York: Appleton.

Spencer, H. (1876). *The principles of sociology*. New York: Appleton.

Spivey, D. (1978). *Schooling for the new slavery: Black industrial education, 1868–1915*. Westport, CT: Greenwood Press.

Stewart, W. R. (1974). *The philanthropic work of Josephine Shaw Lowell*. Montclair, NJ: Patterson Smith.

Sumner, W. G. (1883). *What social classes owe to each other*. New York: Harper & Brothers.

Sumner, W. G. (1966). *Folkways*. Boston: Ginn & Co.

Sumner, W. G., & Keller, A. G. (1927). *The science of society*. New Haven, CT: Yale University Press.

Tarbell, I. M. (1904). *The history of the Standard Oil Company* (Vols. 1 & 2). New York: McClure.

Tarbell, I. M. (1905, July). John D. Rockefeller: A character study. *McClure's Magazine*, 25(3), 227–249, 386–398.

Taylor, F. W. (1911). *The principles of scientific management* (2nd ed.). Mineola, NY: Dover Publications.

Ward, F. L. (1883). *Dynamic sociology*. New York: Appleton.

Watkins, W. H. (1994, Winter). Multicultural education: Toward a historical and political inquiry. *Educational Theory, 44*(1), 99–117.

Watkins, W. H. (1995). Thomas Jesse Jones, social studies, and race. *International Journal of Social Education, 10*(2), 124–134.

Why northern men of money are visiting the south. (1901). *Morning Post* (Raleigh, NC), April 28.

Woodson, C. G. (1933). *The miseducation of the negro*. Washington, DC: Associated Publishers.

# Index

Abels, Jules, 118, 120, 124, 125
Accommodationism, 6, 109, 145, 159, 182;
and Armstrong, 4, 23, 44, 47, 61, 105; and
DuBois, 114, 150; and Hampton, 23, 131–
32, 159; and Jones, 96, 98, 105, 106, 110,
113–14, 117; and Phelps Stokes family, 92–
93, 94, 96, 97; and political sociology, 20,
23; and Rockefellers and associates, 119,
126, 127, 129, 131–32
Africa, 2, 44, 98, 110; as cradle of
civilization, 31, 66, 75; Phelps Stokes
family's interest in, 83, 84, 86, 92, 95;
return of Blacks to, 30, 83, 86. *See also
specific nation*
Agassiz, Louis, 30–32, 33, 34, 57, 172
American Missionary Association, 19, 46, 47–
48, 56–57, 58
American Social Science Association (ASSA),
16, 64, 100, 101, 108
Anderson, James D., 1, 12, 19, 32, 49, 52, 98,
105–6, 110, 126–27, 133, 141, 143, 144,
145–46, 155, 157, 158, 159, 160
Armstrong, Samuel Chapman, 32, 142, 144,
157; biography/early life of, 43–47; on
education of Blacks, 58–59; and Jones, 96,
106; legacy of, 4, 43, 60–61; and
missionary community, 43–44, 47–48, 56–
57, 58; on politics and Blacks, 53–55; on
race, 55–58; unity in diversity outlook of,
57–58; as Washington's mentor, 43, 44,
59–60. *See also* Hampton Institute;
*Southern Workman*; *specific topic*
Arnove, R. F., 19, 21, 22, 98, 111, 173

Baldwin, William Henry, Jr., 2, 93, 161; and
Armstrong, 157; and Conferences for
Education, 145–46, 156; and GEB/
Rockefellers, 122, 126, 128, 133, 134, 136,
154, 158; and Hampton and Tuskegee

Institutes, 136, 146, 157–58, 159, 160;
impact of, 5, 136, 159–60; Ogden compared
with, 154, 159–60; socioracial views of,
159–60; as White supremacist, 125, 133
Berman, Edward, 18–19, 20, 44, 87, 90, 98
Biddiss, M. D., 25, 26, 27
Black education: aim/mission of, 9, 11, 112,
181–82; as means for oppression/control of
Blacks, 1, 6, 78; as model of how to rule,
182–83; motive for involvement in, 141–
42; rationale for, 175; romanticization of,
10. *See also specific person, fund,
institution or topic*
Black radicalism, 94–95
Blacks: culture of, 60–61; as entrepreneurs,
106, 182; as intelligentsia, 150–51. *See also*
Black education; *specific person or topic*
Bolshevism, 85, 89–90, 99. *See also*
Communism
Brain size, 4, 32–33
Brooks, John Graham, 147, 154, 155, 156,
157, 158, 159
Business: Baldwin's views about, 154, 155,
159–60; Ogden's views about, 140, 141,
142, 159–60
Buttrick, Wallace, 96, 119, 122, 125–27, 128,
132, 133, 134, 146

Capitalism, 39, 61, 83, 125; and Armstrong,
45, 60; and corporate philanthropy, 19, 20,
21–22; and Giddings, 69, 70–72; and Jones,
112, 113; and Ogden, 138, 139, 140, 141;
and Phelps Stokes family, 87, 89–90; and
political sociology, 10, 11, 13, 15, 19, 20,
21–22. *See also* Economics
Capon Springs Conference, 129, 144–47,
161
Carnegie, Andrew, 13, 19, 20
Carnegie Foundation, 22, 91

# About the Author

WILLIAM ("BILL") WATKINS was born in Harlem and reared in South Central Los Angeles. Since earning a Ph.D. in 1986, Bill has taught university courses in curriculum theory, the sociology and history of education, and African American studies. His many articles, essays, and lectures have appeared in scholarly journals, books, conference proceedings, the popular press, and the electronic media. A lifelong political activist, Bill has dedicated himself to the pursuit of racial equality and economic justice for all people.